Active Basic English
当代基础英语教程

（下）

（第 2 版）

主　编：徐　斌
副主编：史虹涛　张克军

北京大学出版社
北　京

图书在版编目(CIP)数据

当代基础英语教程.下/徐斌主编. —2 版. —北京:北京大学出版社,2002.9
ISBN 978-7-301-05790-2

Ⅰ.当… Ⅱ.徐… Ⅲ.英语-教材 Ⅳ.H31

中国版本图书馆 CIP 数据核字(2002)第 054229 号

书 名:	当代基础英语教程(下)(第2版)
著作责任者:	徐斌 主编
责 任 编 辑:	徐万丽
标 准 书 号:	ISBN 978-7-301-05790-2/H·0776
出 版 发 行:	北京大学出版社
地 址:	北京市海淀区成府路 205 号 100871
网 址:	http://www.pup.cn
电 话:	邮购部 62752015 发行部 62750672 编辑部 62765014
	出版部 62754962
电 子 信 箱:	xuwanli50@yahoo.com.cn
印 刷 者:	北京大学印刷厂
经 销 者:	新华书店
	890 毫米×1240 毫米 A5 开本 9.125 印张 243 千字
	2001 年 1 月第 1 版
	2002 年 9 月第 2 版 2018 年 8 月第 11 次印刷
定 价:	25.00 元

未经许可,不得以任何方式复制或抄袭本书之部分或全部内容。
版权所有,侵权必究
举报电话:(010)62752024 电子信箱:fd@pup.pku.edu.cn

前 言

随着我国加入 WTO,英语作为国际通用语将会更加普及。由于懂英语的人越来越多,水平也越来越高,因此,从 ABC 起点的基础类教材已不多见。然而,事实上仍有许多在校的大中专学生(包括地方及军队音乐类、艺术类、体育类、财经类等院校的大中专学生;指挥院校、武警院校及各类士官学校中的大中专学生;少数民族地区院校中基础较差的大中专学生),以及有志于学习并掌握英语的各类人员,他们或是未学过英语,或是学过但是不扎实、不系统。这部分人非常渴望能从头学起或重新巩固已有知识。正是基于这样的状况和认识,我们才着手编写这套教材。

本套教材共分上、下两册,其主要特色:
- 起点低,易学易记,适用范围广;
- 取材新,题材广泛,趣味性浓,易激发学生学习兴趣;
- 编排独特,重难点突出,层次分明,符合循序渐进的规律;
- 系统性、实用性强,贯彻学以致用的原则;
- 课内课外相结合,注重学生自学能力和语言综合应用能力的培养。

本套教材中句型、课文、对话、注释、语法、练习均互为补充。语法讲解简明实用,与课文紧密结合。有些语法现象虽不能在语法栏中一一列举,但尽力做到在注释中充分体现;同时,练习的设计强调词汇的复现率,有助于学生复习、巩固和提高。

通过本套教材的学习,学生可掌握语音、基本句型、基本语法现象和 2000 左右常用词汇(其中上册 900,下册 1100),其中课后练习中出现的少量生词及阅读材料中的生词均须掌握。

学生学完本套教材可应用所学知识进行初步的听、说、读、写、译,为日后进入中、高级阶段的学习打下扎实的基础。

为便于教师备课,本套教材还配有教师用书。教参中共设计了六套试卷,其中上册两套,下册四套,并附有答案和听力原文。教师可根据教学进度及学生掌握的情况,选出相应的试题,作为其中和期末的考卷。本套教材还配有录音带(包括试卷中的听力材料)。

本套教材下册共十六个单元。在教学安排上,我们建议每单元至少安排6学时,以保证教学效果。有条件的院校可适当增加课时。

本教材在初稿完成后,我国知名专家、大连外国语大学杨俊峰教授对此书提出了许多中肯的意见。英国著名的语言教育专家、21世纪英文报的专栏作家Neville Grant还专门为本书写了"致学生"。本书在经过了几轮的使用后,许多院校的教师和专家对此书给予了极大的关注,并提出了不少修改意见,这些意见在我们对本书的修订过程中得到了充分的采纳。我们在编写的过程中也汲取了国内外优秀教材的精华,在此不一一罗列。张春诚同志为本书提供了插图。同时在本书出版的过程中,我们还得到了北大出版社英语编辑徐万丽同志的具体帮助,以及郭力等同志的大力支持。在此我们向上述提到的及默默支持和关心我们的所有同志表示最衷心的感谢。

编者

2002年5月22日

目 录

Unit 1 ············ (1)
- Text: A Victim ············ (1)
- Dialogue ············ (4)
- Grammar: 过去进行时 ············ (6)
- Exercises ············ (7)
- Passage Reading ············ (12)

Unit 2 ············ (15)
- Text: World Records ············ (15)
- Dialogue ············ (20)
- Grammar: 形容词和副词的比较级和最高级 ············ (23)
- Exercises ············ (25)
- Passage Reading ············ (31)

Unit 3 ············ (35)
- Text: Setting a Trap ············ (35)
- Dialogue ············ (40)
- Grammar: 过去完成时;不定式 ············ (42)
- Exercises ············ (44)
- Passage Reading ············ (49)

Unit 4 ············ (52)
- Text: The Great Pyramid ············ (52)
- Dialogue ············ (56)
- Grammar: 被动语态 ············ (58)
- Exercises ············ (60)
- Passage Reading ············ (64)

Unit 5 .... (68)
    Text: Victor's Hobby .... (68)
    Dialogue .... (72)
    Grammar: 定语从句(一) .... (74)
    Exercises .... (75)
    Passage Reading .... (80)

Unit 6 .... (84)
    Text: Trains under the Christmas Tree .... (84)
    Dialogue .... (88)
    Grammar: 定语从句(二);感叹句 .... (91)
    Exercises .... (92)
    Passage Reading .... (97)

Unit 7 .... (100)
    Text: Why the Doctor Was Late .... (100)
    Dialogue .... (105)
    Grammar: 名词从句(一) .... (106)
    Exercises .... (108)
    Passage Reading .... (113)

Unit 8 .... (117)
    Text: Learning to Read—in College .... (117)
    Dialogue .... (121)
    Grammar: 名词从句(二) .... (123)
    Exercises .... (125)
    Passage Reading .... (130)

Unit 9 .... (134)
    Text: Doing Favours Can Be Dangerous .... (134)
    Dialogue .... (138)
    Grammar: 状语从句(一) .... (140)
    Exercises .... (141)

    Passage Reading ·· (148)
Unit 10 ·· (152)
    Text: Good Advice ··· (152)
    Dialogue ··· (156)
    Grammar: 状语从句(二) ···································· (157)
    Exercises ·· (159)
    Passage Reading ·· (165)
Unit 11 ·· (168)
    Text: The Flower Effect ···································· (168)
    Dialogue ··· (172)
    Grammar: 现在分词 ·· (174)
    Exercises ·· (176)
    Passage Reading ·· (181)
Unit 12 ·· (185)
    Text: Father Never Got Excited ······················· (185)
    Dialogue ··· (189)
    Grammar: 动名词 ·· (191)
    Exercises ·· (192)
    Passage Reading ·· (197)
Unit 13 ·· (201)
    Text: Chance ·· (201)
    Dialogue ··· (206)
    Grammar: 过去分词 ·· (207)
    Exercises ·· (208)
    Passage Reading ·· (214)
Unit 14 ·· (219)
    Text: A Case of Mistaken Identity ·················· (219)
    Dialogue ··· (222)
    Grammar: 带引导词 It 的常用结构 ················ (224)

Exercises ·· (225)
　　　Passage Reading ··· (230)
Unit 15 ··· (232)
　　　Text: Dolores Silva, Small Business Co-owner ········ (232)
　　　Dialogue ··· (236)
　　　Grammar: 直接引语与间接引语 ························· (237)
　　　Exercises ·· (239)
　　　Passage Reading ··· (244)
Unit 16 ··· (248)
　　　Text: It's Never Too Late ····························· (248)
　　　Dialogue ··· (253)
　　　Grammar: 虚拟语气 ····································· (255)
　　　Exercises ·· (256)
　　　Passage Reading ··· (261)
Vocabulary List 词汇表 ··································· (265)

Unit 1

Text

A Victim

Alfred was the best assistant in a shop. The manager told him to watch people carefully because some thief was taking things from their shop.

At ten o'clock everybody was working hard. Alfred, who was selling meat, saw a man near the shop door. The man had very big pockets. He was taking things from the shelves and putting them back again. When people came near to him he looked away from them. Now he was walking slowly to the other end of the shop. Alfred thought there was something wrong with him.

Three minutes later Alfred saw him coming to the door. He was leaving the shop! Alfred went up to him.

"You can't leave this shop," he said to the man. " Stop!"

But the man did not stop. He put his hand on the door of the shop.

"Stop!" said Alfred again. Then he quickly took a big piece of wet red meat and hit the man in the face with it. The glass door was crushed and the man fell to the ground. There was blood on his face—blood from the meat and from his nose.

A policeman rushed in. He looked carefully into the man's face and told Alfred that this man was from the police station on a special job. He was watching for the thief in the shop.

New Words & Expressions

victim ['viktim] n. 受害者
assistant [ə'sistənt] n. 店员,助手
carefully ['kɛəfuli] adv. 仔细地
thief [θi:f] n. 贼,小偷
sell [sel] vt., vi. 卖,出售
pocket ['pɔkit] n. 小袋,衣袋
slowly ['slouli] adv. 缓慢地
end [end] n. 尽头
later ['leitə] adv. 较迟地,较后地
quickly ['kwikli] adv. 快地,急速地
wet [wet] adj. 湿淋淋的

hit [hit] vt. 打,碰撞
crush [krʌʃ] vt. 压碎
ground [graund] n. 地面,场所
blood [blʌd] n. 血
nose [nouz] n. 鼻子
into ['intu] prep. 到…内,向…里
　　look into 检查
station ['steiʃən] n. 局,所
　　police station 警察局
special ['speʃəl] adj. 特别的,特殊的
watch for 寻找,等待

Proper Name

Alfred [ˈælfred] (人名)艾尔弗雷德

Notes to the Text

1. The manager told him to watch people carefully because some thief was taking things from their shop. 经理要他密切注视着人们,因为有小偷在偷商店里的东西。
   1) tell somebody (not) to do something 告诉某人(不)做某事。例如:
      I told them that I was worried, but she **told me to stop talking about it and not to worry**. 我告诉他们我很担心,但她要我别谈此事并让我不要担心。
   2) some 修饰单数可数名词,表示"某个人或事"。再如:
      Some person may object (反对). 有人可能会反对。
      I'd like to return there some day. 我希望有朝一日回到那儿。

2. Alfred, who was selling meat, saw a man near the shop door. 艾尔弗雷德正在卖肉,看见商店门附近有个人。句中 who 引导的是非限制性定语从句,补充说明 Alfred 在做什么,并不是形容哪一个 Alfred。因此,本句不能译成"正在卖肉的 Alfred",否则会引起误解。

3. put back 意为"放回"。例如:
   Why don't you put your chair back a little to get a better view? 要想看得更清楚些,为什么不把椅子往回放一点呢?

4. Three minutes later, Alfred saw him coming to the door. 三分钟后,艾尔弗雷德看见他正朝门口走来。see somebody doing something 意为"看见某人正在做某事"。例如:
   We saw him crossing the street. 我们看见他正朝街对面走去。

5. Alfred went up to him. 艾尔弗雷德走到他面前。句中"up"是"靠近"的意思。例如：

He was walking up to the other end of the shop. 他正朝商店那头走去。类似的搭配还有：come up to（朝…走来），climb up to（朝…爬去）等。

6. hit the man in the face 打这个人的脸。类似的表达还有：

pat somebody on the shoulder 拍拍某人的肩

catch somebody by the arm 抓住某人的胳膊

7. The glass door was crushed. 玻璃门被压碎了。was crushed 是被动语态(关于被动语态请参见第四单元)。

8. He looked carefully into the man's face. 他仔细地查看这个人的脸部。look into 是短语动词，意为"查看"。例如：

I looked into the room but no one was there. 我仔细查看了房间，但是里面没人。

She looked into my eyes for a long time without speaking. 她一言不发地盯着我的双眼看了好久。

9. watch for the thief 查找小偷。watch for 是短语动词，意思是"寻找、等待"。例如：

Will you watch for the bus while I go into the shop for a moment? 我逛一会儿商店，你等车好吗？

I'm just watching for a chance to punish him in return. 我在伺机惩罚他予以报复。

Dialogue

Whose Students Were They?

A. Where were you this morning?

B. I was in Room 206 all morning.

A. What were you doing at about 10:30?
B. I was teaching an English class. Why?
A. Well, there were quite a few students in Room 204. The students were making a lot of noise. A few of them were just playing cards and talking quietly. The rest of them were laughing and yelling.
B. Whose students were they? Were they mine, by any chance?
A. I don't know whose students they were. Perhaps they were yours, or perhaps they were Paul Allen's.

New Words & Expressions

quite a few 不少
noise [nɔiz] n. 吵闹声
card [kɑ:d] n. 卡片,扑克牌
quietly ['kwaiətli] adv. 静静地

rest [rest] n. 其余
yell [jel] vi. 喊叫
chance [tʃɑ:ns] n. 机会
   by any chance 可能

Proper Name

Paul Allen [pɔ:l 'ælən] (人名) 保尔·艾伦

Notes to the Dialogue

1. There were quite a few students in Room 204. 204 房间有不少学生。quite a few 意为"不少、相当多"。例如:
At that time he knew quite a few people there. 那时他在那儿认识不少人。
2. The rest of them were laughing and yelling. 其余的人又是大笑又是喊叫。the rest 意为"其余的人或物",作主语时如果含有复数概念,谓语动词应用复数。例如:

All the rest are going. 所有其他人都要走了。试比较：

The rest of the money is in the bank. 余下的钱存在银行里。

The first part is hard, but the rest (part) is easy. 第一部分很难，但余下的部分很容易。

The rest of the students are playing football. 其余学生在踢足球。

3. by any chance "也许、碰巧"。例如：

Do you think that by any chance you'd be free for dinner? 你会有空来吃晚饭吗？

Have you got a spare stamp by any chance? 你有多余的邮票吧？

Grammar

过去进行时 (The Past Continuous Tense)

1. 主要表示过去某一时刻(或某一阶段)正在进行的动作,由 was/were + 现在分词构成。例如：

   At ten o'clock everybody was working hard. 十点钟时大家都在辛勤工作。

   He was taking things from the shelves and putting them back again. 他把东西从货架上拿下来，然后又放回去。

   He was watching for the thief in the shop. 他正在寻找商店里的贼。
   Some thief was taking things from their shop. 有贼在偷商店里的东西。
   Something woke me up just as he was going out. 正在他要出去时我被什么弄醒了。

2. 过去进行时与一般过去时的主要差别是过去进行时表示一个动作在某时刻或某阶段正在进行,偏重于动作持续的过程,而一般过去时表示过去某个时候发生过的某个动作。例如：

   I was reading a book last night. 昨晚我在看一本书。(可能没看完)
   I read a book last night. 昨晚我看了一本书。(已经看完了)

但也有少数动词其一般过去时并不表示动作的完成(如:rain, snow, feel, work 等),这时用两种时态意思上差别不大。例如:

It rained all day yesterday.

It was raining all day yesterday.

这两句都是"昨天下了一天雨"的意思。只是在强调延续时间较长时,用过去进行时稍好一点。

Exercises

I. **Choose the best answer a, b, c or d to these questions according to the text.**

1) _____ was the best assistant in a shop.
   a. The manager   b. The thief
   c. The policeman   d. Alfred

2) The manager told Alfred to watch people carefully because _____.
   a. someone was stealing things from the shop
   b. he wanted to leave the shop for a while
   c. he wanted to talk with the policeman
   d. he wanted to send the thief to the police-station

3) Alfred thought that there was something wrong with the man near the shop door because _____.
   a. he had very big pockets
   b. he was taking things from the shelves and putting them back again
   c. when people came near to him he looked away from them
   d. he was walking slowly to the other end of the shop

4) When Alfred saw the man coming to the door, he stopped him because he thought that _____.

a. the man was the policeman

   b. the man was the manager

   c. the man was seriously ill

   d. the man was the thief

5) Alfred stopped the man by _____.

   a. putting his hand on the door of the shop

   b. shouting "stop"

   c. hitting the man in the face with a big piece of meat

   d. all of the above

6) The man fell to the ground with the glass door _____.

   a. opened   b. closed

   c. broken   d. cleaned

7) The man turned out to be (原来是)_____.

   a. a policeman   b. the thief

   c. the manager   d. the butcher (肉商)

8) The man came to the shop to _____.

   a. take things from the shelves

   b. put things back

   c. look for the thief

   d. see the manager

II. Match each word in Column A with a similar meaning in Column B.

A	B
1) crush	a. attack
2) wet	b. in a quick manner
3) sell	c. in a careful way
4) assistant	d. someone who steals things
5) hit	e. not quickly
6) quickly	f. without making much noise

7) carefully   g. a person who helps another, as in a job
8) thief   h. to give something for money
9) slowly   i. not dry
10) quietly   j. to press something so hard that it breaks

III. A. **Fill in the blanks with the words or expressions given below. Change the form where necessary.**

| later | watch for | near | rush | wrong | fall |
| crush | sell | special | look into | end | hit |

1) At first he decided to move to Chicago (芝加哥), but _____ he changed his mind (主意).
2) There is something _____ with my teeth.
3) Joe has a _____ gift (天赋) for music.
4) The man's legs were _____ in a car accident (事故).
5) After she told him to stop complaining (抱怨) he _____ her over the head with a book.
6) There seems to be an electrical (电的) problem. I'll get someone to _____ it.
7) They are _____ the bus to come along.
8) Everyone _____ out into the street to see what was happening.
9) Mary is _____ her car for $1,000.
10) Bob was standing _____ enough to hear what they said.
11) Careful you don't _____. The path (小路) is very icy (滑).
12) He sat at one _____ of the table and I sat at the other.

B. **Fill in each blank with a proper word.**

1) careful, carefully
   a. Be _____ you don't fall off the ladder (梯子).

b. You must be very _____ not to say anything to Paul.

   c. If Bob drove more _____, he wouldn't have so many accidents.

2) quick, quickly

   a. Have we time for a _____ drink?

   b. They ran much more _____ than we had expected.

3) quiet, quietly

   a. Can't you keep the kids (孩子们) _____? I'm trying to be concentrating (集中精力).

   b. He left here _____.

4) slow, slowly

   a. Your watch is three minutes _____.

   b. He is walking _____ to us.

IV. A. **Form questions after the given patterns and answer them.**

1) What were you doing...?

   a. at 7 this morning

   b. last night

   c. from 8 to 10 yesterday

   d. when he met you

2) Why didn't you come to the meeting? (I was attending an English class)

   a. come to join us (prepare for the examination)

   b. come to the film (have a bath)

   c. call me (write a letter)

   d. do your homework last night (watch Olympic Games)

B. **Fill in the blanks with verbs in the proper tenses.**

1) It _____ (rain) hard when we _____ (get) there.

2) At this time yesterday evening we _____ (watch) TV.

3) When I first _____ (meet) her, she _____ (study) in the classroom building.
4) I'm sorry that I _____ (not, come) to your party. I _____ (have) a talk with Bill.
5) Grace: I _____ (have) a wonderful dream last night. I _____ (dream) that I _____ (be) a lady of leisure (清闲) who _____ (not, do) any housework! You _____ (do) it all instead! While I _____ (lie) in the sun, you _____ (cut) the lawn (草坪)! While I _____ (relax 放松) in the bath, you _____ (iron 熨烫) the shirts! While I _____ (take) a swim in the pool (池子), you _____ (hang 挂) out the washing! While I _____ (watch) TV, you _____ (cook) the meal! Wasn't that a marvelous (很好的) dream?
Cavin: And while you _____ (dream), I _____ (have) an even better one: You _____ (become) me and I _____ (become) you.

V. Complete the following sentences.

1) At this time last year _____ (我正在访问日本).
2) When I met him _____ (他正在等公共汽车).
3) _____ (我们不上课) from 3 to 4 yesterday.
4) _____ (我正读一本小说) when he came.
5) While I was relaxing in the bath, _____ (她正做饭).
6) I'm sorry that I didn't come to dinner. _____ (我正在开会).

VI. Translation.

A. **From Chinese to English.**

1) 你看上去非常疲倦, 有什么事吗?
2) 艾尔弗雷德气极了, 朝他脸上打了一拳。

3）他在交卷(hand in the test paper)前,仔细检查了所有答案。

4）她从架子上拿了一样东西,又放了回去。

5）妈妈告诉我天黑前回家。

6）那个人到店里来是查找小偷的。

B. From English to Chinese.

1) A few minutes later, Alfred saw him walking slowly to the other end of the shop.

2) He looked into the TV set, but found there was nothing wrong with it.

3) Alfred rushed into the room and caught the stranger by the arm.

4) The manager told him to watch for the thief because some person was stealing things from the supermarket.

5) The glass door was crushed and the man fell to the ground.

6) When people came near to him, he looked away from them.

Passage Reading

The Wrong Dog

Mr. and Mrs. White were going to the country for their holiday. They had a dog, Blackie. They liked him very much, but they could not take him to the country with them. So they tried to look for a good place to leave him in while they were away. And at last they found a shop. The shop looked after dogs very well while their owners were away. They took Blackie to the shop just before they left for their holiday and said goodbye to him.

At the end of their holiday, they got back home very late at night that day. They thought the shop might be closed at that late hour. They decided to wait until the next morning before going to get Blackie back.

So the next morning Mr. White started his car, got into it and drove off happily to collect Blackie.

When he reached home with the dog, he said to his wife, "Do you know, dear, I don't think Blackie enjoyed his stay at that shop very much. He barked (叫) all the way home in the car as if he wanted to tell me something."

Mrs. White looked at the dog carefully and then answered, "You are quite right, dear. He was certainly trying to tell you something. But he wasn't trying to tell you that he hadn't enjoyed his stay at that shop. He was only saying that you were bringing the wrong dog home. This isn't Blackie!"

New Words & Expressions

at last 最后	close [klouz] vt. 停业,关门
look after 照看	happily ['hæpili] adv. 高兴地
while [wail] conj. 当…的时候	collect [kə'lekt] vt. 拿来,接来
owner ['ounə] n. 主人	bark [bɑ:k] vi. 犬叫

Notes

1. So they tried to look for a good place to leave him in while they were away. 所以他们想在外出期间找个好地方把他留下来。
2. at that late hour 在那么晚的时候。此处"that"作副词,用于强调。
   例如:
   "Did you have to wait long?" "Well, not that long."
   "你得等很久吗?" "不用等那么久"。
3. before going to get Blackie back 相当于 before they went to get Blackie back.

4. I don't think Blackie enjoyed his stay at that shop very much. 我认为Blackie留在那家商店期间不是很开心。
   1) 当think引导一个否定意义的句子时，通常将think变为否定形式。例如：
      I don't think he will come. 我认为他不会来。此类动词还有believe, suppose等。
   2) stay 可做名词。再如：
      We made a short stay in Paris. 我们在巴黎做短暂停留。
5. He barked all the way home in the car as if he wanted to tell me something. 在回家的路上，他在车里一路叫唤，好像有话要告诉我。as if 意为"好像"，后接从句。例如：It looks as if it's going to rain. 看上去天要下雨。

Which of the following statements are true or false? Write T for true and F for false.

( ) 1. The Whites were going to the country to enjoy their holiday.
( ) 2. They had a dog, Blackie and he was dear to them.
( ) 3. They'd like to take the dog with them to the country but they couldn't.
( ) 4. They left the dog alone at home while they were away.
( ) 5. The Whites arrived home early that day after the holiday.
( ) 6. They were afraid that in the shop there might be no one at such a late hour at night.
( ) 7. They decided to get Blackie back at once.
( ) 8. Mr. White went to the shop on foot together with his wife.
( ) 9. Mr. White said that Blackie had had a good time at the shop because the dog was excited all the way home.
( )10. Mrs. White answered "yes" because she saw her dear Blackie again.

Unit 2

Text

World Records

When someone meets a stranger with the same hobby, that person immediately becomes a friend. People enjoy the company of others who share a similar interest. Often they will form a club and travel great distances to attend meetings where they can talk about their hobbies. Other people have such unusual hobbies that no one else can share them. Sometimes they try to do something better, faster or longer than anyone else in order to have their names included in the Guinness Book of World Records.

A lady in Massachusetts may have the world's easiest hobby; she lets her hair grow. Diane Witt has not cut her hair for twelve years. It is now eight feet (2.44 meters) long, and she will soon set a new world record and her name will be placed in the Guinness book. A thirty-year-old man in Pennsylvania played the piano for forty-five days and eleven hours, while a musician in

Connecticut played the flute for forty-three hours.

A teacher in California typed for over 162 hours, and a lady from Iowa spent six years typing the numbers from one to one million. Probably the cleanest people in the world are two young women from England who stayed in the shower for over ninety-eight hour; but a man in Oregon was more than twice as clean after taking a shower that lasted two hundred hours.

Someone said that "records are made to be broken." One record that many young men might enjoy breaking is the one made by Roger Guy English of California. During a period of eight hours Roger kissed three thousand young women.

New Words & Expressions

stranger ['streindʒə] n. 陌生人
same [seim] adj. 同样的
hobby ['hɔbi] n. 爱好
person ['pə:sən] n. 人
immediately [i'mi:diətli] adv. 立即,马上
company ['kɔmpəni] n. 陪伴
share [ʃɛə] vt. 分享
similar ['similə] adj. 相似的
interest ['intrist] n. 兴趣
form [fɔ:m] vt. 形成,组成
distance ['distəns] n. 距离
attend [ə'tend] vt. 参加
unusual [ʌn'ju:ʒuəl] adj. 特别的,不寻常的
else [els] adj. 其余的
include [in'klu:d] vt. 包括

Guinness ['ginis] n. 吉尼斯
record ['rekɔ:d] n. 纪录
meter ['mi:tə] n. (计算单位)米
place [pleis] vt. 放置
piano [pi'ænou] n. 钢琴
musician [mju:'ziʃən] n. 音乐家
flute [flu:t] n. 长笛
number ['nʌmbə] n. 数字
million ['miljən] num. 百万
probably ['prɔbəbli] adv. 可能地
clean [kli:n] adj. 干净的
shower ['ʃauə] n. 淋浴
last [lɑ:st] vi. 延续,持续
break [breik] (broke, broken) vt. 打破
period ['piəriəd] n. 时期,其间
thousand ['θauzənd] num. 千

Proper Names

Guinness Book of World Records 吉尼斯世界纪录大全
Massachusetts [ˌmæsə'tʃuːsits] （美）马萨诸塞州
Diane Witt ['daiæn wit] （人名）黛安·韦特
Pennsylvania [ˌpensil'veiniə] （美）宾夕法尼亚州
Connecticut [kə'nektikət] （美）康涅狄格州
California [ˌkæli'fɔːniə] （美）加利福尼亚州
Iowa ['aiəwə] （美）依阿华州
Oregon ['ɔrigən] （美）俄勒冈州
Roger Guy English ['rɔdʒə; gai; 'iŋgliʃ] （人名）罗杰·盖伊·英格列希

Notes to the Text

1. People enjoy the company of others who share a similar interest. 人们喜欢与有相同兴趣爱好的人交往。who share a similar interest 为定语从句，修饰 others。（关于定语从句，详见第五、六单元。）
2. Often they will form a club and travel great distances to attend meetings where they can talk about their hobbies. 他们常常组成一个俱乐部，长途跋涉去参加他们能讨论业余爱好的会议。where they can talk about their hobbies 也是定语从句，此处，where 相当于 at which。
3. Other people have such unusual hobbies that no one else can share them. 还有一些人，他们的爱好很特别，没有任何人能与之分享。
   1) such...that... 意为"如此…以至于"，a, an 要置于 such 之后。
   　It was such a beautiful night that I wanted to walk. 夜色如此之美，我真想出去走走。

17

It's such a good chance that we mustn't miss it. 这个机会太好了，我们决不能错过。

2) else 意为"别的"，常用于疑问词或不定代词 some, any, no 和与-body, -one, place, thing 合成的词，以及 all, much, little 等词的后面。例如：

We must find somebody else to do the job. 我们必须另外找人来做这项工作。

What else did she say about me? 除此之外她还提到关于我的什么事情？

Not much else is known. 其他都不太清楚。

另外，else 的所有格形式也值得注意。例如：

That must be someone else's ['elsiz] coat; it isn't mine. 那一定是别人的外套，不是我的。

4. Sometimes they try to do something better, faster or longer than anyone else in order to have their names included in the Guinness Book of World Records. 有时他们想把事情做得比别人更好、更快或时间更长，为的是能把他们的名字载入吉尼斯世界纪录大全。

1) in order to 意为"为了，目的是"。例如：

She shut the window in order to keep the insects out. 她把窗户关上，以免虫子飞入。

2) have something done 意为"请(人)把某事情做了"。例如：

I must have my TV fixed. (= I must have somebody fix my TV.) 我得让人把电视机修一下。

5. ... and she will soon set a new world record and her name will be placed in the Guinness Book. 她不久将创造一项新的世界纪录，她的名字将被载入吉尼斯大全。

6. A thirty-year-old man in Pennsylvania played the piano for forty-five days and eleven hours, while a musician in Connecticut played the flute for forty-three hours. 宾夕法尼亚州的一位 30 岁的男士弹钢琴

弹了 45 天零 11 小时,而康涅狄克州的一位音乐家吹了 43 小时的长笛。

1) while 在这类句子中作连词,引起状语从句表示对比。例如:

　　I like tea while she likes coffee. 我喜欢茶,而她喜欢咖啡。

2) a thirty-year-old man 意为"一位 30 岁的男士"。英语中基数词可与名词构成复合形容词,中间应用短线连接。例如:

　　a two-hour meeting　一次两小时的会议

　　a 25-inch TV set　一台 25 英寸的电视

　　a ten-minute walk　一次 10 分钟的步行

7. spend some time doing something 意为"花时间做某事"。再如:"How did you spend your summer vacation?""I spent it (in) reading and fishing.""你是怎样度过暑假的?""看看书,钓钓鱼过的。"

其中的"in"通常可以省略。但如果表示把钱或时间等用于某个方面时,就要用介词"on"。例如:

He spent all his savings on a new car. 他把全部的积蓄用在了一辆新车上。

I spent all my energy on that job. 我把全部的精力投入到那份工作上。

8. ...but a man in Oregon was more than twice as clean after taking a shower that lasted two hundred hours. 而俄勒冈州的一名男士淋浴长达 200 小时,他又比她们干净一倍了。注意:as clean 后省略掉了 as they are。

9. Records are made to be broken. 创纪录就是为了打破纪录。

10. Probably the cleanest people... 句中的 probably 意为"大概,也许,很可能"。例如:

He will probably refuse this offer. 他很可能会拒绝这个建议。

"Will our football team win?""Probably (Probably not).""我们的足球队会赢吗?""大概会(大概不会)。"

注意:probably 不能用于否定词的后面。

我们可以说:Probably he won't come.

也可以说：He probably won't come.

还可以说：He won't come probably.

但不可以说：He won't probably come.

11. One record that many young men might enjoy breaking is the one made by Roger Guy English of California. 一项很多年轻人可能希望打破的纪录是由加利福尼亚州罗杰·盖伊·英格列希创下的。made by Roger Guy English of California 是过去分词短语作定语修饰 one。

Dialogue

A：We need a new television set.

B：Did you have a particular model in mind?

A：No, not really.

B：Well, this is a very popular model.

A：That's not a very clear picture!

B：What about this one? It's a newer model, and the picture is clearer and brighter than the other one.

A：Yes, it is. But the screen is a bit small. It's larger than our old one, of course. But my husband wants a bigger picture screen.

B：I see. Well, look at this one. It has a 25-inch screen. That's the largest one we have. It's the newest and latest model.

A：Yes, that's a perfect size.

B：It's the clearest and brightest picture of all. It's the best one we have.

A：How much is it?

B：It's only $695. It's more expensive than...

A：$695? Is it that much?

B：It's the most expensive one of all. But of course it's an excellent television set. It has the most convenient controls, the most beautiful cabinet, the latest...

A: What's the price of that one?

B: It's $495.

A: Is that the cheapest one you have?

B: No. That one over there sells for $295. That's the least expensive one of all. Also, it has the smallest picture screen.

A: That's about the price range I had in mind. I'll take that one, I guess.

New Words & Expressions

television ['teliˌviʒən] n. 电视
   television set 电视机
particular [pə'tikjulə] adj. 特别的
model ['mɔdl] n. 型号
mind [maind] n. 主意
popular ['pɔpjulə] adj. 受欢迎的
clear [kliə] adj. 清楚的
picture ['piktʃə] n. 图像
than [ðæn] prep., conj. 比
screen [skri:n] n. 屏幕
a bit 一点，一些
large [lɑ:dʒ] adj. 大的
of course 当然
husband ['hʌzbənd] n. 丈夫
inch [intʃ] n. 寸

late [leit] adj. 新近的
perfect ['pə:fikt] adj. 完美的
size [saiz] n. 尺寸
expensive [iks'pensiv] adj. 昂贵的
excellent ['eksələnt] adj. 优秀的，卓越的
convenient [kən'vi:njənt] adj. 方便的
control [kən'troul] vt., n. 控制
cabinet ['kæbinit] n. 外壳
cheap [tʃi:p] adj. 便宜的
price [prais] n. 价格
least [li:st] (little 最高级) adj. 最小的，最少的
range [reindʒ] n. 范围
guess [ges] vt. 猜，认为

Notes to the Dialogue

1. Did you have a particular model in mind? 你考虑好了要买什么型号

了吗? have something in mind 意为"想到,考虑到"。例如:

We always have people's interest in mind. 我们始终考虑到群众的利益。

That's about the price range I had in mind. 这是我所能承受的价格限度。

2. What about this one? 这一台怎么样?

1) What about 用于提出建议,询问观点或征求意见,意为"…怎么样"。例如:

What about (going for) a walk with me? 跟我出去散散步怎么样?

What about your work? You can't leave it to your men. 你的工作怎么办? 你不能把它留给你的部下办吧?

2) one 表示前面已提到过的同种类的可数名词,承接同一个东西则要用 it。例如:

"Do you have a car?" "No, but my father has one. He bought it a few days ago."

如前面提到的名词是不可数名词时,应用形容词承接,不使用 one。例如:

I like red wine better than white.

3. the other 意为(两者之中的)另一个,(三者以上之中)剩下的要用 the others。例如:

He has two sons. One is short and the other is tall. 他有两个儿子,一个矮,另一个高。

Some of the boys went swimming, while the others sat on the beach for sun bathing. 一些男孩在游泳,其余的坐在沙滩上晒日光浴。

4. That one over there sells for ＄295. 那边一台售价 295 美元。此句中 sell 为不及物动词,意为"(以某价格)卖出"。再如:

The bicycle sells for ＄80. 这辆自行车售价 80 美元。

Apples are selling at a high price this year. 今年苹果售价高。

5. I'll take that one, I guess. 句中 guess 意为"想,认为"。例如:

I guess I'll have to go now. 我想我现在就得走了。

Grammar

形容词和副词的比较级和最高级
(The Comparison of Adjectives and Adverbs)

1. 构成：

   形容词和副词的比较级和最高级的构成方法有两种：一种是加后缀-er, -est；一种是在形容词前加副词 more, most。

   1) 单音节和少数双音节词(如以 y 结尾的)在后面加-er, -est。例如：

clean	cleaner	cleanest
small	smaller	smallest
tall	taller	tallest
fast	faster	fastest
long	longer	longest

   注意：

   ① 以-e 结尾的词直接加-r, -st。例如：

   | large | larger | largest |
   | late | later | latest |

   ② 闭音节单音节词末尾只有一个辅音字母要双写这个辅音字母，再加-er, -est。例如：

   | big | bigger | biggest |
   | hot | hotter | hottest |

   ③ 以"辅音＋y"结尾的词把 y 变成 i,再加-er, -est。例如：

easy	easier	easiest
busy	busier	busiest
happy	happier	happiest

   2) 大部分双音节词和所有多音节词,在前面加 more, most。例如：

   beautiful   more beautiful   most beautiful

interesting	more interesting	most interesting
important	more important	most important
clearly	more clearly	most clearly

3) 少数形容词和副词的比较级和最高级有特殊形式。例如：

well / good	better	best
ill / bad	worse	worst
much / many	more	most
little	less	least
far	farther（更远） / further（更进一步）	farthest / furthest
old	older / elder（年长的）	oldest / eldest

2. 用法：

1) 比较级一般用来表示"比…更…"，通常用 than 引起状语从句，说明与什么相比。例如：

Henry is taller than I (am). 亨利比我高。

The picture is clearer and brighter than the other one. 这幅画比另一幅画更清楚更明亮。

Sometimes they try to do something better, faster than anyone else (does). 有时他们努力比别人做得更好、更快。

More people will eat out in restaurants than they do at home today. 将来有更多的人到饭店吃饭，不会像现在这样在家里吃饭。

Tom works harder than we expected. 汤姆工作起来比我们想像的更卖力。

John smoked more expensive cigarettes than he could afford. 约翰抽的香烟其价钱之贵是他买不起的。

有时,由于比较的对象很清楚,因此可以不用带 than 结构。例如:
Are you feeling better? 你(比以前)感觉好点了吗?
Which is longer? 哪一个更长?
比较级前有时可以用表示程度的副词如 much, far, a lot, a little 等进行修饰。例如:
It's much/far/a lot/a little hotter today than it was yesterday. 今天比昨天热得多。
Non-stop flights(直达航班)from country to country will be much cheaper. 从一个国家到另一个国家的直达航班要便宜得多。

2) 使用最高级时,前面一般要用定冠词 the,同时要有相应的定语说明比较的范围。例如:
It is the most expensive one of all. 这是其中最贵的。
This is the most interesting film I've seen. 这是我们看过的最有趣的电影。
A lady in Massachusetts may have the world's easiest hobby: she lets her hair grow. 马萨诸塞州的一位女士可能有世界上最容易的爱好。她任头发自然生长。
Dalian is one of the most beautiful cities in the world. 大连是世界上最美丽的城市之一。
形容词最高级前有物主代词时不加 the。例如:
We are our own biggest enemies because we sometimes destroy(毁坏)our own good health. 我们是自己最大的敌人,因为我们有时损害自己的好身体。

Exercises

I. Choose the best answer a, b, c or d to these questions about the text.
　1) It is _____ for people with similar interest to become friends.
　　　a. strange　　　　　　　　b. easy

    c. difficult   d. unusual

2) Some people have _____ that are not shared by anybody else.
    a. hobbies   b. habits
    c. games   d. records

3) The Guinness Book is a book that records _____.
    a. everything in the world
    b. the best in the world
    c. the worst in the world
    d. world records

4) _____ set a new record by typing the numbers from one to one million.
    a. A teacher from California   b. A lady from Iowa
    c. A man from Pennsylvania   d. A musician from Connecticut

5) A lady may have the world's easiest hobby by _____.
    a. staying in the shower for nearly 100 hours
    b. letting her hair grow
    c. playing the piano for 45 days
    d. placing her name in the Guinness Book

6) _____ often form a club where they can talk about their hobbies.
    a. Those who have similar interests
    b. Those who share the same habits
    c. Those who enjoy breaking records
    d. Those who enjoy traveling great distances

7) "Records are made to be broken" means _____.
    a. Records are easily broken
    b. It is meaningless to make records
    c. It is unnecessary to break records
    d. New records may soon be broken

8) It is _____ who enjoy breaking the records made by Roger Guy English.
   a. young men
   b. young ladies
   c. gentlemen
   d. old men

II. **Match each word in Column A with a similar meaning in Column B.**

A	B
1) include	a. of the same kind
2) attend	b. at once
3) immediately	c. almost certainly
4) popular	d. to have as a part
5) similar	e. of a certain sort
6) probably	f. new, fresh
7) share	g. to go to, to be present at
8) late	h. not common
9) particular	i. to have (with others)
10) unusual	j. well-liked

III. A. **Fill in each blank with a different form of the word given in the bracket.**

1) People with similar interests often travel great distances to attend _____ (meet) where they can talk about their hobbies.

2) It is surprising that the _____ (music) can play the piano for forty-five days.

3) It is _____ (usual) to see snow in Hainan.

4) _____ (strange) immediately become friends if they share the same hobby.

5) _____ (probable) a man in Oregon was more than twice as clean after taking a shower that lasted two hundred hours.

B. Fill in each blank with a proper word according to the initial letter.

1) It's the most e_____ television set, but of course it's an e_____ one.

2) The boy is p_____ with girls. He is very amusing. (有情趣的)

3) The age r_____ is from 25 to 65 years.

4) The television set has the most c_____ controls and the most beautiful c_____.

5) He enjoys the c_____ of others who s_____ a s_____ interest.

C. Fill in the blanks with the words or expressions given below. Change the form where necessary.

enjoy the company	unusual	form	include
place	set	else	attend	travel great distances
in order to	probably	range	the same

1) I'm sure she will _____ a new world record at Sydney Olympic Games.

2) Usually people _____ of others who share similar interests.

3) Mary has such an _____ hobby that no one else can share it.

4) They have been working hard these days _____ pass the coming exam.

5) They often _____ to _____ meetings where they can talk about their hobbies.

6) Zhangjian's name has been _____ in the Guinness Book.

7) They planned to _____ a magic (魔术)club.

8) He has not been _____ person since his wife left him.

9) His interests _____ from soccer (足球) to chess (棋).

10) He can _____ tell us all the details (细节) we want.

11) Our tour party (旅游团) _____ several retired couples (退

28

休夫妇).

12) I've said I'm sorry. What _____ can I say?

IV. A. Given the comparative degree and the superlative degree of the following adjectives and adverbs.

large,   clear,   clearly,   bright,   big,   new,   late,
convenient, expensive, excellent,   beautiful, cheap,   ill,   good,
little,   badly,   interesting, hot,   pretty, busy, great

B. Make sentences after the given patterns.

1) Henry is taller than I.

   a. Tom, John, work, hard

   b. Her grammar, his, good

   c. This job, that one, interesting

2) Summer is hotter in Shanghai than in Beijing.

   a. Henry did well today, yesterday

   b. Days are short in winter, in summer

   c. He behaves (表现) badly this term, last term

3) This is a good TV set. It's the best one we have.

   a. This, a nice room, in the house

   b. This, a modern house, in town

   c. Star, a fast driver, I know

4) Dalian is one of the most beautiful cities in the world.

   a. She, pretty girls, I have ever met

   b. The Great Wall, magnificent (宏伟的) wonders, I have ever visited

   c. Maradona (马拉多纳), great football players, in the world

V. A. Rewrite the following sentences after the model.

Model 1: A lady from Iowa typed the numbers from one to one million for six years.

29

→A lady from Iowa <u>spent</u> six years <u>typing</u> the numbers from one to one million.

1) I read and fished during my summer vacation.
2) The whole morning he tried to solve the math problem.
3) Victor's brother collects butterflies (蝴蝶) during most of his free time.
4) The teacher talked about the story in class for two hours yesterday morning.

Model 2: Other people have unusual hobbies. No one else can share them.

→Other people have <u>such</u> unusual hobbies <u>that</u> no one else can share them.

1) It was a cold dark night. Nobody was out on the streets.
2) It was a difficult task. They didn't know what to do.
3) It is a good chance. We mustn't miss it.
4) They're friendly people. We really enjoyed ourselves.

B. Answer the following questions, using no one else, someone else, something else, somewhere else.

Model: Can anyone share such unusual hobbies?

→ No, no one else can share them.

1) Are you going to watch <u>the football game</u> on TV?
2) Is <u>the old man</u> going to Beijing.
3) Did you go <u>home</u> after the dinner party?
4) Does <u>any one</u> know the truth?

VI. Translation.

A. From Chinese to English.

1) 有着相同爱好的人很容易结成朋友。
2) 整个寒假期间他除了走亲访友之外(besides visiting friends and

retatives),都是看看书或者是吹吹笛子。

3) 我父母喜欢吃完饭以后出去散步。(enjoy)
4) 他的爱好非常特别,以至于无人能与他分享。
5) 为了通过英语考试,他比以前用功多了。
6) 她是我所碰到过的最勤奋的(diligent)女孩子。

B. From English to Chinese.

1) You should not spend hours (in) watching TV. It takes too much of your time.
2) There is such a long line at the cinema that we have to wait before we can get into it.
3) Probably the cleanest people in the world are two young women from England who stayed in the shower for over ninety-eight hours.
4) TV sets sell at a higher price than tape recorders.
5) She didn't attend her classes. She was ill in bed.
6) I'm very happy. I have been included in the football team.

Passage Reading

The World's Greatest Wonders

Three men traveling on a train began a conversation about the world's greatest wonders.

"In my opinion," the first man said, "the Egyptian pyramids are the world's greatest wonder. Although they were built thousands of years ago, they are still standing. And remember: the people who built them had only simple tools. They did not have the kind of machinery that builders and engineers have today."

"I agree that Egyptian pyramids are wonderful," the second man said, "but I do not think they are the greatest wonder. I believe computers are more wonderful than the pyramids. They have taken people to the moon and brought them back safely. They carry out mathematical calculations in seconds that would take a person a hundred years to do."

He turned to the third man and asked, "What do you think is the greatest wonder in the world?"

The third man thought for a long time, then he said, "Well, I agree that the pyramids are wonderful, and I agree that computers are wonderful, too. However, in my opinion, the most wonderful thing in the world is this thermos."

And he took a thermos out of his bag and held it up.

The other two men were very surprised. "A thermos!" they exclaimed. "But that's a simple thing."

"Oh no, it's not," the third man said. "In the winter you put in a hot drink and it stays hot. In the summer you put in a cold drink and it stays cold. How does the thermos know whether it is winter or summer?"

New Words & Expressions

wonder ['wʌndə] n. 奇迹
opinion [ə'pinjən] n. 观点
Egyptian [i'dʒipʃən] adj. 埃及的
Egypt ['i:dʒipt] n. 埃及
pyramid ['pirəmid] n. 金字塔
although [ɔ:l'ðou] conj. 虽然
stand [stænd] vi. 站立
remember [ri'membə] vt. 记得
simple [simpl] adj. 简单的
tool [tu:l] n. 工具
kind [kaind] n. 种类

machinery [mə'ʃi:nəri] n. 机器
builder ['bildə] n. 建设者
agree [ə'gri:] vt., vi. 同意
safely ['seifli] adv. 安全地
mathematical [ˌmæθə'mætikəl] adj. 数学的
calculation [ˌkælkju'leiʃən] n. 计算
second ['sekənd] n. 秒
hold [hould] (held, held) vt. 拿着,握住
  hold up 举起,展示
surprise [sə'praiz] vt. 使吃惊

exclaim [iks'kleim] *vi*. 惊叫
hot [hɔt] *adj*. 热的

whether ['weðə] *conj*. 是否

Notes to the Passage

1. Three men traveling on a train began a conversation about the world's greatest wonders. 三个乘坐火车旅行的人开始谈起世界上最伟大的奇迹。句中 traveling on a train 为现在分词短语作定语修饰 three men。
2. in one's opinion 意为"按某人的观点,依某人的意见"。
   In his opinion, computers are the most wonderful things in the world. 依他之见,计算机是世界上最奇妙的东西。
3. Although they were built thousands of years ago, they are still standing. 虽然他们(埃及金字塔)建于几千年前,他们仍然挺立着。although 意为"尽管,虽然",作连词引导让步状语从句。
4. They carry out mathematical calculations in seconds that would take a person a hundred years to do. 他们(计算机)在几秒钟之内完成了一个人需要100年才能完成的数学计算。
   1) carry out 意为"完成,进行,实现"。例如:
      Can you carry out this plan? 你能实现这一计划吗?
   2) that 引导的是一个定语从句,修饰 mathematical calculations。that 本身又在定语从句中起主语作用,代表 to do mathematical calculations。
   3) 注意"take +时间名词"的用法,请看例句:
      This letter has taken two weeks to get there. 这封信花了两个星期才寄到那儿。
      They took all day to travel ten miles. 他们走十英里花了一整天时间。
      It has taken me all the evening to do my homework. 我花了整整一晚上的时间做家庭作业。

注意 take 和 spend 的区别。后两句可改成：

They spent all day traveling ten miles.

I have spent all the evening doing homework.

5. "In the winter you put in a hot drink and it stays hot."冬天你倒进热饮,热饮还保热。

1) put in 意为"放入"。例如：

Put your hand in and see what's in the box.把手放进去看看盒子里有什么。

2) stay 意为"保持",作系动词,后接形容词。例如：

Try to stay calm.尽量保持冷静。

Answer the questions according to the passage.

1. How did the travelers pass（消磨）their time on the train?
2. Why did the first man think that the Egyptian pyramids are the world's greatest wonder?
3. For what did the second man think that computers were more wonderful than the pyramids?
4. What did the third man think was the most wonderful thing? Why?
5. Do you think that the third man is very clever?

Unit 3

Text

Setting a Trap

(Part I)

One day during the holidays a group of boys decided to set a trap for a thief. There had been several thefts in their neighbourhood. Wallets, transistor radios, jewellery and other small things had mysteriously disap-

35

peared from several houses during the day-time. Nobody had seen the thief and nobody knew how to prevent the thefts from continuing.

It was then that the boys decided to turn detectives. They agreed to watch their group of houses from some nearby trees. They found a suitable tree and started to keep a record of the people who called at each house.

On the fourth day some money was stolen from a handbag in one of the houses. The boys took out their list and found that five people had called at the house but that only two had entered it: a family friend and a man who said he came from the Electricity Company to check the wiring.

"He must be the thief," said David, "There's nothing wrong with the wiring in our house. Shall I ask Father to see whether the Electricity Company did send a man?"

"No," said Peter. "Let's try to catch him ourselves. At least we know who to watch for now."

Two days later, David, Peter and John were nearly asleep as they sat up in their tree on a hot afternoon. They woke up excitedly when they saw a uniformed man approach Peter's house.

"I think that's the same man," said John. "What shall we do?"

The boys got down from the tree and ran to hide behind a hedge outside Peter's house.

"We must get a good look at his face," said Peter. "We can't do anything more. We don't know for sure whether he is the thief."

New Words & Expressions

set [set] *vt*. 设置
trap [træp] *n*. 圈套, 陷阱
several ['sevrəl] *adj*. 几个的

theft [θeft] *n*. 行窃, 偷窃的事例
wallet ['wɔlit] *n*. 钱夹, 皮夹
transistor [træn'sistə] *n*. 晶体管

jewellery, jewelry(美) ['dʒuːəlri] n. 珠宝(总称)
mysteriously [mis'tiəriəsli] adv. 神秘地,难理解地
disappear [ˌdisə'piə] vi. 不见,消失
day-time ['deitaim] n. 白天
nobody ['noubədi] prop. 没有人
prevent [pri'vent] vt. 阻止,预防
detective [di'tektiv] n. 侦探
nearby ['niəbai] adj. 附近的
　　　　　　　　　adv. 在附近
suitable ['sjuːtəbl] adj. 适合的,适宜的
keep a record of 将…记录下来
call at 造访
each [iːtʃ] pron., adj. 每一(个)
steal [stiːl] vt. 偷
handbag ['hændbæɡ] n. 手提袋
list [list] n. 名单表

electricity [iˌlek'trisiti] n. 电,电学
check [tʃek] vt. 检查
wiring ['waiəriŋ] n. 接线,配线工程
nothing ['nʌθiŋ] prop. 没有东西,没有什么
at least 至少
nearly ['niəli] adv. 几乎
asleep [ə'sliːp] adj. 睡着
excitedly [ik'saitidli] adv. 兴奋地
uniformed ['juːnifɔːmd] adj. 穿制服或军服的
approach [ə'proutʃ] vt. 走近,靠近
hide [haid] vi. 躲藏
hedge [hedʒ] n. 树篱(用于田地、花园周围)
sure [ʃuə] adj. 确信的
　for sure 确实,毫无疑问地

Proper Names

David ['deivid] (人名)大卫
Peter ['piːtə] (人名)彼得
John [dʒɔn] (人名)约翰

Notes to the Text

1. day-time 是个复合名词,由名词+名词构成。再如:letter-box 信箱,sea-bird 海鸟,baby-sitter (代人临时)照看婴孩者,ice-cream 冰淇淋等。
2. Nobody had seen the thief and nobody knew how to prevent the thefts from continuing. 没有人见过那个贼,也没有人知道如何阻止这类

37

偷盗行为再度发生。

1) 注意 V. + 疑问词 + to do 结构。再如：

I don't know what/which/whom to choose. 我不知道选择什么/哪一个/谁。

I wondered how/when/where to get in touch with them. 我不知道如何/何时/在何地同他们联系。

2) prevent 是阻止、妨碍、预防的意思，常用于 prevent sb/sth from doing 结构中，意为"阻止某人做某事，预防某事发生"。例如：

Nobody can prevent him from getting married. 没人能够阻止他结婚。

Something must be done to prevent the disease from spreading. 必须采取措施阻止这种疾病的蔓延。

3. It was then that the boys decided to turn detectives. 就在那时孩子们决定当一回侦探。

1) 句中 turn 相当于 become。例如：

The football player turned author later. 那位足球运动员后来当了作家。

2) It is (was)...that (who)是强调句型。被强调部分可以是主语、宾语或状语。例如：

I met Mary in the park yesterday.

→It was I who met Mary in the park yesterday.（强调主语）

→It was Mary whom I met in the park yesterday.（强调宾语）

→It was in the park that I met Mary yesterday.（强调地点状语）

→It was yesterday that I met Mary in the park.（强调时间状语）

4. They agreed to watch their group of houses from some nearby trees. 他们一致同意从附近的几棵树上监视他们的房屋群。agree to do sth 意为"同意做某事"。例如：

They agreed to leave at once. 他们同意立刻动身。注意 agree 的其他一些用法：

1) agree 用在二人或二人以上的情况下，表示他们之间想法一致。

例如：
>The students agreed. 同学们想法一致。

2）agree with + a person 表示"同意另一个人的意见"。例如：
>I hope you will agree with me. 我希望你会同意我的意见。

3）agree on + a noun. 表示"对某件事情表示赞同"。例如：
>We finally agreed on the plan. 最后我们都同意了这个计划。

4）agree that 表示"同意做某事，或一致认为某事要发生"。例如：
>They agreed that they should ask him. 他们都赞成去问问他。

5. keep a record of the people who called at each house 记下造访每一栋房子的人。call at a place 造访、拜访某地。例如：
I called at Mr. Green's house. 我曾到格林先生的府上拜访。
也可以说 call on somebody 拜访某人。例如：
I called on Mr. Green. 我拜访了格林先生。

6. ... but that only two had entered it: a family friend and a man who said he had come from the Electricity Company to check the wiring. 但是仅有两人进入了房间：一个是家人的朋友，还有一位自称是来检查线路的电力公司的人。

7. "He must be the thief." 他一定是那个贼。情态动词 must 表示推测时，暗含有很大的可能性。例如：
He must be ill. He looks so pale. 他一定是病了。他的脸色苍白。
It must be late as the streets are deserted. 时间一定很晚了，街上已空无一人。
表示这个意义时，must 仅用于肯定句，不能用于疑问句或否定句。

8. They woke up excitedly when they saw a uniformed man approach Peter's house. 当他们看到一个穿制服的家伙朝彼得家走去时，睡意顿失，立刻兴奋了起来。
注意：see somebody do something 意为"看到某人做某事"。用不定式 do something 表示动作的全过程。
而 see somebody doing something 意为"看到某人正在做某事"。用

doing something 强调动作正在进行。试比较：

I saw him cross the street. 我看见他横穿马路。

I saw him crossing the street. 我看见他正在过马路。

9. We don't know for sure whether he is the thief. 我们不敢肯定他就是那个贼。

   1) for sure 确定，相当于 for certain。例如：

      I can't say for sure that he is good or not. 我不确知他是好是坏。

   2) whether 意为"是否"，可引导状语从句。例如：

      He asked me whether she was coming. 他问我她是否要来。

Dialogue

Was the Exam Difficult?

A: Hey, Maria! Have you finished your exam?

B: Yes, I have.

A: Was it difficult?

B: Well, it was quite hard.

A: Did you pass?

B: I don't know...she didn't tell me.

A: What questions?

B: First, she asked me what my name was.

A: That was easy, wasn't it?

B: ...then she asked me where I came from, and how long I'd been studying at the school?

A: ...and what else did she ask?

B: She asked when I had begun studying English, and she asked how I would use English in the future.

A: Go on...

B: Then she asked me if I liked the school, and if I lived with my parents.
A: Anything else?
B: Oh, Victor! I'm trying to remember... oh, yes! She asked if I spoke any other languages.
A: Is that all?
B: Oh, there were a lot of other questions. She asked me what my hobbies were, and she asked me to tell her about them. Then she gave me a picture and asked me to describe it. Oh, and then I was asked to read a passage.
A: What did she say at the end?
B: Ah! She asked me to tell you to go in... immediately.

New Words & Expressions

finish ['finiʃ] vt. 完成
exam [ig'zæm] n. 考试
difficult ['difikəlt] adj. 困难的
pass [pɑːs] vt., vi. (考试等)合格，通过
question ['kwestʃən] n. 问题
ask [ɑːsk] vt. 提问
easy ['iːzi] adj. 容易的

how long 多久
study ['stʌdi] vt., vi. 学习
if [if] conj. 是否，如果
describe [dis'kraib] vt. 描述，描写
passage ['pæsidʒ] n. (文章的)一段，一节
at the end 最后

Proper Name

Maria [mə'riə] (人名) 玛丽亚

Notes to the Dialogue

1. What questions? 相当于 What questions did she ask? 她都问了哪些问题？

2. Then she gave me a picture and asked me to describe it. Oh, and then I was asked to read a passage. 接下来她给了我一张图画让我描述，然后又让我读了一段。

Grammar

一、过去完成时(The Past Perfect Tense)

表示过去某时前已经发生的动作或情况要用过去完成时，其形式是 had + 动词过去分词。例句：

Before daybreak we had already wiped out all the enemy troops. 在拂晓前我们已经将敌人全部消灭。

By the end of June they had finished all the work. 到六月底他们已经完成了所有工作。

When I got there it had already stopped raining. 我到那里时雨已经停了。

I hadn't learned any French before I came here. 我来这之前没学过法语。

以上例句中都有明显的时间状语，但在多数情况下，时间是通过上下文表示出来的。这时过去完成时表示的动作较另一过去的动作先发生。例句：

The boys found that five people had called at the house. 孩子们发现有五个人曾造访过这间屋子。

Wallets, transistor radios, jewellery and other small things had mysteriously disappeared from several houses during the day-time. 几间屋子里的钱夹、晶体管收音机、珠宝和一些小东西大白天就神秘地消失了。

二、不定式(The Infinitive)

1. 不定式的形式

   不定式有两种形式：一种是带 to 的不定式,一种是不带 to 的不定式。

2. 不定式的功用

   不定式在句中可以做主语、表语、宾语、定语、同位语、状语、补语。

   1) 用作主语,例如：

      <u>To see</u> is to believe. 百闻不如一见。

      It's important <u>to be responsible for your own acts.</u> 为自己的行为负责很重要。

   2) 用作表语,例如：

      The important thing is <u>to save the girl's life.</u> 救小女孩的命要紧。

   3) 用作宾语,例如：

      A group of boys decided <u>to set a trap for a thief.</u> 一群男孩决定为小偷设置一个陷阱。

      They agreed <u>to watch their group of houses from some nearby trees.</u> 他们同意从附近的几棵树上监视他们的房屋群。

      Nobody knew how <u>to prevent the thefts from continuing.</u> 没人知道如何防止偷窃继续发生。

      At least we know <u>who to watch for now.</u> 至少我们现在知道监视谁了。

   4) 用作定语,例如：

      The next train <u>to arrive</u> was from New York. 下一列火车是从纽约开来的。

      I have nothing <u>to say</u> on this question. 关于这个问题我无话可说。

   5) 用作同位语,例如：

      He gave the order to start the attack. 他发出攻击的命令。

   6) 用作状语

a) 表目的，例如：

He came from the Electricity Company <u>to check the wiring</u>. 他来自电气公司,是来检查线路的。

The boys ran <u>to hide behind a hedge outside Peter's house</u>. 孩子们奔跑着躲到了彼德家外面的篱笆后面。

b) 表原因，例如：

I trembled <u>to think of it.</u> 我想起那件事就不寒而栗。

c) 表结果，例如：

He lifted the rock only <u>to drop it on his own feet.</u> 他搬起石头砸了自己的脚。

7) 用作宾语补语，例如：

The manager told him <u>to watch people carefully</u> because some thief was taking things from their shop. 经理要他密切注视着人们，因为小偷在偷商店里的东西。

后面可带 to do 作宾语补语的动词还有 ask, request, order, want 等。

有些动词后用作宾语补足语的不定式通常不带 to，这种动词分两类，一类是感觉动词，如 feel, see, hear 等，例如：

I saw him <u>cross</u> the street. 我看见他横穿马路。

She saw me <u>lean</u> over to talk to the girl. 她看见我斜过身和那女孩讲话。

另一类是使役动词，如 make, let, have 等，例如：

Let him <u>do</u> it. 让他做吧。

They made the girl <u>go to bed</u> early. 他们让小女孩早点去睡觉。

Exercises

I. Answer the following questions according to the text.

1) What did a group of boys decide to do one day during the holidays?

2) What had happened in their neighbourhood?

3) Had anybody seen the thief? Did anyone know how to prevent the thefts from continuing?

4) What did the boys do to prevent the thefts from continuing?

5) What happened on the fourth day?

6) Was there anything wrong with the wiring of the house?

7) Why were the boys suspicious (怀疑) of the man in uniform?

8) Where did they hide themselves after they got down from the trees?

II. Match each word in Column A with a similar meaning in Column B.

A	B
1) trap	a. go out of sight
2) mysterious	b. right for the purpose
3) detective	c. a clever trick (计谋)
4) disappear	d. stop
5) suitable	e. the act of stealing
6) nearly	f. full of mystery
7) check	g. come nearer to
8) prevent	h. person who finds criminals (犯罪分子)
9) approach	i. examine
10) theft	j. almost

III. A. Fill in each blank with a different form of the word given in the bracket.

1) There have been a number of _____ (thief) in the area.

2) Are there any schools in the _____ (neighbour).

3) We're hoping to find a _____ (suit) hotel.

4) They were nearly _____ (sleep) as they sat up in the tree.

5) "We'll cut off (切断) the _____ (electric) if you don't pay

the bill," said the man.

B. Fill in the blanks with the words or expressions given below. Change the form where necessary.

keep a record of	call at	come from	wake up
for sure	take out	prevent...from	set a trap
turn	nearby	approach	suitable

1) _____ any money you pay out.
2) She _____ a handkerchief and blew her nose.
3) The passage she quoted (引用) _____ Dickens.
4) James usually _____ early.
5) I don't know _____ whether he is the liar (说谎的人).
6) As they _____ the wood, a rabbit ran out of the trees.
7) The boys _____ for the thief.
8) Jane has a back injury (背部受伤) that may _____ her _____ playing in tomorrow's game.
9) Why don't you _____ my house when you are in Dalian.
10) That famous actor _____ politician (政客) at last.
11) We're hoping to find a _____ hotel to stay in.
12) Is there a shop _____ where I can buy some batteries (电池)?

IV. Complete the sentence in past perfect tense.

Model: Did Mr. and Mrs. Jone drive to the beach last weekend?
　　　　No. They had just driven to the beach the weekend before.

1) Did Mr. and Mrs. Henderson see a movie last Saturday night?
　_____ the night before.
2) Did Jeff sit out yesterday evening?
　_____ the evening before.
3) Did you and your friend have a picnic last Saturday?

_____ the Sunday before.

4) Did Henry give a party last weekend?

_____ the weekend before.

5) Did you go window-shopping last Saturday?

_____ the day before.

6) Did Gregory take a geography (地理) course last year?

_____ the year before.

V. A. **Rewrite the following sentences, using "It is (was) ... that (who)..."**

1) <u>Freda</u> phoned Jack last night.

2) <u>A group of boys</u> decided to set a trap for a thief.

3) There had been several thefts <u>in their neighborhood.</u>

4) Wallets and other small things had mysteriously disappeared from several houses <u>during the day-time.</u>

5) <u>Then</u> he quickly took a piece of wet red meat and hit the man in the face with it.

6) The manager told him to watch people carefully <u>because some thief was taking things from their shop.</u>

7) I called on <u>Mr. Green</u> yesterday.

8) <u>Three minutes later,</u> Alfred saw him coming to the door.

B. **Rewrite the following after the model.**

Model: Nobody knew how they could prevent the thefts from continuing.

Nobody knew how to prevent the thefts from continuing.

1) I asked how I could get to the station.

2) She told me what I should do.

3) We are wondering where we shall go.

4) He wanted to know when he would attend the meeting.

47

C. **Explain how the infinitive phrase function in each sentence.**

1) It's my duty <u>to help you.</u>
2) I leaned over <u>to find out that she wanted a pen.</u>
3) The problem is <u>to find a solution.</u>
4) She tried <u>to ask me if I had an extra pen.</u>
5) I can't afford <u>to buy a car.</u>
6) I'm sorry <u>to hear that.</u>
7) It's impossible <u>to get everything ready in time.</u>
8) She was the first person <u>to think of the idea.</u>
9) They came over <u>to welcome the guests.</u>
10) What decided him <u>to give up the job?</u>

VI. **Translation.**

A. **From Chinese to English.**

1) 孩子们决定阻止偷盗行为再次发生。
2) 他们藏在一棵树上,开始记录拜访每一户的人。
3) 没人确切知道他出了什么事。
4) 他一定是病了,你知道怎样与他取得联系(get in touch with)吗?
5) 当他们看到有一个陌生人走近他们设置的陷阱时,他们兴奋不已。
6) 大卫醒来时发现有两人进入了房间。

B. **From English to Chinese.**

1) There had been several thefts in their neighbourhood.
2) I had meant to come, but something happened.
3) I know one person who won't be happy with the decision, that's for sure.
4) Two days later, the boys were nearly asleep as they sat up in their tree on a hot afternoon.

5) They woke up excitedly when they saw the tiger.
6) The boys got down from the tree and ran to hide behind a hedge outside Peter's house.

Passage Reading

Setting a Trap

(Part II)

The boys did not have long to wait. Peter had hardly finished speaking when they heard a shout from inside the house, and the uniformed man came running out. Behind him came Peter's father, shouting angrily, "Stop, thief!"

"Jump on him when I shout 'now!'" Peter said quickly. "Here he comes. Now!"

As the man ran out, the three boys jumped on him and dragged him to the ground. There was a short struggle in which the boys sometimes hit the man and sometimes hit one another in their excitement. Then Peter's father arrived. He pulled the man up and searched him swiftly.

"I thought so!" he exclaimed. "My wallet! You can explain to the police how that got into your pocket."

Peter's father telephoned for the police, and the man was soon taken away. "We know him very well," said the inspector. "He doesn't work for the Electricity Company and never has worked for it. This is a favourite trick of his so that he can get into people's house. You boys have done a good job catching him."

"You certainly have!" agreed Peter's father. "I was dozing in the chair when he slipped in and stole my wallet. Something woke me up just as he was going out. Well, we shan't see him again for a long time."

New Words & Expressions

hardly ['hɑːdli] adv. 几乎不
inside [in'said] prep. 在…里边
drag [dræg] vt. 拖,拽
struggle ['strʌgl] n. 搏斗
sometimes ['sʌmtaimz] adv. 有时
another [ə'nʌðə] pron., adj. 另一个
  one another 互相
excitement [ik'saitmənt] n. 兴奋

pull [pul] vt. 拉
swiftly ['swiftli] adv. 敏捷地
inspector [in'spektə] n. (英)警察巡官
favourite ['feivərit] adj. 最喜欢的
trick [trik] n. 计谋
doze [douz] vi. 打瞌睡,打盹
slip [slip] vi. 悄悄移动,潜行

Notes to the Passage

1. The boys did not have long to wait. 孩子们等了不一会儿。这里 long 是名词化的形容词,表示"长时间"。
2. Peter had hardly finished speaking when they heard a shout from inside the house, and the uniformed man came running out. 彼德的话音刚落就听到房子里传来喊声,那个穿制服的家伙跑了出来。

  1) hardly...when... 一…就…,例如:
    We had hardly got there when it began to rain. 我们刚到那儿就下起雨来。
    使用这种结构,主句往往要用过去完成时。注意:如果将 hardly 置于句首,则后面的主谓语要倒装。如上句话可改为:Hardly had we got there when it began to rain.
    表示这一含义的结构还有 no sooner...than..., scarcely...before...等。

  2) finish + doing something 表示"完成做某事"。例如:
    I haven't finished reading the book yet. 我还没有看完这本书。

3) from inside the house 是介词+介词短语结构,再如:
   from under the table 从桌子底下
   from near the school 从学校附近
4) running out 是分词短语作伴随状语,例如:
   He stood on the step, reading the book. 他站在台阶上看书。
3. Behind him came Peter's father. 彼德的父亲跟在他后面跑了出来。注意介词短语置于句首时,主谓要采用完全倒装。例如:
   From the distance came occasional(偶尔的) shots. 远处偶尔传来枪声。
   After the meeting came a banquet(宴会) in the hall. 在会议之后,大厅内举行了宴会。
4. You boys have done a good job catching him. 你们这群孩子干的漂亮,逮住了他。

Which of the following statements about the text are true or false? Write T for true and F for false.

(　)1. After a long time, the boys saw the man come running out.
(　)2. They jumped on the man and dragged him to the ground as the man ran out.
(　)3. They found the wallet in the man's pocket.
(　)4. Peter's father let him go after he had taken back the wallet.
(　)5. The man was working for the Electricity Company.
(　)6. The man slipped in when Peter's father was sleeping.

Unit 4

Text

The Great Pyramid

(Part I)

The kings of ancient Egypt planned strong tombs to keep their bodies safe after death and to hold their treasures. Over these tombs huge stone pyramids were built. There are over 80 known pyramids in Egypt, but the Great Pyramid is the largest of all.

The Great Pyramid was built thousands of years ago for a king called

Khufu. It is located on the west bank of the Nile River not far from Cairo. In fact, all the pyramids along the Nile are on its west bank. The ancient Egyptians compared the rising of the sun to the beginning of life and the setting of the sun to the end of life. This is why their dead were buried on the west bank of the Nile.

It's very hard to realize just how big the Great Pyramid is. It has over 2,300,000 blocks of solid stone. These huge stone blocks weigh an average of two and a half tons each, as much as a small car. Some even weigh fifteen tons. Without machinery, the ancient Egyptians cut and moved and lifted each of these stones. Many of the blocks came from the east bank of the Nile, and they were taken across the river in boats at flood time. It took more than 100,000 slaves twenty years to build the Great Pyramid.

The Great Pyramid is over 450 feet high today, and it was once higher. Its base covered thirteen acres. Each of the sides of the pyramid is 755 feet long, or about as long as two city blocks. It takes about twenty minutes to walk all the way around the pyramid.

New Words & Expressions

king [kiŋ] n. 国王
ancient ['einʃənt] adj. 古代的, 远古的
strong [strɔŋ] adj. 坚固的
tomb [tu:m] n. 坟, 墓
body ['bɔdi] n. 尸体
safe [seif] adj. 安全的
treasure ['treʒə] n. 金银, 财富
huge [hju:dʒ] adj. 巨大的
known [noun] adj. 著名的

locate [lou'keit] vt. 在…地点设置
   be located on/in 位于
west [west] n. 西方, 西面
bank [bæŋk] n. 河岸
compare [kəm'pɛə] vt. 比较
   compare…to 把…比做
rise [raiz] vi. 升起
rising ['raiziŋ] n. 升起
beginning [bi'giniŋ] n. 开始

set [set] *vi*. 落下
setting ['setiŋ] *n*. 落下
dead [ded] *adj*. 死亡的
bury ['beri] *vt*. 掩埋
realize ['riəlaiz] *vt*. 完全了解，了解
block [blɔk] *n*. (木、石等之)大块
solid ['sɔlid] *adj*. 固体的
weigh [wei] *vt*. 称…的重量
average ['ævəridʒ] *n*., *adj*. 平均，平均的
ton [tʌn] *n*. 吨

without [wið'aut] *prep*. 没有
lift [lift] *vt*. 举起，托起
boat [bout] *n*. 小船
flood [flʌd] *n*. 洪水
slave [sleiv] *n*. 奴隶
foot [fut] *n*. (复 feet [fi:t])英尺
base [beis] *n*. 根基，底面
cover ['kʌvə] *vt*. 遮蔽…的表面，遮盖
acre ['eikə] *n*. 英亩
side [said] *n*. 边，面

Proper Names

the Great Pyramid 大金字塔
the Nile [nail] River (非洲)尼罗河
Khufu [ku:f] (人名)胡佛
Cairo ['kaiərou] (埃及)开罗

Notes to the Text

1. The kings of ancient Egypt planned strong tombs to keep their bodies safe after death and to hold their treasure. 古埃及的历任帝王设计建造了坚固的坟墓用以在他们死后保存尸体和财富。

   1) plan 在这句当中是"设计"的意思 例如：
      plan a house / garden 设计一座房子/ 花园
   2) keep their bodies safe 使尸体保存完好。keep + n. + 形容词/现在分词/过去分词，意为"使某人或某物保持某种状态"。例如：
      This coat will keep you warm. 这件外套可以使你暖和。
      I'll try not to keep you waiting. 我尽量不让你等待。

Please keep the window closed. 请让窗户关着。

2. There are over 80 known pyramids in Egypt. 在埃及有 80 多个著名的金字塔。

   1) over 意为"more than"。再如：

   Over forty people were at the party. 有四十多人参加了聚会。

   I have been waiting for you over an hour. 我已经等了你一个多小时了。

   2) known 意为"著名的、众所周知的"，再如：

   a known actor 一个著名演员

   a known holiday resort 一个著名的度假胜地

3. The Great Pyramid was built thousands of years ago for a king called Khufu. 大金字塔是数千年前为一个叫胡佛的国王建造的。过去分词短语 called Khufu 作 king 的定语。（关于过去分词的用法请参见第十三单元语法部分）

4. It is located on the west bank of the Nile River not far from Cairo. 它位于尼罗河西岸,离开罗不远。

5. The ancient Egyptians compared the rising of the sun to the beginning of life and the setting of the sun to the end of life. 古埃及人把日出比做生命的诞生而把日落比做生命的终结。compare... to.. 意为"把…比做"。如：

   Poets have compared sleep to death. 诗人把睡眠比做死亡。

6. This is why their dead were buried on the west bank of the Nile. 这就是为什么他们的尸体被埋在了尼罗河的西岸。

   1) why 引导的是一个名词从句,在句中作表语。（关于名词从句请参见第七、八单元）dead 意为"死去的人"。这种现象就是形容词的名词化。再如：

   Birds feed their *young* on insects. 鸟儿用虫子喂幼鸟。

   After a storm comes a *calm*. 风暴过后是一片宁静。

   2) 有些形容词可以和冠词连用表示一类人或物,如：the deaf 聋子,

the blind 盲人, the poor 穷人。

7. It is very hard to realize just how big the Great Pyramid is. 要知道大金字塔有多大是很难的。

8. These huge stone blocks weigh an average of two and a half tons each. 这些巨大的石块平均每个重达 2.5 吨。each 置于句尾时，其前面的宾语必须有具体的数量。如：

   He gave us two books each. 他给我们每人两本书。不能说：He gave us books each.

   注意 each 在下面句子中的作用：

   1) **Each** of the players signed his name as he came in. 每一名运动员进门时都签了名。(主语)

   2) **Each** player signed his name as he came in.（定语）

   3) The players **each** signed their names as they came in.（同位语）

9. It took more than 100,000 slaves twenty years to build the Great Pyramid. 建造这座大金字塔动用了十多万奴隶，花了整整二十年的时间。

   It takes (somebody) sometime to do (something) 某人做某事花费多少时间。例如：

   It takes about 20 minutes to walk all the way around the pyramid. 绕金字塔走一圈要用大约 20 分钟时间。

   It took me three hours to finish the homework. 我用了三个小时的时间才做完作业。

10. .... and it was once higher = it was once higher than it is.（过去）曾比现在高。

Dialogue

Visiting a Museum

A: Ah, good. You made it.

B: Yes. It was a bit of rush, though.

A: The museum looks very modern.

B: I really want to see the Fire of London exhibit.

A: What's that?

B: A model of London. You can see what it looked like before and after the Great Fire.

A: Fine. Say, it's very well laid out.

B: Yes. Look, let's leave these things for the moment and see the Fire exhibit first.

A: No, I'm going to take my time. There are so many things to look at. You go ahead.

B: All right. You start here in Roman times and work your way through history as you walk around. See you later. Bye.

New Words & Expressions

rush [rʌʃ] *n.* 仓促,匆忙
though [ðou] *adv.*, *conj.* 尽管,虽然
modern ['mɔdən] *adj.* 现代化的
exhibit [ig'zibit] *n.* 展品

lay out 布局,布置
moment ['moumənt] *n.* 片刻
history ['histəri] *n.* 历史

Proper Name

Roman Times 罗马时代

Notes to the Dialogue

1. You made it. 你总算按时到了。make it 是口语中常用的表达法,意为"及时抵达,赶上"。例如:

There is some time before the train leaves. I think we shall make it if we hurry. 离火车开车还有些时间,我想如果抓紧,我们能赶上。

2. a bit of rush, though. 只是时间紧张了点。

3. You can see what it looked like before and after the Great Fire. 你可以看到大火前后伦敦是什么样子。

4. say 引起话头,以引起注意。如:
   Say, haven't I seen you before somewhere? 喂,我以前是不是在什么地方见过你?

5. Let's leave these things for the moment and ... 眼下先别看这些…

6. No, I'm going to take my time. 不,我要慢慢地看。take one's time 不匆忙,不急,慢慢来。如:
   Take your time over the job, and do it well. 这工作慢慢做,把它做好。

7. You go ahead. 您请吧。go ahead 意为"先请,请"。

8. ... and work your way through history as you walk around. 你边走边回顾历史吧。work one's way through 努力完成或获得;as you walk around 是时间状语从句。

Grammar

被动语态(The Passive Voice)

英语有两种语态:主动语态和被动语态。

当主语是动作的执行者时,其谓语形式称为主动语态;当主语是动作的承受者时,其谓语形式称为被动语态。

主动语态:The ancient Egyptian built the Great Pyramid thousands of years ago. 数千年前古埃及人建造了大金字塔。

被动语态:The Great Pyramid was built by the ancient Egyptian thousands of years ago. 大金字塔是数千年前由古埃及人建造的。

被动语态常由助动词 be 加及物动词的过去分词形式构成。可以有不同的时态。各种时态的被动形式见下表：

	一般时态	进行时态	完成时态
现在	am / is / are } invited	am / is / are } being invited	has / have } been invited
过去	was / were } invited	was / were } being invited	had been invited
将来	shall / will } be invited		shall / will } have been invited

含有情态动词的被动语态，其结构是"情态动词 + be + 过去分词"。如：

What's been done <u>cannot be undone.</u> 覆水难收。

These stairs are very dangerous. They <u>should be repaired.</u> 这楼梯很危险，应该修理了。

被动语态的使用：

1) 当我们不知道或没必要知道动作的执行者时。如：

   Over these tombs huge stone pyramids were built. 石头砌成的巨大的金字塔就被建在这些坟墓的上面。

   Two people were killed in the accident. 有两人死于车祸。

2) 当我们强调或侧重动作的承受者时。如：

   She is liked by everybody. 她为人人所喜欢。

   The Great Pyramid was built thousands of years ago. 大金字塔是数千年前建造的。

3) 当我们出于礼貌避免说出动作执行者时。如：

   Where can you be reached? 哪里可以和你接头？（避免说出"我"）

   You will be contacted. 会和你联系的。（避免说出"我们"）

4) 出于行文需要时。如：

The film was directed by Feng Xiaoning. 该影片由冯小宁导演。

Helen was sent to the school by her parents when she was nine. 海伦九岁时被父母送到这所学校。

Exercises

I. Which of the following statements about the text are true or false? Write T for true and F for false.

(　)1) Only the Great Pyramid was built over the tomb.
(　)2) Some of the pyramids along the Nile are on the west side.
(　)3) The ancient Egyptians compared the rising of the sun to the beginning of life.
(　)4) Slaves lifted great stones to build the pyramids.
(　)5) Many of the blocks were taken across the river in boats at flood time.
(　)6) It took more than 100,000 slaves twenty years to build the Great Pyramid.
(　)7) Each of the sides of the pyramid is about as long as two city blocks.
(　)8) It takes about twenty seconds to walk all the way around the pyramid.

II. Match each word in Column A with a similar meaning in Column B.

　　　A　　　　　　　　B
1) ancient　　a. gold, silver (银), jewels (珠宝) etc.
2) pyramid　　b. say that something is like something else
3) hold　　　c. having a firm (固定) shape (形状), and usually hard
4) average　　d. belonging to a time long ago

5) treasure   e. a large stone building
6) solid   f. the lowest part
7) base   g. find the exact (确切的) position (位置) of sth
8) realize   h. keep
9) locate   i. understand
10) compare   j. not unusually big or small

III. **A. Fill in each blank with a proper word according to the initial letter.**

1) The pirates (海盗) buried their t_____.
2) The a_____ age of the boys in this class is fifteen.
3) When water freezes (结冰) and becomes s_____, we call it ice.
4) She w_____ less than she used to.
5) Do you r_____ your error yet?

B. Fill in each blank with the appropriate form of the word given in the bracket.

1) It is the ancient _____ (Egypt) who cut and moved and lifted each of these stones.
2) All the _____ (machines) is powered electrically.
3) They compared the _____ (rise) of the sun to the _____ (begin) of life and the _____ (set) of the sun to the end of life.
4) There have been several _____ (die) from drowning in the river.
5) Do not go too near the edge, it is not _____ (safety).

C. Fill in the blanks with the words or expressions given below. Change the form if necessary.

| be located on/in | compare...to | in fact | average | realize |
| cover | hold | known | weigh | without | safe | more than |

1) Our new school _____ the center of the city.

61

2) He told me it would be easy but _____ it is very difficult.

3) The _____ age of the students in this class is 18.

4) The territory (领土) _____ an area the size of North Dakota.

5) It's very hard to _____ just how long the Great Wall is.

6) You can't _____ the war in Somalia (索马里) _____ the Vietnam War (越战).

7) They are _____ a room for us.

8) You are getting on weight (发福). Have you _____ yourself lately?

9) Man cannot live _____ air or water.

10) _____ 500 people had to be helped to safety when the stadium (体育场) collapsed (倒塌).

11) Will you feel _____ in the house on your own?

12) Gong Li is a _____ actress.

IV. A. Change the active into passive, using the italicized part as subject.

1) Did you grow *these flowers* in your garden?

2) No one has climbed *this mountain* before.

3) They will send *Jane* to prison.

4) They are discussing *the question* at the meeting.

5) Jane will have finished *the novel* by six o'clock.

6) Someone wants *you* on the phone.

7) They were investigating (调查) *the case* (案子).

8) In this sense (从某种意义上说), we can turn *bad things* into good things.

B. Fill in each blank with the right form of the given verb.

1) These dishes _____ (wash) last night.

2) The door lock _____ (force) open before we got there.

3) A local flower show _____ (hold) on next Monday.
4) Your proposal _____ (discuss) at the moment, sir.
5) Then a long speech on the successes of the past year _____ (make) by the Chairman.

V. A. Answer the following questions with the help of the model and the words given in brackets.

Model: Q: Do you know how big the Great Pyramid is? (hard, realize)
   A: It is hard to realize how big the Great Pyramid is.

1) What do you think of the job? (easy, do)
2) What about the problem? (difficult, explain)
3) What do you think of the language? (hard, learn)
4) What about the water in the river? (unfit, drink)

B. Rewrite the following sentences after the model.

Model: More than 100,000 slaves spent twenty years building the Great Pyramid.
   It took more than 100,000 slaves twenty years to build the Great Pyramid.

1) They took all day to travel ten miles.
2) I have spent all the evening doing my homework.
3) We take about twenty minutes to walk all the way.
4) She spent six years typing the numbers from one to one million.

VI. Translation.

A. From Chinese to English.

1) 大金字塔有450英尺高,每一边有755英尺长。
2) 绕着金字塔走一圈大约需要20分钟。
3) 古埃及人把日出比做生命的诞生。
4) 这衣箱能装得下你所有的衣服吗?
5) 上海位于中国的东部。

6) 这件外套可以保你暖和。

B. From English to Chinese.

1) He won't be able to make it home at Christmas time.
2) The Great Pyramid is located on the west bank of the Nile River.
3) Will you keep these things safe for me?
4) This is now being used in our school as a text-book.
5) This is why the bodies were buried on the west bank of the Nile.
6) These huge stone blocks weigh an average of two and a half tons each, as much as a small car.

Passage Reading

The Great Pyramid

(Part II)

Every king wanted his tomb to be the best. But Khufu outdid them all. The surface of his pyramid used to shine with smooth white limestone, and its top came to a sharp point. Inside, the body of Khufu rested in a great stone coffin. His body was preserved to last forever, and many treasures were buried with him.

Now after many years, the shinning surface is worn away, and men have taken some of the huge stone blocks to build other things. Thieves have stolen the treasures, and they have stolen the body of Khufu himself.

Today, the sides of the Great Pyramid are no longer smooth and white. The limestone is gone. The huge stones are exposed and you can climb them, like steps, to the top. When you have reached the top, you can see for miles about you. You can see the smaller pyramids and the

Sphinx, the great stone statue of the lion with a human head. To the west you can see the Libyan Desert, and to the east you can see the green Nile Valley and the modern city of Cairo.

New Words & Expressions

outdo [aut'du:] vt. 胜过，优于
surface ['sə:fis] n. （任何物体的）表面
used to 过去常常
smooth [smu:ð] adj. 光滑的
white [wait] adj. 白色的
top [tɔp] n. 顶部
sharp [ʃɑ:p] adj. 尖的
point ['pɔint] n. （尖）端
rest [rest] vi. 安息
limestone ['laimstoun] n. 石灰石
coffin ['kɔfin] n. 棺材，柩
preserve [pri'zə:v] vt. 维持，使不损坏

forever [fə'revə] adv. 永远
no longer 不再
expose [iks'pouz] vt. 使暴露
step [step] n. 石阶
mile [mail] n. 英里
statue ['stætju:] n. 雕像
lion ['laiən] n. 狮子
human ['hju:mən] adj. 人的，人类的
head [hed] n. 头，头部
desert ['dezət] n. 沙漠，荒地
valley ['væli] n. 山谷，河谷

Proper Names

the Libyan ['libiən] Desert(非洲)利比亚沙漠
sphinx ['sfiŋks] 狮身人面像
the Nile Valley(非洲)尼罗河谷

Notes to the Passage

1. The surface of his Pyramid used to shine with smooth white limestone, and its top came to a sharp point. 大金字塔的白色石灰石表面过去曾光泽四射，其塔顶呈尖顶形状。

1) used to... 表示过去经常发生但现在不再发生的动作。例如：

He used to travel by sea but now he travels by plane. 过去他常坐船旅行，但现在坐飞机。

It seldom used to rain at the time of year. 过去，每年的这个时候很少下雨。

2) come to... 升至，达到(某一水准、数字、点)。如：

His earnings come to more than ＄20,000. 他的工资达到两万多美元。

2. Today, the sides of the Great Pyramid are no longer smooth and white. 今天，大金字塔的表面已不再如往日般平滑，光泽。no longer 不再...。如：

He is no longer living here. 他已经不住在这了。

He is no longer a student. 他已经不再是学生了。

3. The limestone is gone. 石灰石已经不见了。句中 gone 相当于形容词，表示状态，意为"消失了，不见了"。

4. You can see for miles about you. 你可以看到方圆数英里的地方。about 在…附近，相当于 around。如：

The children ran about/around the house. 小孩子在家里面到处跑。

5. You can see the smaller pyramids and the Sphinx, the great stone statue of the lion with a human head. 你可以看到那些小一些的金字塔和斯芬克斯，即那座巨大的狮身人首雕像。the great stone statue of the lion with a human head 是 the Sphinx 的同位语，用以补充说明。同位语通常放在其说明的名词(代词)之后。例如：

We, *the Chinese people*, are determined to build China into a powerful (强大的) and prosperous (繁荣的) country. 我们中国人民决心将中国建成一个强大繁荣的国家。

I have two little sisters, *Mary and Linda*. 我有两个妹妹，玛丽和琳达。

They *all* went to see the film. 他们都去看那部电影了。

You *two* go first, we *four* stay behind. 你们俩先走，我们四个留下来。

Answer the questions according to the passage.
1. Whose tomb was the best?
2. What was buried with Khufu's body?
3. What did the surface of his pyramid look like thousands of years ago?
4. What happened to the Great Pyramid after many years?
5. Why were the sides of the Great Pyramid no longer smooth and white?
6. What can you see from the top of it?

Unit 5

Text

Victor's Hobby

The class teacher thought that hobbies were very important for every child. She encouraged all her pupils to have one, and sometimes arranged for their parents to come and see the work they had done as a result.

One Friday morning the teacher told the class that those of them who had a hobby could have a holiday that afternoon to get the things they had made as parts of their hobbies ready for their parents to see the following afternoon.

So on Friday afternoon, while those of the pupils who had nothing to show did their usual lessons, the lucky ones who had made something were allowed to go home, on condition that they returned before five o'clock to bring what they were going to show and to arrange it.

When the afternoon classes began, the teacher was surprised to see that Victor was not there. He was the laziest boy in the class, and the teacher found it difficult to believe that he had a hobby. However at a quarter to five, Victor arrived with a beautiful collection of butterflies in glass cases. After his teacher had admired them and helped him to arrange them on a table in the classroom, she was surprised to see Victor pick up again and begin to leave.

"What are you doing, Victor?" she asked. "Those things must remain here until tomorrow afternoon. That's when the parents are coming to see them."

"I know they are coming then," answered Victor, "And I will bring them back tomorrow; but my big brother doesn't want them to be out of our house at night in case they are stolen."

"But what has it got to do with your big brother?" asked the teacher. "Aren't the butterflies yours?"

"No," answered Victor. "They belong to him."

"But Victor, you are supposed to show your own hobby here, not someone else's!" said the teacher.

"I know that," Victor replied. "My hobby is watching my brother collecting butterflies."

New Words & Expressions

encourage [inˈkʌridʒ] *vt*. 鼓励　　　pupil [ˈpjuːpl] *n*. 小学生

arrange [əˈreindʒ] vt. 安排
　　arrange for... 安排…做…
part [pɑ:t] n. 部分
ready [ˈredi] adj. 准备好的
follow [ˈfɔlou] vt. 跟随
following [ˈfɔlouiŋ] adj. 下列的,下述的
show [ʃou] vt. 显示,展示
usual [ˈju:ʒuəl] adj. 平常的,通常的
lesson [ˈlesn] n. 功课
lucky [ˈlʌki] adj. 幸运的
allow [əˈlau] vt. 允许,同意
condition [kənˈdiʃən] n. 条件
　　on condition that 条件是,不过得要

o'clock [əˈklɔk] …点钟
lazy [ˈleizi] adj. 懒惰的
quarter [ˈkwɔ:tə] n. 一刻钟
collection [kəˈlekʃən] n. 收集
butterfly [ˈbʌtəflai] n. 蝴蝶
case [keis] n. 盒子;事例
　　in case 万一
admire [ədˈmaiə] vt. 赞美,称赞
remain [riˈmein] vi. 留下
belong [biˈlɔŋ] vi. 属于,属…所有
　　belong to 属于
suppose [səˈpouz] vt. 设想
　　be supposed to 被期望,应该

Notes to the Text

1. She encouraged all her pupils to have one, and sometimes arranged for the parents to come and see the work they had done as a result. 她鼓励学生们都要有业余爱好,有时还安排家长们来观看他们的成果。

   1) encourage somebody to do something 鼓励某人做某事。例如:
      All the family encouraged me to become a doctor. 全家人都鼓励我当医生。

   2) arrange for somebody to do something 安排…做…
      I have arranged for him to meet our manager. 我已安排他跟我们经理见面。

2. One Friday morning the teacher told the class that those of them who had a hobby could have a holiday that afternoon to get the things they had made as parts of their hobbies ready for their parents to see the following afternoon. 一个周五的上午老师告诉全班:有业余爱好的同学下午可以放假,把他们的部分杰作准备好,以便次日下午家长们来参观。

1) get something ready for 为…做好准备。例如：
We must get the room ready for the new mayor. 我们必须为新市长准备好房间。
2) parts of 意为"有些部分"。例如：
Parts of the book are interesting. 这本书有些部分很有趣。

3. While those of the pupils who had nothing to show did their usual lessons, the lucky ones who had something were allowed to go home, on condition that they returned before five o'clock to bring what they were going to show and to arrange it. 没有作品展示的学生照常做他们的功课，而那些有作品的幸运的学生却可以回到家里，只要五点前带上他们要展示的作品来并且布置好就行了。on condition that 意为"如果，只有在…条件下"。例如：
You may borrow the car, on condition that you do not lend it to anyone else. 你可以把这辆车借走，只要你不把它再借给别人。

4. The teacher was surprised to see that Victor was not there. 老师看到维克托没来上课非常惊奇。be surprised to do 表示"(因)…而感到惊讶"。例如：
He was surprised to hear the news. 听到这个消息，他感到很吃惊。

5. The teacher found it difficult to believe that he had a hobby. 老师感到难以相信他有业余爱好。不定式 to believe... 在句中作真正的宾语，it 为形式宾语。再如：
He found it difficult to understand her. 他觉得难以了解她。

6. Victor arrived with a beautiful collection of butterflies in glass cases. 维克托来的时候带来了一套用玻璃盒子装的漂亮的蝴蝶标本。with a beautiful collection of butterflies in glass cases 是介词短语作状语，表示方式。例如：
He came with a bundle(捆)of books. 他带着一捆书来了。

7. help somebody (to) do something 帮助某人做某事。例如：
I helped her (to) hang the clothes. 我帮她晾衣服。

71

8. That's when the parents are coming to see them. 那时候父母才来看这些作品。此句中 when 引导的是名词从句,在句中作表语。

9. in case 意为"以防,以免",用于引导目的状语从句。例如:
   Take your raincoat in case it rains. 带上你的雨衣,以防下雨。
   Be careful in case it is spotted (弄脏)。小心点,以免把它弄脏。

10. But what has it got to do with your big brother? 但这和你哥哥有什么关系? have (got) something to do with 意为"与…有关系"。例如:
    Hard work had a great deal to do with his achievements. 他取得的成绩与辛勤工作大有关系。
    She had something to do with my decision to study abroad. 我决定出国学习同她是有关系的。

11. "...you are supposed to show your own hobby here, not someone else's!" 你应该展示自己的爱好,而不是其他人的。be supposed to 意为"应该、必须",常用来表示一个期望发生的动作或表示一个责任或义务。例如:
    We are supposed to be there at six. 我们得在六点到达那里。

Dialogue

A: Do you have time for a cup of coffee?

B: I don't know. The cafeteria looks pretty crowded.

A: It's all the people who went to the graduation.

B: Did you go?

A: Oh yes, I went! I wanted to hear the speech that Paul gave.

B: Oh, he's a friend of yours, isn't he?

A: Yes, I've known him for years.

B: Didn't he go to the same high school that you did?

A: Yes, he did. There he is now! I want to congratulate him.

B: Look at all the people who are with him!

A: Those are his parents who are sitting next to him. I'll just go over and say hello.

B: I ought to get on back to the dormitory. I have to catch a bus that leaves at two o'clock.

A: What time is it now?

B: It's one thirty already.

A: I'll only be a minute, I promise. Then I'll walk over to the dorm with you.

New Words & Expressions

cafeteria [ˌkæfi'tiəriə] n. 自助餐馆
pretty ['priti] adv. 相当,非常
crowded ['kraudid] adj. 拥挤的
graduate ['grædjuit] vi. 毕业
graduation [ˌgrædju'eiʃən] n. 毕业典礼,毕业

speech [spi:tʃ] n. 演说
congratulate [kən'grætjuleit] vt. 祝贺
dormitory(dorm) ['dɔ:mitri] n.(集体)宿舍
already [ɔ:l'redi] adv. 已经
promise ['prɔmis] vt. 答应,承诺

Proper Name

Paul [pɔ:l](人名)保罗

Notes to the Dialogue

1. The cafeteria looks pretty crowded. 自助餐厅好像很挤。pretty 意为"相当地,很",修饰形容词或副词。例如:
   He is pretty old now. 他现在很老了。
   I am pretty sure that he will agree. 我深信他会同意的。

2. It's all the people who went to the graduation. 所有的人都是刚参加

完毕业典礼。
3. Oh, he's a friend of yours, isn't he? 哦，他是你朋友，是吗？注意 your friend 和 a friend of yours 在意思上稍有区别，前者意为"你的朋友"（可能只有一个朋友），后者意为"你的朋友之一"。
4. I will just go over and say hello. 我要过去问个好。over 意为"向（这）那边，往…方向"。例如：
She went over to the window. 她往窗户走去。
I have some friends coming over tonight. 今晚我有些朋友要来。

Grammar

定语从句（The Attributive Clause）（一）
关系代词引导的定语从句

1. 由 who 引导的定语从句。例如：
   Those of them **who** had a hobby could have a holiday that afternoon. 有业余爱好的学生那天下午可以放假。
   The lucky ones **who** had made something were allowed to go home. 那些制作了东西的幸运的学生，可以回到家中。
   Those of the pupils **who** had nothing to show did their usual lessons. 那些没有东西可以展示的学生照常做功课。
   (who 在定语从句中作主语，指人)
2. 由 whom 引导的定语从句。例如：
   I don't know anything about the girl **whom**（who, that）you mean. 我对你指的那个女孩一无所知。
   I saw the young woman **whom**（who, that）you'd told me about. 我见到了你告诉过我的那位年轻的女士。
   (whom 在定语从句中作宾语，可以用 who 和 that 替代，亦可省略)
3. 由 whose 引导的定语从句。例如：

I like the room **whose** window looks out over the sea. 我喜欢那间窗户面向大海的房间。

I have a friend **whose** father is a scientist. 我有一个朋友,他父亲是个科学家。

(whose 在定语从句中作定语,既可修饰人也可修饰物)

4. 由 which, that 引导的定语从句。例如:

This is the car **which/that** has been stolen. 这就是那辆被盗的车。

Where is the tape **which/that** I borrowed this morning? 今天上午我借的那盘磁带在哪儿?

He made an electric engine **which/that** looked just like a real one. 他制作了一个看上去像真的一样的电动火车。

(which 和 that 在从句中作主语或宾语,作宾语时可以省略)

注意:

1) 如果关系代词紧跟在介词后面,不能用 who 或 that,只能用 whom 或 which。例如:

The students **with whom** he studied thought he was a bit strange. 同他一起学习的同学都觉得他有点怪。

This is the plan **about which** they have had so much discussion in the past few weeks. 这就是几周来他们反复讨论的那个计划。

2) 如果先行词为 anything, nothing 等不定代词或是被形容词最高级以及 first, only, few 等词修饰时,一般只用 that。例如:

That's all **that** I could find at the time. 这就是我当时所能找到的。

He is the only one **that** was present at the time. 他是当时惟一在场的人。

Exercises

I. Answer the following questions according to the text.

1) What did the class teacher think of hobbies?

75

2) What did the teacher tell the class to do on Friday morning?

3) Did Victor attend the afternoon classes?

4) What did Victor arrive with?

5) Did those things remain there?

6) Whom did the butterflies belong to?

7) What was Victor's hobby?

8) Can you say something about Victor?

II. Match each word in Column A with a similar meaning in Column B.

      A   B

1) usual   a. a thing that happens because of one's effort(努力)

2) encourage b. stay in the same place

3) lucky   c. to have a high opinion of

4) lazy   d. the same as what happens most of the time

5) allow   e. next

6) collect   f. unwilling(不愿意) to work

7) admire   g. having good luck

8) remain   h. give support to

9) result   i. bring together

10) following j. give permission(允许)to

III. A. Fill in each blank with a proper word according to the initial letter.

1) All the family e_____ him to become a soldier.

2) We worked very hard and obtained excellent r_____.

3) Jane was l_____ enough to be selected for the team.

4) People are not s_____ to smoke here, you will be fined.

5) I really a_____ the way she deals with those problems all on her own.

6) The pictures must r_____ here until tomorrow afternoon.

7) Could you please c_____ some branches for a fire?
8) Everything's packed, and we are r_____ to leave.

B. Fill in each blank with a different form of the word given in the bracket.

1) My mother tried her best to _____ (courage) me to apply for the position.
2) You were _____ (luck), you didn't break your legs.
3) Payment must be made in any of the _____ (follow) ways: cheque, cash or credit card.
4) Victor arrived with a _____ (collect) of butterflies.
5) She was even more _____ (beauty) than I had remembered.

C. Fill in the blanks with the words or expressions given below. Change the form where necessary.

on condition that	encourage	pick up	in case
remain	belong to	admire	be supposed to	allow
parts of	arrange for	be surprised to	ready	lucky

1) The teacher _____ see that Victor was not in class.
2) She _____ my decision to study abroad.
3) On Saturday afternoon, parents will see some works as _____ their hobbies.
4) Take a taxi _____ you are late for the exam.
5) I have _____ the window cleaner to come on Sunday.
6) You can go swimming _____ you don't go too far from the river lank.
7) Most of the players _____ the tennis club.
8) I _____ (not) stay out after 10 o'clock when I was a teenager.
9) My parents _____ me to apply for the job.
10) She _____ at home to look after the children.

11) I forgot to _____ her new coat at the party.

12) I need about half an hour to get _____, so I'll see you at eight.

13) Nobody is _____ to smoke in the classroom.

14) Tom was _____ enough to be selected (挑选) for the team.

IV. A. **Complete with who, whom, whose, that or which.**

1) I don't know the young woman _____ was sitting by herself.

2) She is the neighbour with _____ I shared a garden.

3) The lesson _____ we just finished was an easy one.

4) The students copied (抄写) the sentences _____ the teacher wrote on the blackboard.

5) She's returned the books _____ she took out of the library last week.

6) He's the police officer _____ directs (指挥) traffic on this corner.

7) The millionaire (百万富翁) _____ son ran away from home a week ago has made a public appeal (恳请公众援助).

8) The tiles (瓦片) _____ fell off the roof (房顶) caused serious damage (损失).

9) He is the only one _____ was absent at the time.

10) This is the plan about _____ we have had much discussion in the past few weeks.

B. **Combine the sentences, using who, whom, that or which.**

1) They haven't got the office supplies (办公设备). He ordered them last week.

2) I've never met the woman. She has on the yellow sweater (羊毛套衫).

3) The boys are late for school. They are running down the street.
4) He couldn't understand the problems. The teacher had assigned them for homework.
5) I called the woman. She was taking care of the house.
6) The car broke down. I borrowed it from Charles.
7) The homework was very difficult. The teacher assigned it last week.
8) The professor is very popular with the students. Mary and John are talking to him now.

V. Rewrite the following sentences after the model.

Model 1: The teacher found that it was difficult to believe that he had a hobby.

The teacher found it difficult to believe that he had a hobby.

1) We felt that it was necessary to point out (指出) his mistakes.
2) We think that it is important to learn a foreign language.
3) He found that it was difficult to answer the question.
4) She thought that it was easy to finish her homework within (在…之内) 20 minutes.

Model 2: You should show your own hobby here.

You are supposed to show your own hobby here.

1) They should finish their homework in time.
2) You are not allowed to smoke in the classroom.
3) You cannot leave without permission (允许).
4) They expected him to get there before dark.

VI. Translation.

A. From Chinese to English.

1) 如果你想离开教室应该先问老师。
2) 你只有在不远离河岸的条件下才能下水游泳。

3) 轻点儿，免得弄醒孩子。

4) 你认为他心情不好与我说的话有关吗？

5) 他们已安排好让我们明天去游长城。

6) 鼓励孩子们培养业余爱好非常重要。

B. From English to Chinese.

1) You may use the car, on condition that you clean it afterward.

2) Finally, he arrived with a beautiful collection of butterflies in glass cases.

3) After his teacher admired them and helped him to arrange them on a table in the classroom, she was surprised to see Victor pick up again and begin to leave.

4) After the party Jane remained and helped me do the **dishes**（盘碟，餐具）.

5) That is a good book which is opened with expectation（期望）and closed with profit（获益）.

6) I must take the flowers back at night in case they are stolen.

Passage Reading

Debra Miller

The richest and most fashionable section of New York City is between Central Park and the East River. Most of the people in this area live in large apartment buildings, but there are a few private houses too. The area also contains a large number of expensive shops and restaurants.

Debra Miller has just rented a big apartment in this part of the city. Debra is only thirty-five years old, but she is a very successful young woman. A few years ago, she became the editor of a magazine for other young people like herself. Both Debra and the magazine have made a lot of money.

　　Debra is always happy to come home to her apartment. She likes some private time to play the piano and relax. She also likes to have parties on her large terrace, from which there is a wonderful view of the city. The guests at Debra's parties are interesting people who like to listen to music, sing, talk, and have fun.

　　Success has brought Debra the chance to have the possessions she wants. In addition to her piano, she has a car and everything she needs for skiing, tennis, and other activities. She has fallen in love more than once. But she has never got married because she enjoys the freedom to do many different things. She enjoys her work, music, and parties, and she also likes tennis, skiing, and weekend trips to the mountains or the beach.

　　In spite of all the good times she has, Debra has to work very hard. She's in her office every morning at nine o'clock. She herself decides on every article that goes into the magazine. She also checks the magazine sales figures and all of the advertising. She works hard because she wants to continue to be successful. It isn't just luck that's responsible for Debra's success.

New Words & Expressions

fashionable ['fæʃənəbl] *adj*. 高级的, 上流社会的
section ['sekʃən] *n*. 阶层, 地区
between [bi'twi:n] *prep*. 在…之间
central ['sentrəl] *adj*. 中间的, 中心的
area ['ɛəriə] *n*. 地区
private ['praivit] *adj*. 私人的, 个人的

contain [kən'tein] *vt*. 包含, 含有
a large number of 大量的, 许多
rent [rent] *vt*. 租, 租用
succeed [sək'si:d] *vi*. 成功
　succeed in 成功于
successful [sək'sesful] *adj*. 成功的
success [sək'ses] *n*. 成功

editor ['editə] *n*. 编辑
magazine [ˌmægə'ziːn] *n*. 杂志
make [meik] *vt*. 赚(钱),发财
relax [ri'læks] *vi*. 放松,使轻松
terrace ['teris] *n*. 露天平台
view [vjuː] *n*. 看,眺望
guest [gest] *n*. 客人
interesting ['intristiŋ] *adj*. 有趣的
music ['mjuːzik] *n*. 音乐
fun [fʌn] *n*. 快乐,娱乐
possession [pə'zeʃən] *n*. 拥有,所有(物)
addition [ə'diʃən] *n*. 附加物
  in addition to 除了……之外
tennis ['tenis] *n*. 网球
activity [æk'tiviti] *n*. 活动

once [wʌns] *adv*. 一次,一回
free [friː] *adj*. 自由的
freedom ['friːdəm] *n*. 自由
beach [biːtʃ] *n*. 海滨,海滩
in spite of 尽管,虽然
article ['ɑːtikl] *n*. 文章
decide on 选定
sale [seil] *n*. 销售
figure ['figə] *n*. 数字
advertise ['ædvətaiz] *vt*. 做广告
advertising ['ædvətaiziŋ] *n*. 广告
responsible [ris'pɔnsəbl] *adj*. 负责任的,有责任的
be responsible for 对……负有责任的

Notes to the Passage

1. A few years ago, she became the editor of a magazine for other young people like herself. 几年前,她成为一家杂志的编辑,这是一本为像她这样的年轻人办的杂志。

2. Both Debra and the magazine have made a lot of money. 黛博拉和杂志都赚了很多钱。make 意为"赚(钱),发(财)"。例如:
How much do you make from working part-time? 你打零工赚了多少钱?

3. She also likes to have parties on her large terrace, from which there is a wonderful view of the city. 她还喜欢在露天平台上举行聚会,因为从露天平台上眺望全城真是美极了。

4. Success has brought Debra the chance to have the possessions she wants. 成功已经给黛博拉带来了机遇,她可以拥有她想要的东西。

5. in addition to 意为"除了…之外"。例如：

   She can speak French in addition to English. 她除了英语外，也会说法语。

6. She herself decides on every article that goes into the magazine. 她亲自定夺每一篇入选杂志的文章。decide on 意为"选定，决定"。例如：

   Have the committee decided on the prize-winning students? 委员会选出了获奖的学生了吗？

   Have you decided on spending your holiday at home? 你决定在家里度假了吗？

   Have you decided on where to camp? 你们选定了野营的地点了吗？

7. It isn't just luck that is responsible for Debra's success. 黛博拉的成功不仅仅是来自运气。此句中 be responsible for 意为"成为…的原因"，例如：

   What is responsible for the fight? 那场打架的起因是什么？

Answer the following questions according to the passage.

1. What kind of young woman is Debra?
2. What have both Debra and the magazine done?
3. What do the guests at her parties like to do?
4. Has she ever fallen in love?
5. Why has Debra never got married?
6. Why does she work so hard?
7. Is it just luck that is responsible for her success?

Unit 6

Text

Trains under the Christmas Tree

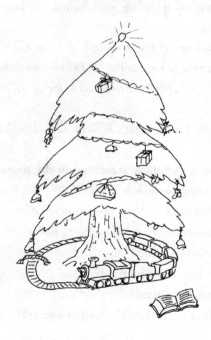

Each year, new kinds of toys are under the Christmas tree. Children are happy to find them there. But one old toy makes children happy, too—the toy electric train.

Mr. J. Lionel Cowen built one of the first toy electric trains, in

1900. In that year, he was just 19 years old. He lived in New York City. There he had a small workroom where he built many new things, such as the first flashlight.

His first toy electric train had only one kind of car, made of wood. The car in front had a small electric motor. The train ran on a track. He sold his train to a toy shop. Soon the shop asked him for many more.

Even today, people stop to watch a toy electric train running in a shop window. But in 1900, they could not stop looking at the new toy. How they loved to watch his train run on its little tracks.

Soon he was making many kinds of cars for his trains. He made all the kinds that real trains have. He made cars to sleep in and cars to carry animals. He made an electric engine that looked just like a real one.

Each year, more and more Lionel trains were sold. But Mr. Cowen went right on making the trains better. He even put electric lights in his trains. At last he did a very surprising thing. He made trains that ran by push button. Now a boy could run his train without going near it. From across a room, he could move the train by pushing a button. He could back it onto a side track. He could drop a car from the train, or pick one up.

Then he did more tricks with push buttons. A boy could now make milk cans or logs go up onto a train. Then by pushing a button he could take them off.

Men as well as children have always liked to play with toy trains. It is men who keep asking for new things. Some even want the food cars to make real ice.

Mr. Cowen worked hard to make his trains please everyone. To make the toy engine whistle sound real, he went to the train yards. For days he listened to engine whistles there. At last he made his train whistle sound like that of a real train.

No wonder most children and their fathers like toy electric trains! Many still think a train is the best thing to find under the Christmas tree.

New Words & Expressions

Christmas ['krisməs] n. 圣诞节
electric [i'lektrik] adj. 电动的,用电的
workroom ['wə:krum] n. 工作室
flashlight ['flæʃlait] n. 手电筒
car [kɑ:] n. 火车车厢
wood [wud] n. 木料,木材
front [frʌnt] n. 前面
   in front 前面
   in front of 在…的前面
track [træk] n. 轨道
   side track (美)(铁路的)侧线,岔道
real [riəl] adj. 真正的
animal ['æniməl] n. 动物

push [puʃ] vt., n. 推,按下
button ['bʌtn] n. 按钮
back [bæk] vt. 使后退
onto ['ɔntu] prep. 到…上
drop [drɔp] vt. 放下,投下
can [kæn] n. 罐子
log [lɔg] n. 圆木
ice [ais] n. 冰
please [pli:z] vt. 使满足,合…之意
whistle ['wisl] n. 汽笛声
yard [jɑ:d] n. 专用围地,工作场
no wonder 难怪,一点都不奇怪

Proper Name

Lionel Cowen ['laiənil; 'kauwin] (人名)赖恩内尔·考文

Notes to the Text

1. ....makes children happy... 使孩子们高兴。注意:make + n. + adj. 结构。例如:
   His present made her very happy. 他的礼物令她非常高兴。

2. There he had a small workroom where he built many new things, such as the first flashlight. 那儿他有一间小工作室,在那间工作室里他建造了许多新东西,如第一只手电筒。

1) where 引导的是一个定语从句,修饰 workroom, 这里 where 相当于 in which。

2) such as 意为"诸如…",一般用于列举事物。例如:
I have been to several cities such as Beijing, Shanghai, and Hongkong. 我去过几个城市,如北京、上海和香港。

3. ...made of wood 用木头制成。make...of...意为"用…做成…"(通常指制造后不改变该材料原来的性质或形状)。例如:
The chair is made of wood. 这把椅子是木制的。
注意同 make...from...的区别。make...from...意为"用…做成…(通常指制造后改变了材料原来的性质和形状)"。例如:
Wine is made from grapes. 葡萄酒是葡萄酿成的。

4. Soon the shop asked him for many more. 很快那家商店就向他要更多的玩具火车。
ask somebody for something 意为"向(某人)索要…"例如:
He asked his father for a radio. 他请求父亲买收音机。
I asked my teacher for help. 我向老师求助。

5. People stop to watch a toy electric train running in a shop window. 人们停下来观看在商店橱窗里奔驰的电动玩具火车。
stop to do...意为"停下一件事来做另一件事"。例如:
He stopped to smoke. 他停下来吸烟。
注意:stop doing...表示"停下正在进行的动作"。例如:
They stopped looking at the new toy. 人们不再看这种新玩具。

6. How they loved to watch his train run on its little tracks! 他们是多么喜欢看他的玩具火车在小轨道上跑啊! 这是一个由 how 引起的感叹句。

7. He made cars to sleep in and cars to carry animals. 他制造了卧铺车厢和装运动物的车厢。to sleep in 和 to carry animals 是两个不定式短语,在句中都是定语,修饰 cars。

8. ...went right on making the train better. 紧接着继续改进火车。...

87

go on doing 表示"继续做某事"。right 用于加强语气。例如：

He went on working without taking a break. 他一直工作,没有休息。

9. by push button 靠按电钮。介词 by 表示"以某种方式,方法"。例如：

The room is lighted by electricity. 房间用电照明。

10. Men as well as children have always liked to play with toy trains. 不仅孩子们,大人们也总是喜欢玩玩具火车。

   1) as well as 意为"除了"。例如：

   Tim was upset (不安) as well as Roger. (Tim as well as Roger was upset.)

   2) play with 意为"玩,玩弄"。例如：

   Play with your own toys, don't take your brother's. 玩自己的玩具,不要拿你弟弟的。

   Whoever plays with fire gets burnt. 玩火者必自焚。

11. It is men who keep asking for new things. 人类总是不断追求新事物。keep doing sth 表示"继续不断地做某事"。例如：

   He kept running after her, trying to catch her. 他一直在追她,想要抓住她。

Dialogue

A Drive in the Country

A: How wonderful it is to get out of the city for a change! And what a lovely day it is! It's so pleasant to feel warm again after a long, cold winter.

B: Yes, and by August you'll be complaining about how hot it is.

A: Well, I don't like it when it's either too hot or too cold. How green all the trees are getting!

B: How do you like the new car?

A: It's pretty nice, Tom. How fast can she go?

B: I don't know. I haven't tried to open her up yet. Let me try now.

A: Isn't that a police siren that I hear?

B: All right. I'll slow down.

A: What a pretty house that is over there! That white one, with all the trees around it. How pleasant it would be to live in the country!

B: When we get married, we'll try to find a house in the suburbs.

A: I said slow down, Tom. I didn't say to stop.

B: I don't know what's wrong. It's the car, not me.

A: We must have run out of gas.

New Words & Expressions

complain[kəm'plein] vi. 抱怨,发牢骚
open up 开足(马力)
siren ['saiərin] n. (警车的)警笛
slow down 放慢速度

suburb ['sʌbəːb] n. 郊区,市郊(常用复数)
run out of 用光,用尽

Notes to the Dialogue

1. How wonderful it is to get out of the city for a change! 到城外去体会一下变化多好啊! change 是名词,意为"改变,变化"。

2. ...and by August you'll be complaining about how hot it is. 到了八月,你又会抱怨天气有多么炎热了。

   1) by 意为"到…时","不迟于…"。再如:
   By the time tomorrow he will be here. 到明天这个时候他就到这里了。

   2) shall (will) be + doing 构成将来进行时,常表示势必要发生的动作,一般不表意愿。例如:

89

  The train will be leaving in a few seconds. 火车马上就要开了。

  They will be meeting us at the air-port. 他们会在机场接我们的。

3. I don't like it when it's either too hot or too cold. 天气太热或太冷我都不喜欢。either...or...意为"(两者之中)…或…(之一)"。再如：

 Either you or I am wrong. 不是你错就是我错。

 Please either come in or go out, don't stand there. 请你要么进来要么出去，不要站在那里。

4. How do you like the new car? 你觉得新车怎么样？How do you like...? 常用于征求对方意见。例如：

 How do you like the book? 你觉得这本书怎么样？

 How do you like eating out? 你觉得出去吃怎么样？

5. How fast can she go? 车能跑多快？she 和下面句中的 her 都是指"汽车"。

6. I haven't tried to open her up yet. 我还从未开足过马力。

 1) open up 意为"开足马力"，例如：

  Once we were on the main road, the car opened up. 我们一上主干道，汽车就飞快地跑起来了。

 2) yet 意为"到那时、至当时"用于否定句中，通常位于句末。再如：

  I have had no news from him yet. 我还没有接到他的消息。

7. We must have run out of gas. 我们的车一定没油了。

 1) run out of 意为"用完，耗尽"。例如：

  We're fast running out of medicine. 我们的药品很快就要用完了。

 2) must have done 表示对过去情况的肯定猜测。例如：

  It is five o'clock. He must have come home. 现在是五点。他一定到家了。

  They look happy, they must have had a good time on their vacation. 他们看上去很快乐，一定是假期里玩得很开心。

Grammar

一、定语从句(The Attributive Clause)(二)
关系副词引导的定语从句

1. 由 when 引导的定语从句。例如：
   December 25 was the time of the year when winter days began to grow longer in the Northern Hemisphere. 12月25日是一年中北半球冬季白天开始变长的时候。
   October is the month when the place is full of tourists. 10月是这个地方游客云集的月份。
   when 在定语从句中作时间状语，其先行词需用表示时间的名词。

2. 由 why 引导的定语从句。例如：
   No one is sure of the reason why this day was chosen. 谁也不知道为什么选择这一天。
   He refused to tell the reason why he was late. 他拒绝说出他迟到的原因。
   That is not the reason why you should tell a lie. 那不是你必须说谎的原因。
   why 在定语从句中作原因状语，其先行词是 reason。

3. 由 where 引导的定语从句。例如：
   I know of a shop where we can get batteries. 我知道有一个可以买到电池的商店。
   There he had a small workroom where he built many new things. 在那里，他有一间小工作室，许多新东西就是在那里制造的。
   where 在定语从句中作地点状语，其先行词是表示地点的名词。

二、感叹句 (The Exclamatory Sentence)

用以表示说话时的喜、怒、哀、乐等强烈情感的句子被称为感叹句。这类句子常以 what 或 how 引起，what 后接名词，how 后接形容词、副词，也可修饰动词。

1. what 引起的感叹句。例如：

   What a lovely day it is! 多好的天啊！

   What a pretty house that is over there! 那边的房子多漂亮啊！

   What a beautiful picture that is! 那是一幅多么漂亮的画啊！

2. how 引起的感叹句。例如：

   How they loved to watch his train run on its little tracks! 他们多么喜欢看他的火车在小轨道上跑啊！

   How wonderful it is to go out of the city for a change! 到城外去体验一下变化多好啊！

   How green all the trees are getting! 树木变得多绿啊！

Exercises

I. **Choose the best answer a, b, c or d to these questions about the text.**

1) Each year children are happy to find _____ under the Christmas tree.

   a. toys   b. fries(油煎食品)   c. candies   d. apples

2) When Mr. J. Lionel Cowen built one of the first toy electric trains in 1900, he was _____ years old.

   a. 18   b. 19   c. 20   d. 21

3) He built many new things in a small _____.

   a. room   b. factory   c. workroom   d. laboratory

4) The car of his first toy electric train was made of _____.

a. plastic   b. wood   c. steel   d. paper

5) At last he made trains that ran by _____.

   a. electricity b. spring   c. push button d. battery

6) In order to make the toy engine whistle sound real, he went to the _____.

   a. station   b. factory   c. laboratory   d. train yards

7) Mr. Cowen went right on making the train better, he even put _____ in his train.

   a. tables   b. electric lights
   c. logs   d. cans

8) Mr. Cowen then did more _____ with push buttons.

   a. improvements (改进)   b. works
   c. tricks   d. changes

II. Match each word in Column A with a similar meaning in Column B.

    A   B

1) electric   a. unexpected
2) flashlight   b. make (someone) happy
3) workroom   c. garden
4) track   d. press (挤, 压) against with force
5) surprising   e. move backwards (往后)
6) please   f. sound made by forcing air
7) yard   g. operated by electricity
8) back   h. set of rails (轨道) for trains, etc.
9) whistle   i. a room where work is done
10) push   j. electric hand-light

III. A. Fill in each blank with a proper word according to the initial letter.

1) The toy e_____ train makes children very happy.

93

2) It is in a small w_____ where he built many new things.
3) I'll d_____ your bags at the hotel.
4) Jane only got married to p_____ her parents.
5) The man managed to jump o_____ the truck while it was running.
6) It is not s_____ that only Tony came tonight.
7) Now a boy could b_____ it onto a side track.
8) He made all kinds of cars that r_____ trains have.

B. Fill in the blanks with the words or expressions given below. Change the form where necessary.

go on doing	be made of	ask...for...	no wonder
go up onto	play with	many more	pick up	open up
run out of	slow down	complain	at last	surprising

1) Remember to buy me the white blouse (短上衣) which _____ silk (丝).
2) The young man _____ one of our guides (向导) _____ directions (方向) to post-office.
3) _____ that he has failed in the examination.
4) You can't _____ (work) too late, it is not doing yourself any good.
5) You should not allow your children to _____ fire.
6) Now a boy could make milk cans or logs _____ a train.
7) We have some people volunteering (志愿) to help out (帮助脱离困境), but _____ are needed.
8) Now a boy could drop a car from the train or _____ one _____.
9) What will the world use for power, when it has _____ oil?
10) Can't you _____ the engine a little more?
11) There's a police car ahead. Will you _____?

12) Mary _____ that she couldn't find a job anywhere.

13) He hesitated (犹豫) for a long time, but _____ he decided to go.

14) It was _____ that so many students showed up (来到) for the lecture.

IV. A. Complete the sentences after the model.

Model: This is the room _____ (我以前工作的).

This is the room <u>where I worked</u>.

1) Do you remember one day five years ago _____? (我到你办公室送信)

2) Is there a train yard around _____. (在那我们可以听到发动机的汽笛声)

3) The reason _____ is that he was ill. (他被打败的原因)

4) There he had a small workroom _____. (在那他建造了许多新东西)

5) Tell me the time _____. (比赛开始的)

B. Fill in each blank with "what or how".

1) _____ wonderful a time we ever had together!

2) _____ good wine it is!

3) _____ a foolish mistake I have made!

4) _____ empty and pedantic (迂腐的) a thinker (思想家) she is!

5) _____ delightful (令人高兴的) weather we are having!

V. A. Rewrite the following sentences after the model.

Model: Not only children but also men have always liked to play with toy trains.

Men as well as children have always liked to play with toy trains.

1) I think you were not only rude (粗鲁), but also foolish.

2) Your mother was very angry. I was angry, too.

3) I'm studying biology (生物) and chemistry (化学). I'm studying history, too.

4) He speaks English and France (法语). He also speaks Spanish (西班牙语).

B. Complete the following sentences, using "go on + V-ing", or "keep + V-ing".

1) _____ (他们继续在田地工作) though it was getting dark.

2) Since everything is over, _____ (你为什么还哭个没完)?

3) _____ (你不能再喝这么多酒了). You are not doing yourself any good.

4) I could not bear it because _____ (他反复问些愚蠢的问题).

VI. Translation.

A. From Chinese to English.

1) 你不能再喝下去了,那会对你的健康有害。

2) 他的这件衬衫是由丝绸(silk)制作的。

3) 难怪你这么困,昨晚你睡的太晚了。

4) 不要让小孩子玩火,那很危险。

5) 很显然五个人是不够的,我们需要更多的帮手。

6) 他们看上去很快乐,一定是假期里玩得很开心。

B. From English to Chinese.

1) Tim, as well as Roger, was upset (不安).

2) Listen! I can't keep repeating things.

3) I hope it won't go on snowing all day.

4) The book-store where he works is the largest one in China.
5) At last he made his train whistle sound like that of a real train.
6) It's difficult to please all the customers.

Passage Reading

Christmas

December 25 is celebrated as the birthday of Christ. No one is sure of the reason why this day was chosen. It was probably because, according to the calendar then in use, December 25 was the time of the year when winter days began to grow longer in the Northern Hemisphere. The people had celebrated this day as the promise of spring.

Over the years a number of special customs associated with Christmas have grown up. Many of these have been introduced from Europe, while others have their origins in America.

Christmas is coming again. The radio stations are playing Christmas music, and the stores are very busy. At this time in past years, we made or bought presents for our family. This year I am going to buy a recorder for my elder brother. He is very fond of music. I am going to make a toy for my little sister and buy a present for my mother.

My family usually has a reunion on Christmas Day. My elder brother lives in another town, but he always drives his car here. I hope we are going to be together again this year. Then we are going to put up the tree in the living room on Christmas Eve. The Christmas tree is the symbol of the spirit of Christmas in many homes. We are going to decorate it with small electric lights and other decorations. Christmas trees, songs, bells, and merry music each has been a part of Christmas for centuries.

New Words & Expressions

celebrate ['selibreit] vt. 庆祝
Christ [kraist] n. 基督
be sure of 知道,确信
reason ['ri:zn] n. 理由
choose [tʃu:z] (chose, chosen) vt. 选择
according to 根据
calendar ['kælində] n. 日历
in use 在使用的,在用的
northern ['nɔ:ðən] adj. 北部的,
hemisphere ['hemisfiə] n. 半球
promise['prɔmis] n. 征兆,征候
custom ['kʌstəm] n. 习惯
associate[ə'souʃieit] vt. 把…联系在一起
 associate...with 与…有关,把…联系在一起
grow up 成长,发展

introduce [ˌintrə'dju:s] n. 介绍
Europe ['juərəp] n. 欧洲
origin ['ɔridʒin] n. 起源
radio station 广播站
present ['preznt] n. 礼物
recorder [ri'kɔ:də] n. 录音机
elder ['eldə] adj. 年长的
fond [fɔnd] adj. 喜欢
 be fond of 喜欢
reunion['ri:'ju:njən] n. 团聚
put up 搭起
eve [i:v] n. 前夜,除夕
symbol ['simbəl] n. 象征
spirit ['spirit] n. 精神
decorate['dekəreit] vt. 装饰
decoration[ˌdekə'reiʃən] n. 装饰品
merry ['meri] adj. 欢乐的,快乐的

Notes to the Passage

1. ... the calendar then in use 当时所使用的日历。in use 意为"在使用着的,在用的"。例如:
   This textbook is still very much in use. 这课本还在广泛使用。
2. the promise of spring 期待(预示)春天的来临。
3. Over the years a number of special customs associated with Christmas have grown up. 许多年来已经形成了许多与圣诞有关的特别的风俗习惯。

1) a number of 意为"许多,若干",修饰可数名词。例如:

A number of people are waiting for you there. 许多人正在那儿等你。

2) associate...with... 意为"与…有联系"。例如:

I always associate the smell of those flowers with my childhood. 我一闻到那些花就想起我的童年。

He refused to associate himself with cheats. 他拒绝参与欺骗行为。

3) grow up 在文中意为"形成,发展"。例如:

New cities grew up in the desert. 沙漠中兴起了新的城市。

grow up 还有"长大,成熟"之意。例如:

What do you want to be when you grow up? 你长大想干什么?

4. Christmas trees, songs, bells, and merry music each has been a part of Christmas for centuries. 几个世纪以来,圣诞树、歌声、钟声、以及欢快的音乐,所有这些都已成为圣诞节的一部分。

Which of the following statements are true or false? Write T for true and F for false.

( )1. No one knows why December 25 is celebrated as the birthday of Christ.

( )2. The people had celebrated this day as a sign(象征)of coming spring.

( )3. The radio stations only play Christmas music on Christmas day.

( )4. The author's family live together.

( )5. People do their Christmas shopping before Christmas.

( )6. The author's elder brother likes music very much.

( )7. The Christmas tree is the sign of the spirit of Christmas in each family.

( )8. The Christmas trees have been a part of Christmas recently.

Unit 7

Text

Why the Doctor Was Late

One night, a little before nine o'clock, the doctor answered his telephone. "Glens Falls calling Dr. Van Eyck," said the voice on the telephone.

"This is Dr. Van Eyck speaking," said the doctor.

A moment later Dr. Van Eyck heard another voice: "This is Dr. Haydon at the hospital in Glens Falls. We have a very sick boy here in our hospital. He has just been brought in with a bullet in his brain. He is very weak and may not live. We should operate at once, but I'm not a surgeon, you know."

"I'm 60 miles from Glens Falls," said Dr. Van Eyck. "Have you called Dr. Mercer? He lives in Glens Falls."

"He is out of town," said Dr. Haydon. "I am calling you because the boy comes from your city. He was visiting here and shot himself while playing with a gun."

"You say that the boy is from Albany?" asked Dr. Van Eyck. "What is his name?"

"Arthur Cunningham."

"I don't think that I know him. But I'll get there as soon as I can. It's snowing here, but I think that I can get there before 12 o'clock."

"I should tell you that the boy's family is very poor. I don't think that they can pay you anything."

"That's all right," said Dr. Van Eyck.

A few minutes later, the surgeon's car had to stop for a red light at the edge of town. A man in an old black coat opened the door of the car and got in.

"Drive on," he said. "I've got a gun."

"I'm a doctor," said Van Eyck. "I'm on my way to the hospital to operate on a very sick—"

"Don't talk," said the man in the old black coat. "Just drive."

A mile out of town he ordered the doctor to stop the car and get out. Then the man drove on down the road. The doctor stood there for a moment in the falling snow.

A half hour later Dr. Van Eyck found a telephone and called a taxi. At the railway station he learned that the next train to Glens Falls would not leave until 12 o'clock.

It was after two o'clock in the morning when the surgeon arrived at the hospital in Glens Falls. Dr. Haydon was waiting for him.

"I did my best," said Van Eyck, "but I was stopped on the road and my car—"

"It was good of you to try," said Dr. Haydon. "The boy died an hour ago."

The two doctors walked by the door of the hospital waiting room. There sat the man in the old black coat, with his head in his hands.

"Mr. Cunningham," said Dr. Haydon to the man, "this is Dr. Van Eyck. He is a surgeon who came all the way from Albany to try to save your boy."

New Words & Expressions

Dr. ['dɔktə] (医生 doctor 的) 缩写
voice [vɔis] n. 声音
bullet [bulit] n. 子弹
brain [brein] n. 脑,脑髓
weak [wiːk] adj. 虚弱的,脆弱的
operate ['ɔpəreit] vi. 动手术
   operate on 给…动手术

gun [gʌn] n. 枪,炮
edge [edʒ] n. 边缘
black [blæk] adj. 黑色的
order ['ɔːdə] vt. 命令
taxi ['tæksi] n. 出租车
waiting room 候诊室
save [seiv] vt. 挽救

Proper Names

Glens Falls [glens fɔːls] (美) 格雷恩斯·福尔斯
Van Eyck [væn aik] (人名) 凡·艾克

Haydon [ˈheidən] (人名) 黑登
Mercer [ˈməːsə] (人名) 摩瑟
Albany [ˈælbəni] (美) 艾尔巴尼
Arthur Cunningham [ˈɑːθəˈkʌniŋəm] (人名) 亚瑟·坎宁安

Notes to the Text

1. "This is Dr. Van Eyck speaking," 此句为电话用语,可译为"我是凡·艾克医生"。在电话中一般不说"I am...",而应说"This is...speaking."
2. He has just been brought in with a bullet in his brain. 他被子弹击中了头部,刚刚被送进医院。此句中 with 表示原因。
   My grandfather is in bed with a bad cold. 我祖父患重感冒卧病在床。
3. He is out of town. 他不在城里。out of 意为"在…的范围外,在…之外"。例如:
   He is out of the room. 他不在房间。
   We live a few miles out of the city. 我们住在离市区数英里之外的地方。
4. ...shot himself while playing with a gun. 在玩枪的时候开枪打中了自己。
5. ...the surgeon's car had to stop for a red light at the edge of the town. 这位外科医生到达市区边上的时候,由于红灯,不得不把车停下来。
   for a red light 由于红灯,介词 for 表示原因。例如:
   I'm sorry for bothering you. 打扰你我很抱歉。
   Thank you for all you have done. 感谢你所做的一切。
6. A man in an old black coat opened the door of the car and got in. 一个身着破旧黑色上衣的男子打开车门上了车。
   1) in an old black coat 介词 in 意为"穿着、戴着"。例如:

the woman in furs 穿着皮大衣的那位女士。

the old man in sweat suit 穿运动服的那位老人。

2) get in 意为"坐进(上、进入)轿车、出租车"。in 是副词。

7. "I'm on my way to the hospital to operate on a very sick—." 我正要赶往医院去给一个生命垂危的(男孩)动手术。operate on ... 意为"为…动手术"。例如：

   The surgeon decided to operate on the boy at once. 医生决定立刻给那孩子动手术。

8. ...he ordered the doctor to stop the car and get out. 他命令医生停下车并把他赶了下去。order somebody to do something 意为"命令某人做某事"。例如：

   The soldier ordered me to go away. 那个士兵命令我走开。

9. At the railway station he learned that the next train to Glens Falls would not leave until 12 o'clock. 到了火车站他得知下一列开往格雷恩斯·福尔斯的火车要到12点才开车。not ... until ... 意为"直到…才…"，例如：

   The noise of the square didn't stop until midnight. 广场上的噪音一直到深夜才停止。

10. I did my best. 我尽力了。do one's best 意为"竭尽全力"。例如：

    I will do my best to complete the work. 我将尽全力来完成这项任务。

11. There sat the man in the old black coat, with his head in his hands. 那个穿破旧黑上衣的男士就坐在那里，双手抱着头。

    1) 注意本句中的倒装结构。在英语中，状语是 there, now, then 或介词短语，并位于句首，句子需要完全倒装，即谓语置于主语之前。例如：

       There comes the bus. 汽车来了。

       There goes the bell. 铃声响了。

       Then followed eight years of Anti-Japanese War. 接下来是八年

抗战。

After them came in the teacher. 在他们后面进来的是老师。

如果主语是人称代词,句子仍用正常语序。例如:

There he comes. 他来了。

2) 注意 with + n. + 介词短语构成的独立结构。例如:

He stood there with his hands in his pockets. 他站在那里,两手插在兜里。

Dialogue

A: How many hours are you taking this semester?
B: Eighteen, plus two hours of lab.
A: Does that mean you are taking 19 credits?
B: Uh-huh.
A: When do you have your mid-term exams?
B: They'll be next week. I think I'll have to cram.
A: Do you have Professor Min this semester?
B: Yes, she's teaching me History of American Literature.
A: She is so tough. A lot of students flunked her course last semester.
B: Oh, yeah? I'd better watch out for her, then.

New Words & Expressions

semester [si'mestə] n. 半学年,一学期
plus [plʌs] prep. 加
mean [mi:n] vt. 意思是
credit ['kredit] n. (学科的)学分
mid-term [mid tə:m] adj., n. 期中的,期中
cram [kræm] vi. (为考试)死记硬背
literature ['litəritʃə] n. 文学,文艺
tough [tʌf] adj. 倔强的,难对付的
flunk [flʌŋk] vt. 通不过(考试)

Notes to the Dialogue

1. How many hours are you taking this semester? 你这学期选了多少个小时的课?
2. I think I'll have to cram. 我想我得临时抱佛脚了。
3. Do you have Professor Min this semester? 这学期你有明教授的课吗?
4. She is so tough. A lot of students flunked her course last semester. 她不好对付,上学期有很多学生没有通过她的课程。
5. I'd better watch out for her, then. 那我可得小心点儿了。
   1) had better 表示建议某人做某事,后接原形动词。例如:
      You'd better hurry, or the shops will be shut. 你最好抓紧时间,否则商店要关门了。
      注意 had better 的否定形式。例句:
      You'd better not take a walk after dark. 你最好不要在天黑以后散步。
   2) watch out for 意为"当心,提防"。例如:
      I'm always watching out for mistakes that I may have missed before. 我总是注意以前可能没有注意到的错误。

Grammar

名词从句(The Noun Clauses)(一)

由 that 引起的名词从句在句中的功能相当于名词,可作主语、表语、宾语或同位语。

1. 作主语。如:
   That he didn't come is strange. 他没来,真奇怪。
   That you missed such a good film is a pity. 你没有看这样一部精彩

的影片,真是可惜。

注:that 引起的主语从句常被放到句子后部,而用代词 it 做形式主语。如上两句可改成:

It is strange that he didn't come.

It is a pity you missed such a good film.

2. 作表语。例如:

The fact is that I have lost my passport. 事实是我把护照弄丢了。

What's surprising me is that you are so careless. 让我吃惊的是你竟然如此粗心。

My idea is that we can get some water from the lake. 我的意思是我们可以从湖里取水。

3. 作宾语。例如:

I don't think that I know him. 我想我不认识他。

He learned that the next train to Glens Falls would not leave until 12 o'clock. 他得知下一列开往格雷恩斯·福尔斯的火车要到 12 点才发车。

The boys found that five people had called at the house. 这些孩子们发现有五人曾来过这间房子.

注意:有时 that 引起的从句还跟在一些形容词,如:aware, proud, afraid, sorry, glad 后面做宾语。例如:

I am afraid that I can not help you. 恐怕我不能帮你。

4. 作同位语(用于对名词作进一步解释和说明)。例如:

The news that we are invited to the banquet is very surprising. 我们被邀请参加宴会的消息令人吃惊。

We got a message that the chairman could not see him that morning. 我们得到消息,主席那天上午不能同他会面。

注意同位语从句与定语从句的区别:定语从句中的 that 在从句中充当某一成分(主语或宾语),而同位语从句中 that 是连词,起连接作用,不可充当句子成分。例如:

The proposal <u>that he put forward</u> is applicable. 他提出的建议是可行的。(定语从句, that 在从句中作宾语)

The proposal <u>that we should improve the quality of the products</u> is applicable. 我们应当提高产品质量的建议是可行的。(同位语从句, that 在从句中不作任何成分)

Exercises

I. Choose the best answer a, b, c or d to these questions about the text.

1) Why did Dr. Haydon ask Dr. Van Eyck to come to Glens Falls?

    a. The boy came from his city.

    b. The boy knew Dr. Van Eyck.

    c. The boy needed the help of a surgeon.

    d. The boy wanted to talk with Dr. Van Eyck.

2) Why has the boy been sent into a hospital?

    a. He had shot himself with a gun.

    b. He had broken one of his legs.

    c. He had a bad headache.

    d. He suddenly fell ill.

3) What happened when the surgeon's car had to stop for a red light?

    a. A man in an old black coat opened the door of the car and got in.

    b. He was running out of fuel.

    c. His car was stopped by a policeman.

    d. The surgeon jumped out of the car.

4) What did Dr. Van Eyck do after his car was taken?

    a. He telephoned Dr. Haydon.

    b. He went back home.

    c. He called a taxi.

d. He stood there.

5) What happened to the boy before Dr. Van Eyck got to the hospital?

   a. He got better.

   b. He died.

   c. He was sent to another hospital.

   d. He left the hospital.

6) Who had taken the doctor's car?

   a. The boy's father.

   b. A thief.

   c. A robber.

   d. A policeman.

7) How did the surgeon get to Glens Falls?

   a. He got there by train.

   b. He got there by taxi.

   c. He got there on foot.

   d. He got there by plane.

8) When did the surgeon arrive at the hospital?

   a. Two o'clock.

   b. After two o'clock.

   c. Before two o'clock.

   d. In the morning.

II. Match each word in Column A with a similar meaning in Column B.

A	B
1) weak	a. not physically strong
2) operate	b. perform (实施) a surgical (外科的) operation
3) surgeon	c. doctor who performs operation
4) edge	d. boundary (边界)
5) order	e. give an order

6) brain f. make sb/sth safe from danger
7) moment g. ill, unwell
8) sick h. track on which trains run
9) save i. very brief period of time
10) railway j. grey (灰色的) matter in the head

III. A. **Fill in each of the blanks with a word according to the initial letter.**
1) He is too w_____ to walk. He must have a good rest.
2) We must send for (派人去请) a s_____ to operate on the boy.
3) After the doctor was o_____ to get out of his car, he called a taxi to take him to the railway station.
4) We have a very s_____ boy, who has just been brought in with a b_____ in his brain.
5) Grass grew at the e_____ of the road.

B. **Fill in the blanks with the words or expressions given below. Change the form where necessary.**

edge	surgeon	operate on	play with	as soon as	out of
on one's way to		bring in	pay	do one's best	

1) A _____ is a doctor who operates on a person.
2) It was at the _____ of town where the doctor had to stop.
3) I met Jane _____ the market.
4) _____ the light switch (开关) is very dangerous.
5) After a few minutes, he is _____ sight.
6) We'll _____ to finish it on time.
7) He has his left knee _____ last Monday.
8) I'll ring (打电话) again _____ I can.
9) Could I just _____ some members of the audience to get their view?

10) The boss _____ me a cheque of $100 for my suggestions.

IV. A. **Complete each of the following sentences with the noun clauses given below.**

   a. that we can get some water from the lake
   b. that he will be able to reach the top
   c. that such things happened
   d. That he failed in the entrance examination
   e. The fact that many people have nothing to eat
   f. The news that he was sentenced to death

1) _____ is entirely (完全) understandable (可以理解的).
2) It is not your mistake _____.
3) My idea is _____.
4) We believe _____.
5) _____ must concern (令…担心) all of us.
6) _____ proved to be incorrect.

B. **Rewrite the following sentences after the model.**

Model: I can't afford a car.
   (afraid) I am <u>afraid that I can't afford a car</u>.

1) I locked the door.
   (sure) I am _____.
2) David is in hospital again.
   (sorry) I am _____.
3) You can come to the dinner party.
   (happy) I feel _____.
4) I might make a mistake.
   (afraid) I am _____.
5) Computers will be used increasingly (不断地) in the English teaching.
   (confident) Mr. Brown is _____.

C. **Complete the following sentences.**

1) My opinion is _____ (孩子们如今有太多的零花钱（pocket money）).

2) I expect _____ (情况会有好转).

3) It was evident (显然) _____ (他在这一点上是错误的).

4) I'm afraid _____ (这次考试通不过).

5) _____ (他已出国的消息) is untrue.

V. A. **Rewrite the following sentences after the model.**

Model 1: The next train to Glens Falls would leave only after 12 o'clock.

      The next train to Glens Falls would not leave until 12 o'clock.

1) He's coming only after next Wednesday.

2) He wore glasses only after he was ten.

3) She came only after the meeting was over.

4) Victor went to bed only after he had finished his homework.

Model 2: You were good to try.

      It was good of you to try.

1) You were kind to help me with my studies.

2) You are good to offer your seat to the old man.

3) He was wrong not to prepare his lessons.

4) You were rude (粗鲁的) to talk like that.

B. **Combine the following sentences after the model.**

Model: There sat the man in the old black coat. He held his head in his hands.

      There sat the man in the old black coat with his head in his hands.

1) Sam entered the dark room. He had a gun in his hand.

2) The professor rested against the blackboard. He had chalk (粉笔)

in one hand and a textbook in the other.

3) The man stood there. He put his hands in his pockets.

4) He ran to Daddy. He had tears (眼泪)in his eyes.

VI. Translation.

A. From Chinese to English.

1) 医生们决定立刻为他动手术。

2) 我认为他们不能给你付任何报酬。

3) 这位外科医生直到凌晨两点多才赶到医院。

4) 他是从奥尔巴尼一路赶来救你儿子的外科医生。

5) 他两手插在口袋里站在那里。

6) 穿黑色上衣的那个男子是他父亲。

B. From English to Chinese.

1) A few minutes later, the surgeon's car had to stop for a red light.

2) I met her on my way to the station.

3) It was after two o'clock in the morning when the surgeon arrived at the hospital in Glens Falls.

4) There sat the man in white.

5) It was good of you to invite me to the dinner party.

6) The trouble is that we are short of medicine.

Passage Reading

Why the Poor Man Moved Back to the Park Bench?

Every morning at about eleven o'clock, a bright new car ran through Central Park in New York City, inside the car sat a driver and his boss, a well-known millionaire.

Almost each morning the millionaire noticed a poorly-dressed man sitting on a park bench. The man always sat there staring at the hotel in which the millionaire lived.

One day the millionaire was so curious about the man that he asked his driver to stop the car and he walked towards the bench. He said to the poor man, "But I just have to know why you sit here staring at my hotel every day."

"Sir," said the poor man, "I'm a failure. Now I have no job, no family and even no home. I sleep on this bench, and every night I dream that one day I will sleep in that hotel."

The millionaire said to the poor man, "Tonight your dream will come true. I'll pay for the best room in that hotel for you for a month." So the poor man moved to the best room in the hotel.

But a few days later, the millionaire went by the poor man's room, and he wanted to ask him how he enjoyed himself in such a nice room. To his great surprise, the millionaire found that the poor man had moved out of the hotel, back to the park bench.

When the millionaire asked the reason, the poor man said, "You see, when I'm down here sleeping on the bench, I always dream I am up there in the hotel, it is a wonderful dream. But when I was up there in the hotel, I dreamed I was back here on this cold bench, it was a terrible dream. I could not get any sleep at all, though I was lying in the soft bed."

New Words & Expressions

boss [bɔs] *n*. 老板,上司
millionaire [ˌmiljəˈnɛə] *n*. 百万富翁
poorly-dressed [ˈpuəlidrest] *adj*. 衣着破旧的
stare [stɛə] *vi*. 盯着,凝视

stare at 盯着看,目不转睛
curious [ˈkjuəriəs] *adj*. 好奇的
failure [ˈfeiljə] *n*. 失败者
dream [driːm] *vi*. 做梦,梦见
      n. 梦

dream of 梦见
terrible ['terəbl] *adj*. 糟糕的,很坏的

soft [sɔft] *adj*. 柔软的

Notes to the Passage

1. ...a well-known millionaire 一个著名的百万富翁。英语中副词+过去分词可以合成形容词。再如:poorly-dressed 破衣烂衫的,well-educated 受到良好教育的。
2. Almost each morning the millionaire noticed a poorly-dressed man sitting on a park bench. 几乎每天早上这个富翁都可以看到那个衣着破烂的人坐在公园里的椅子上。notice sb. doing 意为"注意到(某人)正在做某事"。例如:
   We noticed a stranger breaking open the window. 我们看到一个陌生人正在撬开窗户。
3. The man always sat there staring at the hotel in which the millionaire lived. 那个人总是坐在那里盯着富翁居住的酒店。
4. be curious about 意为"对…感到好奇"。例如:
   Children are always curious about things around them. 孩子们总是对周围的事充满了好奇心。
5. Tonight your dream will come true. 今晚你的梦想便会实现。
6. I'll pay for the best room in that hotel for you for a month. 我将为你租下酒店中最好的房间,让你住上一个月。
7. enjoy oneself 意为"过得快乐,玩得痛快"。例如:
   Did you enjoy yourself last night? 你昨晚玩得愉快吗?
8. To his great surprise…使他吃惊的是…。类似的结构还有:
   to one's disappointment 令人失望的是
   to one's regret 令人遗憾的是
   to one's relief 令人放心的是

Which of the following statements are true or false? Write T for true and F for false.

(   )1. Inside the car sat a driver and a well-dressed man.
(   )2. Only on holidays was the man noticed sitting on a park bench.
(   )3. The millionaire wanted to drive him off so he asked his driver to stop the car.
(   )4. The millionaire paid for the best room in the hotel for him for a month.
(   )5. The poorly-dressed man enjoyed his time in the hotel.
(   )6. The poorly-dressed man moved out of the hotel, back to the park bench again.
(   )7. The millionaire was surprised to see that the man was not in the room.
(   )8. The man could not get any sleep on the cold bench.

Unit 8

Text

Learning to Read—in College

(Part I)

The Timkens sent their child Laura off to college with a check for $7,000 in tuition and thought that was the end of it. But soon after they received a letter from the dean of studies.

"We are happy to announce that we have started a remedial reading class for college freshmen and strongly advise that your daughter Laura participate in it. If she doesn't, it is our opinion that Laura will not be able to keep up with her studies. The cost will be $250."

Timken read the letter. "I thought Laura could read," he said to his wife.

"So did I. I think the problem is she can read, but she does not understand what she reads."

"What did they teach her in public school and high school?"

"I have no idea, but if the college says she needs remedial reading we'd better see that she gets it or $7,000 will be thrown away."

A few days later they got another letter from the dean.

"The English Department has informed us that your daughter cannot write. They have suggested that she enroll in the remedial writing class. We started it two years ago when we discovered this was a common problem for most college students. If you agree that Laura should get this special help, please send a check for $250."

Timken was angry now.

"How did she get in college if she can't write?"

Mrs. Timken was much more optimistic about it. "Laura can write. She just can't write complete sentences."

"She went to school for 12 years and she can't write a sentence?" Timken said. "They made an illiterate out of our daughter!"

New Words & Expressions

check [tʃek] *n.* 支票
tuition [tjuːˈiʃən] *n.* 学费
dean [diːn] *n.* 系主任
   dean of studies 教务主任
soon after 不久
announce [əˈnauns] *vt.* 宣布

remedial [riˈmiːdjəl] *adj.* 补救的
freshman [ˈfreʃmən] *n.* 大学一年级学生
strongly [ˈstrɔŋli] *adv.* 强烈地
advise [ədˈvaiz] *vt.* 建议
participate (in) [pɑːˈtisipeit] *vi.* 参加
cost [kɔst] *n.* 费用

problem ['prɔbləm] n. 问题
understand [ˌʌndə'stænd] vt. 理解
public ['pʌblik] adj. 公共的
throw away 扔掉
English Department 英语系
inform [in'fɔ:m] vt. 告知
suggest [sə'dʒest] vt. 建议

enroll (in) [in'roul] vi. 参加
discover [di'skʌvə] vt. 发现
common ['kɔmən] adj. 普通的
optimistic [ɔpti'mistik] adj. 乐观的
complete [kəm'pli:t] adj. 完全的
sentence ['sentəns] n. 句子
illiterate [i'litərit] n. 文盲

Proper Names

Timken ['timkən] (人名)蒂姆肯
Laura ['lɔ:rə] (人名)劳拉

Notes to the Text

1. The Timkens sent their child Laura off to college with a check for $7,000 in tuition and thought that was the end of it. 蒂姆肯夫妇以一张 7,000 美元的支票付了学费,将女儿劳拉送进大学,以为此事就这样结束了。thought 往往含有"误以为"之意。再如:
I thought Laura could read. 我原以为劳拉的阅读没问题。
He thought he had found the right answer, but that was not the case. 他以为他找到了正确答案,但事实并非如此。

2. We are happy to announce that we have started a remedial reading class for college freshmen and strongly advise that your daughter Laura participate in it. 我们很高兴地宣布,已经为大学新生开办了一个阅读补习班,并竭力建议你们的女儿劳拉参加补习。注意:一些表示建议、命令、劝告等的动词作谓语时,其后面的宾语从句中谓语动词要用原形动词。例如:
They have suggested that Laura enroll in the remedial writing class.

他们建议劳拉报名参加写作补习班。

He ordered that the prisoners be shot. 他命令开枪打死犯人。

除了 advise, suggest, order 以外, 类似的动词还有 propose(提议), ask(要求), insist(坚持), demand(要求), request(请求), urge(催促)等。

3. keep up with 赶上, 跟上。例如:

   I have to work hard to keep up with the other students. 我得努力学习以赶上其他同学。

4. So did I. 相当于 "I also thought that Laura could read", 意为"我也是这样想。"在英语中, 如赞同别人对某人某事的评论或与某人有相同的感受, 可以用 so 开头, 并采用倒装。例如:

   "I <u>am</u> hungry."   "So <u>am</u> I."

   "They <u>can</u> both play the piano."   "So <u>can</u> I."

   "They'<u>ll</u> enjoy it."   "So <u>will</u> you."

   如果前一句用的是行为动词, 后面一般用 "do"来代替, 其时态必须与第一句的时态一致。例如:

   "I love to go swimming."   "So do I."

   "She plays tennis everyday."   "So does he."

   "They went to Australia last year."   "So did he."

   如果前一句是个否定句, 后面则用 neither 开头。例如:

   "I can't hear him."   "Neither can she."

   "You're not listening."   "Neither is Paul."

   "I don't want to go there."   "Neither do they."

5. ...but she does not understand what she reads. 但她对她所阅读的东西理解不了。what she reads 为名词从句, 做动词 understand 的宾语。

6. I have no idea, but if the college says she needs remedial reading we'd better see that she gets it or $7,000 will be thrown away. 我不知道, 但如果校方说她需要补习阅读, 我们还是设法让她参加, 不然那7,000美元就白扔了。

   1) idea 意为"想法、猜想", 后面可接 of 短语、that 从句和 what 从句。例如：

Have you any idea of the price? 你知道这个价格吗？

I had an idea that you were there. 当时我还以为你在那儿。

Have you any idea (of) what it's going to cost? 你知道这将要付出什么代价吗？

He had no idea what was likely to happen next. 他无法预料接下来会发生什么事。

2) see 在句中意为"make sure"（务必使…，设法），也可用 see to it 表示。例如：

We'll see (to it) that the boy is properly educated. 我们一定设法使这个孩子受到良好的教育。

See (to it) that you're not late for work again. 你务必上班不能再迟到了。

3) gets it 在此句中意为"参加补习班"。

4) or 意为"不然，否则"。例如：

You'd better hurry, or you'll be late. 你最好赶紧点，否则就要迟到了。

5) throw away 意为"丢弃，扔掉"。例如：

Let's throw the old TV set away, and get a new one. 我们把旧电视机扔掉吧，弄台新的。

7. They made an illiterate out of our daughter! 他们把我的女儿培养成了文盲。此句中 make 意为"成为，培养成"。再如：

make good citizens out of the students 把学生培养成好公民。

Dialogue

A: May I help you?
B: Yes, I'd like to see Mr. Jackson. I have an appointment at four o'clock.

121

A: Just a moment, please. I'll see if he is still in his office. I thought I saw him leaving about an hour ago... would you mind waiting here for a moment?

B: No, not at all. Thank you.

A: I'm sorry. Mr. Jackson is in conference at the moment but he should be back here before long. You're welcome to wait if you wish.

B: Yes, I will. Thank you.

New Words and Expressions

appointment [əˈpɔintmənt] n. 约会
mind [maind] vt. 介意
not at all 根本不
conference [ˈkɔnfərəns] n. 会议

before long 不久
welcome [ˈwelkəm] adj. 受欢迎的
wish [wiʃ] vt. 希望

Proper Name

Jackson [ˈdʒæksən] (人名) 杰克逊

Notes to the Dialogue

1. I'll see if he is still in his office. 我看一看他是否还在办公室里,这里 if 意为"是否",引导的是宾语从句。

2. Would you mind waiting here for a moment? 你介意在这儿等一会吗? mind doing something 意为"介意做某事"。例如:
   Do you mind opening the window? 把窗户打开你介意吗?

3. Mr. Jackson is in conference at the moment but he should be back here before long. 杰克逊先生现在在开会,但他一会儿就会回来。before long 意为"不久以后",常用于将来时态。例如:

The fog will disappear before long. 不久雾就会消散。

Grammar

名词从句(The Noun Clauses)(二)

Ⅰ. 用连接代词和连接副词引导的名词从句。

1. 作主语

   <u>What they saw and heard in China</u> made a deep impression on them. 他们在中国的所见所闻给他们留下了深刻印象。

   <u>Who will chair the meeting</u> has not yet been decided. 谁将主持这个会议还未决定。

2. 作宾语

   She doesn't understand <u>what she reads.</u> 她对所阅读的东西理解不了。

   The millionaire wanted to ask him <u>how he enjoyed himself in such a nice room.</u> 百万富翁想问问他住在这样好的房间里过得怎么样。

   I don't know <u>where I can find Jim.</u> 我不知道在哪儿能找到吉姆。

3. 作介词宾语

   Your success will depend on <u>how you work.</u> 你的成功将取决于你如何工作。

   Were you surprised at <u>what eventually happened?</u> 你对最终发生的事情感到惊讶吗?

4. 作表语

   She is not <u>what she was ten years ago.</u> 她不再是十年前的她了。

   This dictionary is just <u>what I have been looking for.</u> 这本词典正是我一直在寻找的。

   注意:1) 用连接代词和连接副词引导的名词从句前面不再加that。例如:

不能说：No one could understand that what he was talking about.

只能说：No one could understand what he was talking about.

2) 在用连接代词和连接副词引导的名词从句中，主语和谓语应按陈述句的语序排列。例如：

不能说：Where did Mary go is none of your business.

只能说：Where Mary went is none of your business.

Ⅱ．用连接词 if, whether 引导的名词从句

1．作主语

<u>Whether he is coming</u> remains a question. 他会不会来还是个问题。

2．作宾语

I wonder <u>whether/if you have finished your homework</u>. 我不知道你们是否已经做完了家庭作业。

3．作表语

The question is <u>whether you can do this in some other way</u>. 问题是你是否能用别的方法做这件事。

注意：1) whether 后面能紧接 or not, if 后面一般不接 or not。例如：

可以说：I wonder whether or not there will be a live broadcast from Sydney tonight. 我不知道今晚是否有来自悉尼的现场报道。

也可以说：I wonder if there will be a live broadcast from Sydney tonight or not.

但不能说：I wonder if or not there will be a live broadcast from Sydney tonight.

2) if 引导的名词从句只能作动词的宾语，不能做主语或表语。例如：

可以说：Whether (or not) you go is your decision.

但不能说：If you go is your decision.

Exercises

I. **Which of the following statements are true or false? Write T for true and F for false.**

( )1) The Timkens thought that was the end of it after sending their daughter off to college and paying the tuition.

( )2) A remedial class is a class for college freshmen.

( )3) The dean of studies strongly advised in his letter that the Timkens' daughter attend the remedial class.

( )4) From what the dean says in his letter we know for sure that Laura is very good at reading.

( )5) From what the dean says in his second letter we learn that Laura cannot write.

( )6) Laura is only one of the very many students who fail to write well.

( )7) An "illiterate" means a person who is unable to read.

( )8) The story took place before Laura entered the college.

II. **Match each word in Column A with a similar meaning in Column B.**

A	B
1) tuition	a. take part
2) freshman	b. get rid of
3) participate	c. the money paid for being taught
4) keep up with	d. thinking that good things will happen in the future
5) inform	e. a student in his first year
6) throw away	f. a person who cannot read or write
7) enroll	g. catch up with, follow

8) optimistic   h. formally tell someone about something

9) illiterate   i. shared by everyone in a society

10) common   j. make oneself officially a member of a group

III. A. **Fill in the blanks with the words or expressions given below. Change the form where necessary.**

send...off	keep up with	participate in	had better
throw away	soon after	optimistic about	enroll in
remedial	advise	cost	inform

1) Mary complained about getting up early in the morning to _____ her husband _____ to work.

2) You _____ hurry or you will be late.

3) The teacher _____ that he go there at once.

4) It's time we _____ the old furniture _____.

5) I had to run to _____ the girls.

6) He built the house without regard to (不考虑) the _____.

7) The small boy wanted to _____ the youth club, but he was too young.

8) I like the whole school to _____ the sports.

9) He thought that he had accomplished his work but _____ he found that was not the case.

10) "Some money is missing." "Have you _____ the police?"

11) In spite of all the problems we remain _____ the company's future.

12) The government is taking _____ measures against unemployment (失业).

B. **Fill in the blanks with a proper word according to the initial letter.**

1) They sent their daughter off to a private school with a check for

126

$8,000 in t_____.

2) The dean of studies says she should p_____ in a r_____ writing class.

3) This was a c_____ problem for most college f_____.

4) They strongly a_____ that he e_____ in an English training class.

5) The boy is now ten years old, but he cannot write a c_____ sentence.

6) The team manager sounded quite o_____ when we asked him about tomorrow's game.

7) The dean of studies has i_____ them that their daughter cannot write.

8) They are determined to help those i_____ learn to read and write.

IV. A. **Complete each of the following sentences using a "what" clause.**

1) (they, see)_____ in Tibet made a deep impression on them.

2) Don't put off till tomorrow _____(we, can, do, today).

3) This is just _____(we, should, always, keep in mind).

4) (cause, forest fire)_____ is a complete mystery (完全是个迷).

5) (you, say) _____ does not surprise me.

B. **Complete the following sentences with either "whether" or "if" clauses.**

1) "Can you make less noise?"
   I only asked _____.

2) "Does Mary actually want to come?"
   It isn't very clear _____.

3) "Have you got any letters for me?"

I wonder _____.

4) Can you finish your homework in time?

The question is _____.

5) Does he want to go?

He doesn't seem to know _____.

C. Put the following Chinese into English by using noun clauses.

1) _____ is a mystery. （她为什么要离开这里）

2) _____ is unknown to us. （他们什么时候到）

3) We always had to live _____. （我父亲工作的地方）

4) I'll never forget _____. （我们第一次是如何在大雨中见面的）

5) It's a secret _____. （谁给了她这本书）

6) Do you know _____? （这是谁的辞典）

7) I don't remember _____. （我已经说过多少遍了）

8) I wonder _____. （你喜欢哪本书）

V. A. Answer the following questions after the model.

Model: What did they strongly advise?

  (Laura, participate in, a remedial reading class)

  → They strongly advised that Laura participate in a remedial reading class.

1) What have they suggested in the letter?

  (Laura, enroll in, a remedial writing class)

2) What did he propose?

  (the discussion, put off)

3) What did they advise?

  (we, go there, at once)

4) What did they insist?

(this novel, make into a film)

B. Rewrite the following sentences after the model.

Model 1: Timken thought that Laura could read. His wife also thought that Laura could read.

→ Timken thought that Laura could read. So did his wife.

1) I was late for class. She was late, too.

2) They came to Dalian last summer. She came here, too.

3) She can swim. Her sister can swim, too.

4) Bob plays tennis. Mary plays tennis, too.

Model 2: It would be a good idea for us to see that she gets it.

→ We'd better see that she gets it.

1) It would be a good idea for her to attend the remedial class.

2) It would be a good idea for us to get more exercise.

3) It would be a good idea for him not to sing the same song.

4) It would be a good idea for me not to be late for class again.

C. Make sentences after the model, using the pattern "see (to it) that" and the given words and expressions.

Model: Laura, get it

→ See to it that Laura gets it.

or: We'll see (to it) that Laura gets it.

or: Will you please see (to it) that Laura gets it?

1) you, not, late for work, next time

2) all the windows, close, before you leave

3) such accidents, never happen, again

4) you, throw away, the old TV set, and, get, a new one

VI. Translation.

A. From Chinese to English.

1) 他极力建议我参加为大学新生开设的写作补习班。

2) 在这一点上蒂姆肯太太要比她丈夫乐观多了。
3) 这是许多大学生的通病,都不会写作。
4) 我们认为她年龄尚小,无法跟上学业。
5) 我们最好负责让她报名参加一个舞蹈班。
6) 我错过了(miss)两次会议,她也错过了。

B. From English to Chinese.

1) It was the school's responsibility(责任) to make good citizens out of the students.
2) The dean of studies has informed them that Laura should get this special help.
3) The problem is she can read, but she doesn't understand what she reads.
4) Listening carefully to what the teacher says in class means less work later.
5) What most surprised her teachers was the fact that she passed her examination despite her absence from school.
6) Hurry up, or you'll be late for school.

Passage Reading

Learning to Read—in College

(Part Ⅱ)

"Oh, I believe that's a bit strong, I'm sure, anyway, the college can help her learn to write. After all, it is an institution of higher learning."

"So now we have to pay $250 for something they should have taught her in grammar school?"

"Don't you remember what the principal said years ago? It was the school's responsibility to make good citizens out of the students, and the parents' responsibility to teach the children to read and write. It seems that we're the ones who failed."

Timken sent in the check, and was not surprised to find another letter waiting for him a week later.

It read: " We have found that no one in freshman class can add, multiply, subtract or divide simple sums. We feel it is urgent that this deficiency be corrected early in a student's college career. Therefore, we are setting up a special remedial arithmetic course. The fee will be $250. If you do not want your daughter to take this course we cannot guarantee she will graduate."

Once again Timken flew into a rage. "I thought Laura got A's in math in high school."

Mrs. Timken said, "That was conceptional math. She never could add or subtract. Don't you remember when you complained once about it and Laura's teacher told you, 'she can always learn to add and subtract when she gets to college.'?"

New Words & Expressions

anyway ['eniwei] adv. 无论如何
after all 毕竟
institution [ˌinsti'tjuːʃən] n. 惯例,制度
higher learning 高等教育
grammar school 小学
principal ['prinsəpəl] n. 校长
responsibility [risˌpɔnsə'biliti] 责任
citizen ['sitizn] n. 公民
fail [feil] vi. 失败
add [æd] vt. 加法

multiply ['mʌltiplai] vt. 乘法
subtract [səb'trækt] vt. 减法
divide [di'vaid] vt. 除法
sum [sʌm] n. 数目
urgent ['əːdʒənt] adj. 紧急的
deficiency [di'fiʃənsi] n. 缺陷
career [kə'riə] n. 生涯
arithmetic [ˌæriθ'metik] adj. 数学的
fee [fiː] n. 费用
guarantee [ˌgærən'tiː] vt. 保证

rage [reidʒ] *n*. 生气
fly into a rage 勃然大怒

conceptional [kən'sepʃənəl] *adj*. 理想的

Notes to the Passage

1. I believe that's a bit strong. 我觉得你这么说未免有些言过其词。

   1) that 指 Timken 说的 "They made an illiterate out of my daughter" 这句话。

   2) strong 含有"夸夸其词,夸张"之意。

2. "So now we have to pay ＄250 for something they should have taught her in grammar school?" "所以说为了那些他们本该在小学里就教会她的东西,我们现在得破费 250 美元?"

   1) should have done 表示过去某动作应该发生而实际并未发生,有"本来应该"的意思。例如:

   He should have let us know his plans. (＝ but he did not) 他应该让我们了解他的计划。(但他没有)

   2) 否定形式表示过去发生了在说话人看来本不应该发生的动作。例如:

   You look so pale. You shouldn't have eaten those seafood yesterday. 你看上去脸色苍白,你昨天不应该吃那些海鲜。(但你吃了)

3. We feel it is urgent that this deficiency be corrected early in a student's college career. 我们认为这一缺陷必须在学生的大学生涯早期得到纠正。注意 It is ＋ adj. ＋ that 结构,在这一结构中,从句中的谓语动词要用原形动词。例如:

   It is important that we take notes on his lecture. 我们在听他的课时作笔记很重要。

   类似的形容词还有: necessary, desirable (值得的), advisable (明智的), etc.

Answer the questions according to the passage.

1. By saying "oh, I believe that's a bit strong", did she mean that her husband was exaggerating (夸大)?
2. How much did the parents have to pay for the remedial writing course?
3. What was the school's responsibility according to the principal?
4. Was Timken surprised to find another letter waiting for him a week later?
5. What was the letter about?
6. Did Timken get very angry?
7. How many letters did the parents receive from the college according to the whole passage?
8. What does the title "Learning to Read—in College" imply?

Unit 9

Text

Doing Favours Can Be Dangerous

I found out one time that doing a favour for someone could get you into a lot of trouble. I was in the eighth grade at the time, and we were having a final test. During the test, the girl sitting next to me whispered something, but I didn't understand. So I leaned over her way and found out that she was trying to ask me if I had an extra pen. She showed me that hers was out of ink and would not write. I happened to have an extra one, so I took it out of my pocket and put it on her desk.

Later, after the test papers had been turned in, the teacher asked me to stay in the room when all the other students were dismissed. As soon as we were alone she began to talk to me about what it meant to grow up; she mentioned how important it was to stand on your own two feet and be responsible for your acts. For a long time, she talked about honesty and emphasized the fact that when people do something dishonest, they are really cheating themselves. She made me promise that I would think seriously about all the things she had said, and then she told me I could leave. I walked out of the room wondering why she had chosen me to talk about all those things.

Later on, I found out that she thought I had cheated on the test. When she saw me lean over to talk to the girl next to me, it looked as though I was copying answers from the girl's test paper. I tried to explain about the pen, but all she could say was it seemed awfully strange to her that I hadn't mentioned anything about the pen the day she talked to me right after the test. Even though I tried to explain that I was just doing the girl a favour by letting her use my pen, I am sure she continued to believe that I had cheated on the test.

New Words & Expressions

grade [greid] n. 年级
dangerous ['deindʒrəs] adj. 危险的
final ['fainl] adj. 最后的
test [test] n. 考试
   test paper 试卷
whisper ['wispə] vi. 小声说
lean [li:n] vi. 倾斜,倚
extra ['ekstrə] adj. 额外的

happen to 碰巧
turn in 上交,交出
dismiss [dis'mis] vt. 解散
alone [ə'loun] adj. 独自一人
mention ['menʃən] vt. 提及
own [oun] adj. 自己的
act [ækt] vi., n. 行为,行动
honesty ['ɔnisti] n. 诚实

135

emphasize ['emfəsaiz] vt. 强调
dishonest [dis'ɔnist] adj. 不诚实的
cheat [tʃi:t] vt., vi. 欺骗
seriously ['siəriəsli] adv. 严肃地,严重地

copy ['kɔpi] vt. 抄
awfully ['ɔ:fuli] adv. 非常
strange [streindʒ] adj. 奇怪的

Notes to the Text

1. I found out one time that doing a favour for someone could get you into a lot of trouble. 有一次我发现帮助别人可能会使你陷入困境。doing a favor for someone 是动名词短语,在这里做从句中的主语。do somebody a favour 或 do a favour for somebody 意为"施惠于,帮助"。get somebody into trouble 意为"使某人陷入困境"。

2. During the test, the girl sitting next to me whispered something, but I didn't understand. 考试时,坐在我旁边的女孩小声说了什么,但我没明白。sitting next to me 是现在分词短语作定语,修饰 the girl。

3. So I leaned over her way and found out that she was trying to ask me if I had an extra pen. 所以我向她那边靠了靠,发现她原来是在问我有没有多余的笔。

4. She showed me that hers was out of ink and would not write. 她向我示意,她的笔没墨水了,写不了字。would 是情态动词,在本句中意为"不起作用"。例如:
   The drawer would not shut. 抽屉关不上。

5. I happened to have an extra pen, so I took it out of my pocket and put it on her desk. 我碰巧有枝多余的笔,就从口袋里掏出笔,把它放在她的桌上。happen 意为"碰巧,刚好",后跟不定式。例如:
   I happened to meet him yesterday. 我昨天刚好碰见他。

6. As soon as we were alone she began to talk to me about what it meant to grow up; she mentioned how important it was to stand on your own two feet and be responsible for your acts. 别人一走完,她就开始

跟我讲起长大意味着什么,并提起自立自强,对自己行为负责有多么重要。该句中,两个 it 都是形式主语,真正的主语是不定式 to grow up 和 to stand on your own feet and be responsible for your own acts。再如:

It is difficult to finish the work without help. 在没有别人帮助的情况下完成工作很困难。

7. For a long time, she talked about honesty and emphasized the fact that when people do something dishonest, they are really cheating themselves. 很长时间,她一直谈论着诚实,强调当人们做了不诚实的事,他们实际上是在欺骗自己。

8. She made me promise that I would think seriously about all the things she had said, and then she told me I could leave. 她让我许诺要认真考虑她所说的话,然后让我走了。

9. I walked out of the room, wondering why she had chosen me to talk about all these things. 我走出房间,琢磨着她为什么选择我谈论这些事。wondering why she had chosen me to talk about all these things 是现在分词短语,在句中作伴随状语。

10. When she saw me lean over to talk to the girl next to me, it looked as though I was copying answers from the girl's test paper. 她看到我斜过去和旁边的女孩讲话,看上去好像我在抄袭女孩试卷上的答案。as though(if) 意为"看起来好像"。例如:

It sounds as though she's been really ill. 听起来她好像真的病了。
as though (if) 后面还可以跟非真实的情况,这时,后面的从句要用虚拟语气。例如:

I can not move my legs—it is as if they were stuck to the floor. 我的腿动不了了,它们好像被钉在了地板上。

11. ...but all she could say was it seemed awfully strange to her that I hadn't mentioned anything about the pen the day she talked to me right after the test. 但她说考试后她找我谈话时我却没提笔的事,

实在太奇怪了。

Dialogue

A: There's a lot of noise coming from the picnic area. I hope Laddie didn't get in trouble.

B: I hope not, either, but you know Laddie.

A: Well, he's not here in the picnic area. Maybe he's over there by the lake.

B: There he is! That man is holding him.

Man: Is this your dog?

A: Yes, sir. I'm really sorry. He's a bad dog. He ran away.

Man: He's not a bad dog. He's a good dog. That little girl over there fell in the lake. Your dog barked and barked until someone came to get her. He saved that little girl's life.

A: Good dog. Laddie! Helping someone is better than winning a Frisbee contest!

New Words & Expressions

hope [houp] vt. 希望
get in trouble 惹麻烦
maybe ['meibi:] adv. 也许
run away 逃跑

lake [leik] n. 湖
win [win] vt. 赢得
Frisbee ['frizbi:] n. 飞盘
contest ['kɔntest] n. 比赛

Notes to the Dialogue

1. There's a lot of noise coming from the picnic area. 从野餐区传来许多嘈杂声。coming from the picnic area 是现在分词短语作定语, 修饰

noise。

2. I hope not, either, but you know Laddie. 我也希望莱蒂不会惹麻烦,但你知道他。I hope not 是个省略句,完整的句子应为 I hope that Laddie didn't get in trouble。not 可用来替代上文提到的事物。例如:

"Will it rain?" 会下雨吗?

"I hope not." (= I hope that it will not rain.) 我希望不会下雨。

I'll try to get home by six, but if not (= if I can't get home by six), go to the theatre without me. 我会尽量赶在六点钟之前回来,如果我回不来,你们就自己去戏院吧,别等我了。

如果是肯定句,则用 so 代替上文提到的内容。例如:

He hopes he'll win, and I hope so. 他希望自己能赢,我也这样希望。

Are you tired? If so(= If you are tired), please have a rest. 你累了吗? 如果累了,休息一下吧。

3. Your dog barked and barked until someone came to get her. 你的狗一直叫,一直叫,直到有人把她(小女孩)救起。until 作为连词,引起表示一段时间的状语,分三种情况:

1) 如果主句的谓语动词是延续性动词,主句要用肯定式。例如:

She stood there until he left. 她站在那里,直到他离开。

2) 如果主句的谓语动词是非延续性动词,主句要用否定式。例如:

He didn't enter the room until I returned. 直到我回去他才进屋。

3) 有的动词既可用作延续性动词,又可用作非延续性动词,因此其肯定式和否定式均可和 until 连用,但表示的意思不同。例如:

He ate until it was dark. 他一直吃到天黑。

He did not eat until it was dark. 天黑了他才吃饭。

4. Helping someone is better than winning a Frisbee contest! 帮助别人比赢得飞盘比赛要好。

Grammar

状语从句(The Adverbial Clause)(一)

状语从句是由从句充当状语。作状语的从句通常由一个连词或一个起连词作用的词组引起,状语从句可用来表示时间、地点、条件、原因、让步、目的、结果、比较和方式。

1. 时间状语从句

   常见的引导时间状语从句的连词有:when, while, as, before, after, as soon as, until, till, since。例如:

   When she saw me lean over to talk to the girl next to me, it looked as though I was copying answers from the girl's test paper. 她看到我斜过去和旁边的女孩讲话,看上去好像我在抄女孩试卷上的答案。

   They looked for a good place to leave him in while they were away. 他们在外出期间找了个好地方给他留下来。

   They took him to the shop just before they left for their holiday and said goodbye to him. 就在他们去度假并向布莱克告别以前,他们把他带到了那个商店。

   After the test paper had been turned in, the teacher asked me to stay in the room. 试卷交上去后,老师让我留在教室里。

   As soon as we were alone she began to talk to me about what it meant to grow up. 别人一走完,她就开始跟我讲起长大意味着什么。

   The children didn't go to bed until their mother came back. 直到妈妈回来孩子们才去睡觉。

   Since he graduated from the college, he has worked in this city. 他大学毕业后一直在这个城市工作。

2. 地点状语从句

   表示地点的状语从句由 where 或 wherever 引起。例如:

There are plenty of sheep <u>where I live.</u> 我住的地方有很多羊。
<u>Where there is a will,</u> there is a way. 有志者事竟成。
<u>Wherever I am</u> I'll miss you. 无论我到了哪里,我都会想你的。

3. 条件状语从句

常见的引导条件状语从句的连词有：if, unless（除非,如果…不), in case, so (as) long as, so far as, on condition (that) 等。例如：

<u>If I were you,</u> I will take this job. 如果我是你,我就会干这份工作。
<u>If you agree that Laura should get this special help,</u> please send a check for ＄250. 如果你同意劳拉应该得到这份特殊的帮助,那么请寄一张250美元的支票。
We'll be late <u>unless we hurry up.</u> 如果我们不快点,就会迟到的。
Send us a message <u>in case you have any difficulty.</u> 万一有什么困难,给我们一个信。
I tried to bear all this <u>as long as I could.</u> 我尽可能地忍受这一切。
<u>So far as I know,</u> he is a good teacher. 据我所知,他是个好老师。

4. 原因状语从句

表示原因的状语从句可以由 as, because, now that, since 引导。例如：
I do it <u>because I like it.</u> 我做这事因为我喜欢。
<u>As he wasn't ready in time,</u> we went without him. 因为他未及时准备好,我们没有等他就先走了。
<u>Since (now that) no one is against it,</u> we'll accept the suggestion. 既然没人反对,我们就接受这个建议。

Exercises

I. Choose the best answer a, b, c or d to these questions about the text.

1) During the test, the girl sitting next to the boy whispered something, because _____.

    a. she wanted to copy the answer from the boy

b. she wanted to borrow a pen
   c. she wanted to borrow some ink
   d. She wanted to ask the time
2) As the boy didn't understand the girl, he _____.
   a. told her to be silent
   b. asked the teacher for help
   c. tried to find out what she meant
   d. paid no attention to her
3) After the test, the teacher _____.
   a. asked the boy to stay
   b. dismissed all the students as usual
   c. asked the boy and the girl to stay
   d. asked the boy why he cheated
4) The thing(s) the teacher emphasized was(were) _____.
   a. sense of duty   b. honesty
   c. seriousness   d. all of the above
5) The boy was _____ when the teacher talked to him.
   a. ashamed   b. puzzled
   c. happy   d. sad
6) The teacher _____.
   a. told the boy not to do the same thing next time
   b. criticized the boy for his dishonesty
   c. asked him to explain why he cheated on the test
   d. said whispering in the test was wrong
7) The boy knew what the teacher meant _____.
   a. when he left the room
   b. when the teacher asked him to stay
   c. when the teacher talked to him
   d. a few days later

8) When the boy tried to explain about the pen, the teacher _____.
   a. realized that she was wrong
   b. said sorry to the boy
   c. still believed that the boy had cheated on the test
   d. said nothing about it

II. Match each word in Column A with a similar meaning in Column B.

A	B
1) final	a. speak very quietly
2) whisper	b. not honest
3) alone	c. taking the duty
4) understand	d. more of something
5) dishonest	e. give special importance to something
6) extra	f. last, coming at the end
7) responsible	g. on one's own; by oneself
8) dismiss	h. very much
9) emphasize	i. ask somebody to leave
10) awfully	j. know the meaning of something

III. A. Fill in each of the blanks with the suitable form of the word given. Change the form if necessary.

1) dangerous
   a. Do you know the _____ of smoking?
   b. Sky-diving (空中滑翔) is a _____ game.
2) honesty
   a. Tom is an _____ boy. He never tells a lie.
   b. The teacher talked about _____ all the time.
3) choose
   a. Will you help me _____ a coat?

    b. I have no _____; I must do all the work.
4) act
    a. You must stop your foolish _____.
    b. We must _____ to save the girl's life.
5) responsible
    a. Who is _____ for breaking the window?
    b. As you have grown up, you must know your _____.

B. Fill in each of the blanks with a word according to the initial letter.

1) It is d_____ for women to walk alone at night.
2) Jill m_____ something about the party on Sunday.
3) You must be r_____ for your own acts.
4) It should be e_____ that flying is a safe way to travel.
5) Daddy p_____ that he will take me to the zoo on Saturday.

C. Fill in the blanks with the words or expressions given below. Change the form where necessary.

find out	do somebody a favor	seriously	lean over
turn in	be responsible for	alone	whisper	awfully
happen to	extra	emphasize	copy	dismiss

1) It's very important to stand on your own feet and _____ your acts.
2) Did you ever _____ why he cheated on the test?
3) Students _____ the papers and left the room.
4) The teacher _____ her class early because she felt uncomfortable.
5) I _____ have an extra pen so I gave it to her.
6) He _____ to hear what she said.
7) Could you get an _____ loaf (片) of bread?
8) _____ and turn off the radio.

9) It should be _____ that flying is a very safe way to travel.

10) I _____ the article and gave it to the class to read.

11) Suddenly they found themselves _____ together in the room.

12) Stop _____ in the corner; say whatever it is out loud.

13) It's _____ cold here. Please turn the heater (暖气) on.

14) I think it's about time we talked _____ about our relationship.

IV. A. Make sentences after the given patterns.

1) We didn't leave <u>until</u> the rain stopped.
   a. he, finish the work, his father came back
   b. I, know the reason, the teacher told me
   c. baby, stop crying, his mother came back

2) I'll let you know <u>as soon as</u> it is arranged.
   a. Tom, begin to write his homework, he came back home
   b. we, set off, the rain stopped
   c. I, give the letter to you, it arrives

3) Don't leave the room <u>unless</u> I tell you to.
   a. I, go, he calls me
   b. we, go there next Sunday, it rains
   c. she, die, the doctor operates at once

4) <u>Now that</u> you are all here, let's try to make a decision.
   a. John, arrive, we can begin
   b. they, know each other better, get along fine
   c. you, a student, you must work hard

B. Combine each pair of sentences using the connecting words in brackets after the models.

Model 1: It will be close to midnight. He'll leave his office.
         (when)

→ He'll leave his office when it is close to midnight.
1) She will take a vacation. She'll be able to rest. (when)
2) He'll see a ship. He'll continue swimming. (until)
3) She'll check the computer. She'll answer their questions. (after)
4) They'll have a sale (销售). They'll advertise (打广告) in the newspaper. (before)
5) She'll look in her purse. She'll find some cigarettes. (if)

Model 2: Why have they cut back on space programs? They have proved to be very expensive. (because)
→ They have cut back on space programs because they have proved to be very expensive.

1) Why did they close the factory? It was releasing (释放) too much pollution (污染) into the air. (because)
2) Why did he take a gun with him? He thought the job was dangerous. (since)
3) Why didn't they ask her to attend the meeting? She was working on another project (项目). (as)
4) Why do they depend on their computers? They need a great deal of information (信息). (as)

C. Fill in the blanks with a suitable conjunction.

where	as	because	so long as	in case
if	before	now that	unless	since

1) You wouldn't had a bad time at all _____ you weren't seasick (晕船).
2) Sit _____ you like.
3) He had only spoken that word _____ he came back.
4) _____ she has no car, she can't get there easily.
5) He did not come _____ he was ill.

6) _____ you have come you may as well stay.

7) Sometimes it gets out _____ I can stop it.

8) _____ the weather is fine tomorrow, we shall have a picnic (野餐).

9) He won't finish his work in time _____ he works hard.

10) _____ it rains, I'll not come.

V. **Rewrite the following sentences after the model.**

Model 1: It happened that I had an extra one.

→ I happened to have an extra one.

1) It happened that I met him in the street.

2) It happened that the famous actor was her brother.

3) It happened that there was a doctor at the meeting.

4) It happened that I was just passing, so I thought I'd call and see you.

Model 2: I was copying answers from the girl's test paper. (look)

→ It looked as though I was copying the answers from the girl's test paper.

1) She's been really ill. (sound 听起来)

2) Tenny is hungry. (look)

3) This milk is fresh. (smell 闻起来)

4) These puddings (布丁) are homemade (自己制作的). (taste 尝起来)

VI. **Translation.**

A. **From Chinese to English.**

1) 汤姆只有4岁,让他一个人在家很危险。

2) 他一直强调说他有很重要的事情告诉老师。

3) 天很阴,好像要下雨。

4) 你长大了,应该为自己的行为负责。

5) 尽管我尽力解释我只是借给她笔用,老师还是不相信我。

6) 你不应在朋友有困难时逃走。

B. From English to Chinese.

1) I happened to see Mary when I was shopping.

2) When friends are in trouble, we should try to do them a favour.

3) I didn't start my meal until Mum came back.

4) The manager accepted the suggestion that we should cut down the price.

5) "I think Laddie will win the contest." "I think so."

6) Saving the girl's life is better than winning the Frisbee contest.

Passage Reading

Getting away from Work and Enjoying Yourself

There's another American saying, "All work and no play makes Jack a dull boy." But Jack and Jill too, now do have more than enough time for play —leisure time activities, to use the current expression. Most Americans work only forty hours a week. They have evenings and weekends free to enjoy themselves. There are also a few long weekends during the year since some holidays now fall on Monday. In addition, many men and women have two or more weeks of vacation time every year. Thousands of people work at filling up all this leisure time; they work while others play.

Not so many years ago, people used to have to go out for entertainment if they didn't stay home and read. They could go to the movies, the theater, the ballpark, wherever there was something happening. Now they can stay home, but instead of curling up with a good book, they usually watch television. Television brings not only the latest news but also just about anything you can imagine in the way of entertainment right into your home. You can see movies, concerts, entertainment programs, and spectator sports like football, basketball, and baseball without getting up from your chair. Only a few thousand people can watch a football game right there in the stadium, but millions can see it on TV. And now you can see movies only a year or so old on a VCR.

  Hobbies are another way in which people can fill up their leisure time. A hobby is just something that someone likes to do away from work. Some people collect stamps or watch birds, others go hunting or fishing. Many men and women are amateur artists; that is, they aren't trying to make their living in the arts. They paint pictures, play a musical instrument, or make pottery just for their own enjoyment. That's what leisure time is for—to get away from work and to enjoy yourself.

New words & Expressions

saying ['seiiŋ] *n*. 谚语
dull [dʌl] *adj*. 呆笨的
leisure ['leʒə] *n*. 空闲
current ['kʌrənt] *adj*. 现代的,时下的
express [iks'pres] *vt*. 表达
expression [iks'preʃən] *n*. 表达
fall on 落到
fill up 填满
entertainment [,entə'teinmənt] *n*. 娱乐
theater ['θiətə] *n*. 戏院
ballpark ['bɔːlpɑːk] *n*. 棒球场
instead of 而不是
curl [kəːl] *vi*. 卷曲
 curl up 蜷缩
imagine [i'mædʒin] *vt*. 想象

program ['prougræm] *n*. 节目
spectator [spek'teitə] *n*. 观众
sports [spɔːts] *n*. 运动
 football sports 足球运动
 basketball sports 篮球运动
baseball ['beisbɔːl] *n*. 棒球
stadium ['steidiəm] *n*. 体育馆
VCR 摄像机
stamp [stæmp] *n*. 邮票
amateur ['æmətə] *n*., *adj*. 业余爱好者,业余的
art [ɑːt] *n*. 艺术
paint [peint] *vt*. 画画
musical ['mjuːzikəl] *adj*. 音乐的
instrument ['instrumənt] *n*. 乐器

pottery [ˈpɒtəri] *n*. 陶器　　　　enjoyment [inˈdʒɔimənt] *n*. 娱乐

Notes to the Dialogue

1. There's another American saying, "All work and no play makes Jack a dull boy."美国有一句谚语"只学习不玩耍，聪明孩子也变傻"。
2. But Jack and Jill too, now do have more than enough time for play—leisure time activities, to use the current expression. 但是，杰克，还有吉尔，现在确实有足够的时间去玩，用句时髦的话来说，叫休闲。do 在这里表示强调。再如：
   I did see him on the street yesterday. 我昨天在街上的确看见过他。
3. Thousands of people work at filling up all this leisure time; they work while others play. 数以千计的人却以工作来填补所有这些空闲时间。fill up 意为"填满"。例如：
   The room was soon filled up with people. 房间里很快挤满了人。
4. Now they can stay home, but instead of curling up with a good book, they usually watch television. 现在他们可以呆在家里，但是他们不是捧本好书躺在沙发上，而是看电视。instead of 意为"而不是"。例如：
   I want a cup of coffee, instead of a cup of tea. 我想要一杯咖啡，而不是茶。
   I should be at school, instead of lying here in bed. 我应该在学校，而不是躺在床上。
5. Television brings not only the latest news but also just about anything you can imagine in the way of entertainment right into your home. 电视里不仅有最新的消息，而且可以把一切你所能想象到的娱乐带到家中。in the way of 意为"以…方式"。例如：
   You should talk to the children in the way of tenderness. 你应该温和地跟孩子讲话。

Answer the questions according to the passage.
1. What does the saying "All work and no play makes Jack a dull boy" mean?
2. Do Americans have enough time for play now?
3. When do Americans do leisure time activities?
4. What did people use to do if they didn't stay home?
5. What do people do now if they stay home?
6. What can people get from television?
7. What's a hobby?
8. What does "amateur artist" mean?

Unit 10

Text

Good Advice

When I was about 12, I had an enemy, a girl who liked to point out my shortcomings. Week by week her list grew: I was very thin, I wasn't a good student, I talked too much, I was too proud, and so on. I tried to bear all this as long as I could. At last, I became very angry. I ran to Daddy with tears in my eyes.

He listened to me quietly. Then he asked, "Are the things she says true—or not? Allen, didn't you ever wonder what you're really like? Well, you now have that girl's opinion. Go and make a list of everything she said and mark the points that are true. Pay no attention to the other things she said."

I did as he told me. To my great surprise, I discovered that about half the things were true. Some of them I couldn't change (like being very thin), but a good number I could—and suddenly I wanted to change. For the first time I got a fairly clear picture of myself.

I brought the list back to Daddy. He refused to take it. "That's just for you," he said. "You know better than anyone else the truth about yourself. But you have to learn to listen, not just close your ears in anger and feeling hurt. When something said about you is true, you'll find it will be of help to you. Our world is full of people who think they know your duty. Don't shut your ears. Listen to them all, but hear the truth and do what you know is the right thing to do."

Daddy's advice has returned to me at many important moments. In my life, I've never had a better piece of advice.

New Words & Expressions

advice [əd'vais] n. 建议
enemy ['enimi] n. 敌人
point [pɔint] vi. 指, 指出
    n. 要点
 point out 指出
shortcoming [ʃɔːt'kʌmiŋ] n. 缺点
thin [θin] adj. 瘦弱的
proud [praud] adj. 骄傲的
bear [bɛə] vt. 忍受
as long as 只要, 在某条件下
tear [tiə] n. 眼泪

mark [mɑːk] vt. 做记号
attention [ə'tenʃən] n. 注意
 pay attention to 注意
fairly ['fɛəli] adv. 相当地
refuse [ri'fjuːz] vt. 拒绝
truth [truːθ] n. 真相
anger ['æŋgə] n. 生气
full of 充满
duty ['djuːti] n. 职责
shut [ʃʌt] vt. 关上

Proper Name

Allen [ˈælən]（人名）阿伦

Notes to the Text

1. When I was about 12, I had an enemy, a girl who liked to point out my shortcomings. 我大约12岁时，有个女孩喜欢挑我毛病，我视她为敌人。
2. I tried to bear all this as long as I could. 我曾试图尽可能地忍受这一切。as long as 意为"只要，在某条件下"，引导条件状语从句。例如：
As long as you work hard, you will pass the exam. 只要你努力，就会通过考试。
I'll help you as long as I can. 我会尽可能帮助你。
3. I ran to Daddy with tears in my eyes. 我眼含泪水，扑在爸爸怀里。
4. Go and make a list of everything she said and mark the points that are right. Pay no attention to the other things she said. 去把她所说的列个清单，标出正确的，别理会其他的。
5. I did as he told me. 我照他(爸爸)说的做了。as 在这里引导的是方式状语从句，意为"像，如"。as 作为连词时用法比较灵活，除可引导方式状语从句外，还可以引导：
1) 时间状语从句，意为"当…时"。例如：
I saw him, as he was getting off the bus. 当他下车时我看见了他。
2) 原因状语从句，意为"因为"。例如：
As it was late, we had to go back home. 因为天晚了，我们得回家了。
3) 比较状语从句，意为"和…一样"。例如：

It isn't as large as you think it is. 它不如你想象的那么大。

6. Some of them I couldn't change (like being very thin), but a good number I could—and suddenly I wanted to change. 有些我改不了（比如我很瘦），但有很多我能够改正，而且我突然想要改变。a good number 意为"相当多的"，后面省略了 of them (shortcomings)。

7. But you have to learn to listen, not just close your ears in anger and feeling hurt. 不过你得学会听取意见，不要愤然闭耳不听或感到受伤害了。句中 hurt 是过去分词，意为"受伤害"。

8. When something said about you is true, you'll find it will be of help to you. 当所说的关于你的事是对的，你会发现它对你很有帮助。

   1) said about you 是过去分词短语作定语，修饰 something。
   2) be of help 相当于 be helpful, 意为"有帮助的"。类似的短语还有：
      be of use = be useful
      be of importance = be important
      be of harm = be harmful

9. Listen to them all, but hear the truth and do what you know is the right thing to do. 去听所有意见，但要听取对的，做那些你认为是正确的事。all 是 them 的同位语。注意 all 的位置：
   1) all 作形容词时，放在所修饰的词的前面。例如：
      All men have equal rights. 所有的人都有平等的权利。
   2) all 作代词时，放在代词的后面，或采用 all of + 名词/代词的结构。例如：
      可以说：They all laughed at the joke.
             All of them laughed at the joke.
      但不能说：All they laughed at the joke.
      可以说：The students all agreed to make a trip.
             All of the students agreed to make a trip.
             All students agreed to make a trip.

10. In my life, I've never had a better piece of advice. 在我的一生中，

再也没得到比这更好的建议了。a piece of advice 意为"一则建议"，类似的有：

a piece of information　　一则信息
a piece of gossip　　　　一则流言蜚语
a piece of news　　　　　一则消息

Dialogue

A: (talking to his father) They offered me a job at the restaurant, but it doesn't sound very interesting.

B: How much will they pay you?

A: $ 175 a week.

B: I'd take it if I were you. You've been looking for a job for two months, and this is the first one you've found.

A: But it doesn't sound interesting.

B: Maybe not. But you need a job, don't you? If I were you, I'd consider trying it anyway.

A: But I might find a better job somewhere.

B: It's possible. But it might take a long time. In the meantime, I don't think you can afford to pass up a job opportunity like this one. I advise you to take it. Then, later, you can always move to another job if you don't like this one.

A: I don't know, Dad. I'll think about it.

New Words & Expressions

offer ['ɔfə] vt. 提供
meantime ['miːntaim] n. 在这期间
pass up 错过
opportunity [ɔpə'tjuniti] n. 机会

Notes to the Dialogue

1. I'd take it if I were you. 如果我是你, 我就会干这份工作。此句用的是虚拟语气。关于虚拟语气的用法详见 Unit Sixteen。
2. You've been looking for a job for two months, and this is the first one you've found. 你已经找了两个月工作了, 这是你找到的第一份工作。have been doing 为现在完成进行时, 表示发生在过去的动作一直持续到现在, 还有可能继续下去。例如：
   I have been working hard all day. 我一整天都在勤奋工作。
   He's been working on those repairings for a week. (and he's still working on them) 一个星期以来, 他一直在做些修理工作。
3. I don't think you can afford to pass up a job opportunity like this one. 我认为你承受不起错过这个工作的机会。pass up 意为 "错过"。例如：
   Never pass up a chance to improve your English. 不要错过提高英语的机会。
4. Then, later, you can always move to another job if you don't like this one. 以后如果你不喜欢这份工作, 还可以跳槽。

Grammar

状语从句(The Adverbial Clause)(二)

1. 目的状语从句
   表示目的的状语从句可以由 so that, in order that, lest, in case 等引导。例如：
   We sent the letter by airmail <u>in order that it might reach them in good time.</u> 这封信我们航空寄去, 以便她们能及时收到。
   He wrote the name down <u>lest he should forget it.</u> 他把名字写下来免

得忘了。

Better take more clothes <u>in case the weather is cold.</u> 最好多带点衣服以防天冷。

2. 结果状语从句

表示结果的状语从句可以由 so...that, such...that, so that 引导。例如：

The question is <u>so</u> difficult <u>that I can't make it out.</u> 这个问题太难了我做不出来。

We left in <u>such</u> a hurry <u>that we forgot to lock the door.</u> 我们走得太匆忙,门都忘锁了。

3. 比较状语从句

表示比较的状语从句可以由 than, as 引导。例如：

The project was completed earlier <u>than we had expected.</u> 工程完成的比我们预料的还要早。

He works as fast as a skilled worker (does). 他干得像熟练工人一样快。

4. 方式状语从句

表示方式的状语从句可以由 as, as if 等引导。例如：

I did <u>as he told me.</u> 我照他说的做了。

I remember the whole thing, <u>as if it happened yesterday.</u> 整件事我都记得,就仿佛昨天发生似的。

5. 让步状语从句

表示让步的状语从句可以由 though, although, even though(if), however, no matter 等引起。例如：

<u>Even though I tried to explain that I was just doing the girl a favour by letting her use my pen,</u> I was sure the teacher continued to believe that I had cheated on the test. 尽管我尽量解释我只是帮女孩忙,借她笔用,但我确信老师还是认为我作弊。

We'll try to finish the work <u>though (although) we are short of hand.</u> 虽然我们人手不够,我们还会尽力完成工作的。

He will never be dishonest <u>even though he should be very poor.</u> 即使他一贫如洗，也决不会不诚实。

<u>No matter who he is,</u> he must pay the ticket. 无论他是谁，都必须买票。

Exercises

I. Which of the following statements are true or false? Write T for true and F for false.

1) When I was about 12, I had a good friend who always praised me.
2) I accepted what the girl said pleasantly.
3) The father asked me to write a list of everything the girl said.
4) All that the girl said was wrong.
5) I never wanted to change myself.
6) Somebody knows better than you the truth about yourself.
7) When some advice is true, it's helpful to you.
8) You must listen to others and do everything they tell you.

II. Match each word in Column A with a similar meaning in Column B.

A	B
1) opinion	a. in the time between two events
2) shortcoming	b. not to accept or do something
3) list	c. tell somebody what one think should be done
4) discover	d. weak point
5) refuse	e. a chance to do something
6) interesting	f. find
7) meantime	g. a set of words written one below another
8) opportunity	h. ideas about a subject
9) advise	i. give
10) offer	j. exciting, keeping one's attention

159

III. A. Choose the one in which the italicized word has the same meaning as it does in the sentences quoted from the passage.

1) I had an enemy, a girl who liked to *point* out my shortcomings.
   a. "Look!" said a soldier, and *pointed*.
   b. They walked into the car park and Cook *pointed* out his new car.
   c. He *pointed* out the dangers of smoking.

2) I tried to *bear* all this as long as I could.
   a. She *bore* her husband three sons.
   b. Please don't leave me alone, I could not *bear* it.
   c. Will the ice on the lake *bear* your weight?

3) Allen, didn't you ever *wonder* what you're really like?
   a. I *wonder* what they are going to do now.
   b. I *wonder* to see him looking so cheerful.
   c. I *wonder* at his rudeness.

4) Pay no *attention* to the other things she said.
   a. Old cars need a lot of *attention*.
   b. "*Attention*!" ordered the officer.
   c. John gives too much *attention* to TV.

5) For the first time I got a *fairly* clear picture of myself.
   a. He *fairly* raced past us on his motorcycle.
   b. I felt I hadn't been treated *fairly*.
   c. The house has a *fairly* large garden.

6) For the first time I got a fairly clear *picture* of myself.
   a. May I take your *picture*?
   b. You can't get a clear *picture* on this site.
   c. This book gives a good *picture* of life in England 200 years ago.

7) Our world is full of people who think they know your *duty*.

a. It's my *duty* to help you.

   b. When I am off *duty* I play tennis.

   c. The *duty* on wine has gone up.

8) Don't *shut* your ears.

   a. The shops *shut* at 8:30.

   b. *Shut* the door so that the dog can't get out.

   c. He *shut* himself in his room to think.

B. Fill in the blanks with the words or expressions given below. Change the form where necessary.

in the meantime	pass up	pay attention to	make a list of
to one's surprise	get a clear picture of	in anger	be of help
refuse	point out	full of	bear

1) The teacher asked me _____ my spelling.

2) _____, I passed the exam!

3) Don't _____ a chance like that.

4) Some advice may _____ to you.

5) We can't go out for the rain, so let's play a game _____.

6) He _____ their names.

7) His advice helps me _____ myself.

8) The car absolutely (完全) _____ to start. There must be something wrong with it.

9) He shut the door _____.

10) The theatre is _____ the audience. I'm afraid you'll have to wait for the next show.

11) The pain was almost more than she could _____.

12) I must _____ further delay (延误) would be avoided.

IV. A. Choose the best suitable answer to complete the sentence.

1) You can start the work _____ we agree on your plan.

a. unless   b. as soon as   c. then   d. since

2) _____ he had gone, I did not begin work.

a. Until   b. Till   c. After   d. As

3) I was reading a book _____ he was writing.

a. as   b. when   c. while   d. then

4) Make a mark _____ you have questions.

a. where   b. everywhere   c. in where   d. somewhere

5) _____ we have finished the work, we'll leave for home.

a. For now   b. As long as   c. Now that   d. When

6) She has a lot of books, _____ she is still a young girl.

a. although   b. but   c. since   d. so that

7) You'd better take a note _____ you forget it.

a. unless   b. in case
c. in order that   d. now that

8) It was _____ a hundred people looked lost in it.

a. such large a room that   b. so large a room that
c. a such large room that   d. so a large room that

9) _____ I know, he will be away for two months.

a. As long as   b. By far   c. Unless   d. As far as

10) _____ we could afford it, we will not buy a new car.

a. Even if   b. In case
c. As long as   d. Now that

B. Combine each pair of sentences after the model.

Model 1: She went to the university. She wanted to study engineering.

→ She went to the university so that she could study engineering.

1) They listened to the tape in silence. They wanted to hear every word.

2) He took a government job. He wanted to have security (保险).
3) She opened a savings account (储蓄账户). She wanted to save some money for a vacation.
4) They're going to choose the factory. They want to cut down on (降低) pollution.

Model 2: There was a lot of noise. I couldn't hear what she was saying.
→ There was so much noise that I couldn't hear what she was saying.

1) He was driving very fast. I was sure he was going to have an accident.
2) There was a great deal of fog (雾). She could hardly see the road ahead of her.
3) The building was very old. They tore it down.
4) She spoke very fast. I couldn't understand her.

C. Change the following sentences after the model.

Model: She wasn't feeling well, but she wouldn't go to the clinic. (though)
→ she wouldn't go to the clinic though she wasn't feeling well.

1) I turned off the lights, but I forgot to lock the door. (though)
2) The boat was cut in half, but several of the men were able to swim to safety. (although)
3) The assignment was dangerous, but she wasn't afraid. (although)
4) They've installed a new computer, but they still have just as many employees as before. (even though)

V. A. **Rewrite the following sentences after the model.**

Model: I was greatly surprised to discover that about half the things were true.

→ To my great surprise, I discovered that about half the things were true.

1) She was surprised to find that her father knew very little about it.

2) I was disappointed that our team had lost the game. (disappointment)

3) I was delighted (高兴) to see my parents in good health. (delight)

4) I deeply regret (遗憾) that I won't be able to attend the meeting. (regret)

B. **Fill in the blanks with the following.**

be of (some) help   be of (no) use
be of (much) importance   be of (no) value
be of (no) harm

1) You'll find this map _____ in helping you to get round London.

2) This kind of medicine _____ to my cold, so I have to go to see the doctor.

3) Smoking _____ to health.

4) The dictionary _____ to our studies.

5) Preventing pollution _____ to the development of our country.

VI. **Translation.**

A. **From Chinese to English.**

1) 这里太吵了,我实在受不了了。

2) 我想知道你为什么迟到。

3）我们必须关注污染问题。

4）这本书介绍了第二次世界大战的情况。

5）不要闭耳不听,父亲的话对你有好处。

6）如果你不愿意做这份工作,还可以换一份。

B. From English to Chinese.

1）She ran to us with a hat in her hand.

2）The teacher's advice is of great importance to us.

3）You know better than anyone else the truth about yourself.

4）They offer us $ 25,000 for the house.

5）You'll pass up the opportunity unless you work hard.

6）The world is full of people who think they know your duty.

Passage Reading

The Most Useful Thing and Useless Thing in the World

Jim was sitting with some of his old friends. They were drinking coffee and talking the worth of things in the world.

After a few minutes, one of Jim's friends said to him, "Well, Jim, you are a bright man, but you have said nothing on this matter yet. Jim, I wonder, what is the most useful thing in the world?"

"I think Advice is the most useful thing in the world," Jim replied immediately.

Jim's friends thought about it for a few minutes, and then one of them asked him, "And what is the most useless thing in the world?" "I think it is also Advice," the same answer was immediately given by Jim again.

"Really?" said one of Jim's friends, "are you all right? A moment ago you said that Advice is the most useful thing in the world, and now you say it is the most useless thing in the world? How can it be both?"

"Well," answered Jim, "if you think about the matter carefully, you'll see that I am quite right. You see, when you give someone good advice, and he takes it, now Advice is the most useful thing in the world. However, when you give a person advice, and he doesn't take it, then it is the most useless thing in the world."

New Words & Expressions

useful ['juːsful] adj. 有用的
useless ['juːslis] adj. 没用的

worth [wəːθ] n., adj. 价值；值得
bright [brait] adj. 聪明的

Notes to the Passage

1. They were drinking coffee and talking the worth of things in the world. 他们喝着咖啡,谈论着世界上事物的价值。worth 在这里是名词,意为"价值"。它还可以用作形容词,意为"值得,有…的价值",后跟名词或动名词。例如：
   The book is worth reading. 这本书值得一读。
   Life is not worth living without friendship. 人生若没有友情便不值得活下去了。
   It isn't worth two pounds. 它不值两英镑。
   It's not worth the paper it's printed on. 它的价值比用来印它的纸还不如。

2. …you are a bright man, but you have said nothing on this matter yet. 你很聪明,但你还未对这件事发表过意见。

3. Jim's friends thought about it for a few minutes 吉姆的朋友想了一会儿。think about 意为"思考"。注意它与 think of 的区别：think about 指对某一计划、观念仔细考虑,看它是否可行；而 think of 意

为"打算,有意,想"或"持某种念头",常与 could, should, not, never 连用。例如:

She is thinking about emigrating(移居)to Canada. 她在考虑移居加拿大。

I did think of visiting him, but I have changed my mind. 我确曾想拜访他,不过我已改变注意。

He would never think of giving up. 他从未想过放弃。

4. How can it be both? 这怎么可能既是最有用的又是最没用的呢？it 指的是 advice, both 指的是 the most useful thing in the world 和 the most useless thing in the world。

Answer the questions according to the passage.

1. What were Jim and his friends talking about?
2. In Jim's opinion, what's the most useful thing in the world?
3. What did Jim think is the most useless thing in the world?
4. Why did Jim think Advice is the answer to the both questions?
5. Do you agree with Jim?

Unit 11

Text

The Flower Effect

Miss Nancy had just got a secretary's job in a big company to work in the sale department. Monday was the first day she went to work, so she was very excited. She got up very early and arrived at the office at twenty to eight.

She pushed the door open and found nobody there. "I am the first to arrive." She thought and came to the desk which was to be hers. She was surprised to find a large bunch of flowers on it. They were fresh. She picked up the flowers from the desk and smelled them. "Oh, how lovely!" Miss Nancy cried joyfully. She then looked round for a vase to put them in. "Somebody has sent me flowers the very first day!" she thought happily. "But who could it be?" She began to wonder.

Just then, the manager came in. He greeted Miss Nancy morning and caught sight of the flowers on her desk.

"Like the flowers, Miss Nancy?" he asked.

"Yes, I like them very much." She answered and looked into his face, expecting to find some clues. But the manager walked away to his own desk and began his work.

The day passed very quickly and Miss Nancy did everything with great interest and enthusiasm. During the lunch time, the manager sat with her at the same table, talking and joking freely while eating.

The colleagues were very friendly. Almost every one gave the new secretary a kind smile when they passed by. Nothing unusual, and nothing happened for the rest of the day.

For the following days of the week, the first thing Miss Nancy did was to change water for the flowers. And then she buried herself in her work.

Then came another Monday. That morning she arrived at the office at the usual time. When she came near her desk she was overjoyed to see a new bunch of flowers there. She quickly put them in the vase, replacing the old ones.

The same thing happened again the next Monday. Miss Nancy felt it strange and this time she began to think of ways to find out the sender.

Tuesday afternoon, she was sent to hand in a plan to the general manager's office. She had to stay for a while at his secretary's desk waiting for his directives. She happened to see on the desk a big note book marked "Minutes of managers' meetings", and glanced at the half-opened pages. Suddenly her eyes fell on these words: "In order to keep the secretaries in high spirits, the company has decided that a bunch of fresh flowers should be sent to each secretary's desk."

She looked up and saw right before her on the very desk, standing a vase of flowers just like hers. "Why didn't I notice it just now?" she was amazed.

Later, she was told that their general manager was a business management psychologist.

New Words & Expressions

bunch [bʌntʃ] n. 束
fresh [freʃ] adj. 新鲜的
smell [smel] vi. 闻
joyfully ['dʒɔifuli] adv. 高兴地
vase [vɑ:z] n. 花瓶
greet [gri:t] vt. 问候
sight [sait] n. 看见
   catch sight of 看见
expect [iks'pekt] vt. 期望
clue [klu:] n. 线索
enthusiasm [in'θjuziæzəm] n. 热情
enthusiastic [in,θjuzi'æstik] adj. 热情的
joke [dʒouk] vi. 开玩笑
freely [fri:li] adv. 自由地
colleague ['kɔli:g] n. 同事

overjoyed [,ouvə'dʒɔid] adj. 非常高兴的
replace [ri'pleis] vt. 代替
sender ['sendə] n. 赠送者
hand in 递交
general ['dʒenərəl] adj. 总的
   general manager 总经理
directive [di'rektiv] n. 指示
minutes ['minits] n. 会议记录
glance [glɑ:ns] vi. 瞥
   glance at 瞥见
keep in high spirits 保持高昂情绪
amazed [ə'meizd] adj. 惊奇的
management ['mænidʒmənt] n. 管理
psychologist [sai'kɔlədʒist] n. 心理学家

Notes to the Text

1. She thought and came to the desk which was to be hers. 她边想边走到将要属于她的桌子旁。be to 表示将要发生的动作或情况,尤指按计划安排要发生的事。例如:
   Am I to go on with the work? 这工作我是不是接着干下去?
   She said that she was to be married in June. 她说她将于六月份结婚。

2. "But who could it be?" 但可能是谁呢?
   1) 当不知所指对象的性别时,就用 it 代替。例如:
   It's a lovely baby. Is it a boy or a girl? 宝宝真可爱,是男孩还是女孩?
   2) could 在本句中表示猜测,意为"可能"。例如:
   It could be my mother. 可能是我母亲。
   He could arrive tomorrow. 他可能明天到。

3. During the lunch time, the manager sat with her at the same table, talking and joking freely while eating. 吃午饭时,经理和她坐在同一张桌边,一边吃一边说笑。talking and joking, eating 均是现在分词,在句中作状语。

4. And then she buried herself in her work. 然后她就埋头工作。句中 bury 意为"使…沉浸在"。例如:
   He was buried in thoughts. 他陷入了沉思。
   He buried himself in his books. 他埋头看书。

5. Miss Nancy felt it strange and this time she began to think of ways to find out the sender. 南希小姐觉得很奇怪,因此这次她开始想办法要找到送花的人。句中 it 代替"送花"这件事。

6. She happened to see on the desk a big note book marked "Minutes of managers' meetings" 她碰巧看到桌上有个大笔记本,上面写着"经理会议记录"。marked "Minutes of managers' meetings"是过去分词短

语,在句中作定语,修饰 a big note book。

7. In order to keep the secretaries in high spirits, the company has decided that a bunch of fresh flowers should be sent to each secretary's desk. 为了使秘书们保持高昂的精神状态,公司决定给每个秘书的桌子上送一束鲜花。decide 作谓语,其后的宾语从句的谓语动词应用 should+原形动词,或用原形动词。例如:

It was decided at the meeting that a special committee (should) be set up at once. 会议决定应立即成立一个特别委员会。

8. half-opened 半开着的。

9. She looked up and saw right before her on the very desk, standing a vase of flowers just like hers. 她抬起头,看到就在她正前方的桌子上,放着一瓶花,和她的一样。

1) very 在本句中是形容词,用于加强语气,意为"正是那个,恰好的"。例如:

Somebody has sent me flowers the very first day. 刚刚上班第一天,就有人给我道歉。

You are the very person I'm looking for. 你正是我要找的那个人。

Police arrived at the very moment. 恰恰在那个时候警察赶到了。

2) 在短语 right before her on the desk standing a vase of flowers just like hers 中,因为介词短语 right before her on the desk 提前,短语用了倒装语序,正常语序应为 a vase of flowers just like hers standing on the desk right before her, 其中 standing 是现在分词,作宾语 a vase of flowers 的补语。

Dialogue

A: What have you got there?
B: My books from night school. Whenever I get a chance, I take a look at them, I don't believe in killing time by just sitting around and do-

ing nothing.

A: Oh, always studying, studying, studying.

B: The only way to get ahead is by studying, by working hard, and by learning as much as possible.

A: Oh, I don't know. You can get ahead by playing up to the boss or by pretending to work, instead of reading and doing homework all the time.

B: You're a fine person to talk like that. You always do your work conscientiously.

A: But I don't believe in grinding away, day in and day out.

B: Not having gone to college, like you, I have to finish my education at night. And, not being married, I have more free time than you have.

New Words and Expressions

whenever [wen'evə] conj. 无论何时
kill [kil] vt. 消磨
play up to 拍马屁
pretend [pri'tend] vt. 假装
conscientiously [ˌkɔnʃi'enʃəsli] adv. 谨慎地

grind [graind] vi. 刻苦
day in and day out 整日整夜
education [edju'keiʃən] n. 教育

Notes to the Dialogue

1. I don't believe in killing time by just sitting around and doing nothing. 我认为只坐在那无所事事地消磨时间没什么好处。

   1) believe in 在本句中意为 "认为…有价值"。例如：

      He believes in getting plenty of exercise. 他相信充分的运动有益处。

      believe in 另一个意思是 "信任"。例如：

      I can help you only if you believe in me. 只要你信任我，我就能帮助你。

2) killing time 意为"消磨时间",是动名词短语,在句中作宾语。

3) by doing something 表示通过某种方式。例如:

He earns his living by teaching. 他以教书为生.

2. The only way to get ahead is by studying, by working hard, and by learning as much as possible. 超过别人的惟一办法是学习,努力工作,学的东西越多越好。get ahead (of somebody) 意为"超过(某人)"。例如:

Tom has got ahead of all the other boys in the class. 汤姆胜过了班上其他的男孩子。

3. You can get ahead by playing up to the boss or by pretending to work, instead of reading and doing homework all the time. 你可以靠拍上司马屁或假装工作超过别人,而不是靠整天读书写作业。

4. But I don't believe in grinding away, day in and day out. 但我认为整日整夜拼命读书没什么价值。grind away (at) 意为"刻苦,用功"。例如:

He grinded away at his studies. 他用功读书。

5. Not having gone to college, like you, I have to finish my education at night. 没能像你一样上大学,我不得不在晚上完成学业。not having gone to college 是现在分词短语,在句中作状语,表示原因,相当于 because I have not gone to college。like you 是插入语。

6. Not being married, I have more free time than you have. 没有结婚,我的空闲时间比你多。not being married 是现在分词短语,在句中作状语,表示原因,相当于 because I am not married.

Grammar

现在分词(The Present Participle)

现在分词在句中可以用作表语、定语、状语、补语等。

1. 用作表语。例如：
   This book is very *interesting*. 这本书很有趣。
2. 用作定语。例如：
   This is a *moving* film. 这是部感人的电影。
   China is a *developing* country. 中国是发展中国家。
   现在分词短语作定语一般置于其所修饰词的后面，相当于定语从句。例如：
   The girl *sitting next to me* asked if I had an extra pen. (= who sat next to me)
   坐在我旁边的女孩问我有没有多余的笔。
   Do you know the number of people *coming to the party*? (= who will come to the party) 你知道来参加晚会的人数吗？
3. 用作状语，可表示时间、原因、结果、条件、让步、方式或伴随情况。例如：
   Walking through the park, we saw a lovely girl. 穿过公园时，我们看见一个可爱的女孩。（时间）
   Being sick, I stayed at home. 由于生病了，我呆在家里。（原因）
   Not having gone to college, I have to finish my education at night. 因为我没上过大学，所以不得不在晚上完成学业。（原因）
   Not being married, I have more free time than you have. 因为没有结婚，我的空闲时间比你多。（原因）
   Her husband died, *leaving* her with five children. 她丈夫死了，给她丢下五个孩子。（结果）
   She answered and looked into his face, *expecting* to find some clues. 她回答说，盯着他的脸，希望能发现一些线索。（伴随）
   The manager sat with her at the same table, *talking* and *joking* freely while *eating*. 经理和她坐在同一张桌边，一边吃一边谈笑。（伴随）
4. 用作补语。例如：
   She looked up and saw right before her on the very desk, *standing* a

175

vase of flowers just like hers.她抬起头,看到恰恰就在她正前方的桌子上,放着一瓶花,和她的一样。

I felt the house *shaking*.我感觉房子在晃。

He was seen *going* upstairs.有人看见他上楼。

Exercises

I. **Choose the best answer a, b, c or d to these questions about the text.**

1) When Miss Nancy went to work on the first day, she was _____.

    a. upset   b. excited   c. nervous   d. calm

2) Miss Nancy came into office and found _____.

    a. she was the first to arrive

    b. the manager had been there

    c. all the colleagues had been there

    d. she was the last to arrive

3) When Miss Nancy came to her desk, she was very surprised, because _____.

    a. she found a letter there

    b. she found a vase there

    c. she found a bunch of flowers there

    d. somebody had taken her seat

4) When Miss Nancy saw the flower, _____

    a. she was happy, but didn't know who was the sender

    b. she was happy and knew who was the sender

    c. She was upset because she didn't know the sender

    d. She was excited and knew who was the sender

5) When Miss Nancy worked _____.

    a. she felt very tired

b. she was interested in everything

   c. she was puzzled and didn't know how to do her job

   d. she had to ask others for help

6) The next Monday morning, Miss Nancy was overjoyed, because _____.

   a. the flowers disappeared

   b. the flowers were still fresh

   c. the old flowers were replaced by new ones

   d. she had a new bunch of flowers

7) Miss Nancy did not know who was the sender until _____.

   a. the general manager told her

   b. one of her colleagues told her

   c. she saw the minutes of managers' meetings

   d. she caught the sender on the spot

8) Why did Miss Nancy get a bunch of flowers every Monday morning?

   a. Somebody wanted to make her happy.

   b. It's the way to keep secretaries in high spirits.

   c. The general manager was fond of her.

   d. Miss Nancy's friend wanted to give her a pleasant surprise.

II. **Match each word in Column A with a similar meaning in Column B.**

A	B
1) colleague	a. take the place of
2) overjoyed	b. something that helps to find the answer
3) replace	c. order
4) greet	d. someone you work with
5) glance	e. a person who studies the mind
6) minutes	f. very pleased and happy

7) clue g. very surprised
8) directive h. give a quick look
9) amazed i. say hello to someone
10) psychologist j. a written record at a meeting

III. A. **Study the meaning of the following words with the help of the dictionary and fill in the blanks with them.**

overwork   overgrown   overflow   overseas   overtake

1) The bathtub (浴缸) is _____. Who left the water running?
2) They are _____ students.
3) You have been _____. Why don't you have a rest?
4) A car _____ me although I drove very fast.
5) The garden is _____ with weeds (草).

B. **Not all the words ending with -ly are adv. Point out which are adj., which are adv., among the following words, and fill in the blanks with suitable words.**

lovely   freely   friendly   joyfully   fairly

1) He came into the room and everybody gave him a _____ smile.
2) Mary cried _____ when she saw her present.
3) I got a _____ clear picture of myself.
4) She got a _____ doll on her birthday.
5) At the club people can talk about their hobbies _____.

C. **Fill in the blanks with the words or expressions given below. Change the form where necessary.**

look up	keep...in high spirits	have to	hand in
glance at	catch sight of	put in	think of
bury	pretend	grind away	play up to
believe in	kill		

1) She _____ and saw nothing before her.

2) He _____ his watch.

3) We cannot get ahead of others by _____ the boss.

4) Please _____ your books at the end of the lesson.

5) After the divorce (离婚), she _____ herself in her work.

6) These songs are helpful to _____ soldiers _____.

7) Father firmly _____ doing morning exercise every day.

8) We must _____ ways to find out the thief.

9) It's late. We _____ go back home.

10) Don't _____ to know what you don't know.

11) I _____ her hurrying away.

12) The old couple _____ their time by just watching TV.

13) He _____ the money _____ the drawer.

14) They have been _____ in the library for months.

IV. Make sentences after the examples with the given words.

1) They were busy <u>repairing</u> farm tools.

    a. make paper flowers for May Day

    b. prepare for the test

2) When he got there, he found them <u>working at their reports.</u>

    a. play football

    b. watch TV

3) Just then she heard someone <u>whispering.</u>

    a. sing in the next room

    b. call her name

4) I like to watch people <u>dancing.</u>

    a. play chess

    b. skate

5) She caught the boys <u>stealing apples.</u>

    a. smoke

b. cheat on the test.

V. A. Replace the attributive clause in each of the following sentences with a participial phrase.

1) She has a daughter who was living with her.
2) The train that stands at platform is for Wuhan.
3) Any student who does not work hard should be criticized.
4) Is there anyone in your class who wish to go to the show?
5) The man who is shaking hands with that lady is a famous artist.

B. Rewrite these sentences, turning the part in italics into a participial phrase.

1) Look around *when you cross the street*.
2) He walked down the hill. *He sang softly to himself*.
3) *Because Tom had arrived too early*, he had to wait.
4) He talked to me for two hours. *He tried to persuade me to change my mind*.
5) A good rain followed. *It turned leaves green*.

VI. Translation.

A. From Chinese to English.

1) 我们用电脑取代了老式的加法计算器(adding machine)。
2) 我们必须在星期五之前把作业交上。
3) 玛丽瞥了瞥半开的书,突然发现她的名字。
4) 在剩下的一天里,她一直埋头工作。
5) 他四下看看,看到墙上的画。
6) 为了使秘书们保持高昂的情绪,他每周送给她们一束花。

B. From English to Chinese.

1) Who is to be on duty today?
2) On the table stands a vase of flowers.
3) The last thing I want to do is to leave you.

4) I went on standing there, waiting for something to happen.
5) Miss Nancy did everything with great interest and enthusiasm.
6) The nurse gave the patient a friendly smile when she passed by.

Passage Reading

Say It with Flowers

There's nothing like bouquet of fresh flowers to brighten up a room. But flowers are more than just decorations. Flowers can make someone's day better. They say, "I'm thinking of you." A dozen red roses can even tell somebody, "I love you." Flowers have become beautiful messengers of our deepest feelings. But how can you be sure you are sending the right message to that special someone? By arranging the flowers yourself.

Though many people like receiving flowers, giving them is expensive. Arranging your own flowers can save you money. Go to a local flower market to buy the freshest flowers. Arrive early—around 5 a.m.—to get the best buys.

You also need a few tools. Get some sharp scissors, containers for holding the flowers and some small rubber bands. Then, with a little creativity and these helpful tips, go for it! Tell someone you care—with flowers!

Some "do's and don'ts":
- Think about the occasion. Is it casual or formal? About what size should the bouquet be?
- Use the freshest flowers you can. Pick ones with buds or the flowers still half-open. Put them into water as soon as possible.
- Don't use flowers all of one length. Cut stems to different

lengths for variety.

• Make your longest flower stem about one and a half times the height of your container.

• Follow a basic plan. Keep larger, darker flowers near the center.

• Don't mix equal amounts of different flowers. Try to have a variety of shapes and colors to make the bouquet look natural.

• Don't put flowers near or in drafty places, such as by a window. And keep containers full of clean water.

New Words and Expressions

bouquet [buˈkei] n. 花束
brighten [ˈbraitən] vt. 点亮,使生辉
  brighten up 使…生辉
dozen [ˈdʌzn] n. 一打,十二个
rose [rouz] n. 玫瑰花
messenger [ˈmesindʒə] n. 信使
feeling [ˈfiːliŋ] n. 感觉
message [ˈmesidʒ] n. 信息
local [ˈloukəl] adj. 本地的
market [ˈmɑːkit] n. 市场
buy [bai] n. 便宜货
scissor [ˈsizə] n. 剪刀
container [kənˈteinə] n. 容器
rubber [ˈrʌbə] n. 橡皮
band [bænd] n. 带,箍带
creativity [ˌkriːeiˈtiviti] n. 创造力
helpful [ˈhelpful] adj. 有帮助的
tip [tip] n. 提示

do's and don'ts 注意事项
formal [ˈfɔːməl] adj. 正式的
bud [bʌd] n. 花蕾
length [leŋθ] n. 长度
stem [stem] n. 花茎
variety [vəˈraiəti] n. 变化
  a variety of 各种各样的
time [taim] n. 倍数
height [hait] n. 高度
basic [ˈbeisik] adj. 基本的
dark [dɑːk] adj. 黑的,颜色深的
equal [ˈiːkwəl] adj. 同样的
amount [əˈmaunt] n. 数量
shape [ʃeip] n. 形状
natural [ˈnætʃərəl] adj. 自然的
drafty [ˈdrɑːfti] adj. 通风的
such as 例如

Notes to the Passage

1. There's nothing like bouquet of fresh flowers to brighten up a room. 没有什么能比一束鲜花更能增添一室的光彩了。

2. But flowers are more than just decorations. 但花朵不仅仅是用来装饰的。more than 在句中意为"不仅仅,不只是"。例如:
What we need is more than money. 我们需要的不仅仅是钱。

3. Though many people like receiving flowers, giving them is expensive. 虽然许多人喜欢收到花束,但送花并不便宜。receiving flowers 是动名词短语,作 like 的宾语;giving them 也是动名词短语,在句中作主语。

4. Arranging your own flowers can save you money. 自己插花可以省钱。arranging your own flowers 是动名词短语,在句中作主语。

5. Then, with a little creativity and these helpful tips, go for it! 然后,用些创造力和以下有用的建议,开始动手吧!

6. Pick ones with buds or the flowers still half-open. 挑选带有花苞或仍是半开的花。

7. Make your longest flower stem about one and a half times the height of your container. 最长的花茎应是你容器高度的1.5倍。倍数的表达法有3种:

    1)基数词 + times + n. + of
    The earth is 49 times the size of the moon. 地球的大小是月球的49倍。

    2)基数词 + times + as + adj. + as
    It's four times as big as Europe. 它是欧洲的四倍大。

    3)基数词 + times + 形容词比较级 + than
    Their garden is four times larger than ours. 它们的花园比我们的大四倍。

Fill in the blanks according to the passage.

1. Flowers are very important in our daily life.
   1) A bouquet of fresh flowers can _____ a room.
   2) Flowers can _____ someone's day _____.
   3) Flowers are _____ of our deepest _____.
2. In order to _____ money and send the right _____ to others, you can _____ flowers yourself. How to arrange flowers?
   1) Go to a _____ flower market early.
   2) Get a few _____, such as _____, containers and _____ bands.
   3) Some tips are helpful.
      a. Think about the _____.
      b. Pick flowers with _____ or flowers still _____.
      c. Cut _____ to different _____.
      d. Make the longest stems about one and a half times the _____ of your container.
      e. Follow a _____ plan.
      f. Have a _____ of shapes and colors.
      g. Don't put flowers near a _____ or in a _____ place.

Text

Father Never Got Excited

My father was a lawyer in a small city in Illinois. In one way he was different from most other lawyers: there were times when he didn't have much to say. He was friendly, but he was also a wonderful man for keeping his mouth shut.

One year we spent part of the summer in a big house in Michigan. At midnight my mother woke us up screaming: "There's a bat in this bedroom! Robert! Get up! Get up!"

Father said something in a sleepy voice, but we couldn't quite hear his words. Then my mother's voice, excited and mad, came clearly into our bedroom. "Well, if you aren't going to do anything about it, I'm going to spend the rest of the night down in the living room."

We were all asleep when she screamed again: "There's another bat down here!" This time we could hear my father's answer. "I could have told you that," he called out. "I saw it before I came up to bed."

Yes, father was a wonderful man for keeping his mouth shut.

One September day, I remember, the minister of our church came to visit us. He wanted to find out why my father hadn't gone to church for a long time. We were in the garden when he arrived and started talking.

Father didn't say much, but the minister kept right on talking. He was still talking when he started to leave, walking backward as he talked. He couldn't see where he was going. All at once he fell head over heels into a little ditch.

The minister wasn't hurt, but his clothes were dirty and he was red in the face when he got to his feet again. Then Father remembered that the minister was very proud of knowing Latin, so he comforted him in that language: "*Facilis descensus Averno*"—"Easy is the road down to Hell." Then Father sent me to get the clothesbrush.

New Words & Expressions

in one way 某种程度上
midnight ['midnait] *n.* 午夜
scream [skri:m] *vi.* 尖叫
bat [bæt] *n.* 蝙蝠

sleepy ['sli:pi] *adj.* 昏昏欲睡的
mad [mæd] *adj.* 疯狂的
minister ['ministə] *n.* 牧师
church [tʃə:tʃ] *n.* 教堂

keep on 一直，继续
backward [ˈbækwəd] adv. 向后
all at once 突然
heel [hiːl] n. 足跟
ditch [ditʃ] n. 小沟

dirty [ˈdəːti] adj. 肮脏的
Latin [ˈlætin] n. 拉丁语
hell [hel] n. 地狱
clothesbrush [ˈklouðbrʌʃ] n. 衣服刷

Proper Names

Illinois [ˌiliˈnɔiz] （美国）伊利诺斯州
Michigan [ˈmiʃigən] （美国）密歇根州

Notes to the Text

1. In one way he was different from most other lawyers: there were times when he didn't have much to say. 在某种程度上他和其他大多数律师不一样：他常常无话可说。

   1) in one way 意为"在某种程度上"。例如：
      In one way, you are right, but it's not as simple as that. 在某种程度上你是对的，但事情并没那么简单。

   2) be different from 意为"与…不同"。例如：
      This picture is different from the one we saw yesterday. 这幅画与我们昨天看到的不一样。

   3) have something to do 意为"自己有某事要做"。例如：
      I have a lot of work to do this Sunday so I can't go swimming with you. 星期天我有许多工作要做，所以不能和你去游泳了。
      但 have something done 意为"让别人做某事"。例如：
      I'll have my hair cut this afternoon. 今天下午我去剪头发。
      I'll have my radio repaired tomorrow. 明天我得找人修收音机。

2. He was friendly, but he was also a wonderful man for keeping his

mouth shut. 他平易近人，但又十分有趣，因为他常常缄口不言。

3. One year we spent part of the summer in a big house in Michigan. 有一年夏天我们在密歇根的一座大房子里过了一段时间。part 意为"部分"，常和 of 连用。在 part 前通常不用加冠词，句中的谓语随 part 后的名词变。例如：

Part of the house was burnt in the fire. 房屋的部分地方在大火中烧毁了。

Part of the passengers were injured in the accident. 部分乘客在事故中受伤。

4. Then my mother's voice, excited and mad, came clearly into our bedroom. 然后我妈妈歇斯底里的喊叫声清楚地传到我们的卧室。excited and mad 在句中起补充说明的作用。此句可以变为：Then my mother's voice became excited and mad and it came clearly into our bedroom.

5. "I could have told you that," he called out. "I saw it before I came up to bed." "我本该告诉你的"，他大声说，"我在上楼睡觉之前就看见它了。" could have done 意为"本来能够做某事，但没有做"。例如：
You could have passed the exam if you had worked hard. 如果你努力学习的话，你本来是可以通过考试的。

6. One September day, I remember, the minister of our church came to visit us. 我记得九月里的一天，我们这儿教堂的牧师来到我们家。I remember 在句中作插入语。

7. We were in the garden when he arrived and started talking. 牧师到的时候，我们正在花园里，他便开始高谈阔论。

8. Father didn't say much, but the minister kept right on talking. 父亲没说什么，但牧师却喋喋不休地说个没完。keep on doing something 意为"持续做某事"。例如：
It kept on raining. 雨一直没停。

right 在句中是副词，意为"直接地，一直"。例如：

Go right back to your seat. 直接回到你的座位上去。

9. All at once he fell head over heels into a little ditch. 突然他一下子头朝下跌到沟里。head over heel 是俗语,意为"头朝下"。

10. The minister wasn't hurt, but his clothes were dirty and he was red in the face when he got to his feet again. 牧师没有受伤,但他的衣服弄脏了,当他站起来时,满脸通红。get to one's feet 意为"站起来"。

11. Father remembered that the minister was very proud of knowing Latin, so he comforted him in that language 父亲记得牧师以懂拉丁语为傲,他便用拉丁语安慰他。

12. Easy is the road down to Hell. 要下地狱是件很容易的事。实际可译成:倒霉的事是难免的。此句是倒装句,把表语 easy 提到句首,表示强调,正常语序应为:The road down to Hell is easy.

Dialogue

A: Hi, Henry. How was the game yesterday?

B: Great. Why did you miss it?

A: I had a fever.

B: Too bad you weren't there. We all went together—Jenny, Jim and I.

A: It must have been freezing sitting outside, I suppose.

B: It was very cold. We were all bundled up in blankets and heavy coats.

A: I hear it started snowing in the middle of the game.

B: It did. But it didn't stop the game.

A: Did you see Jim Pullman make his touchdown?

B: That was the most exciting moment. When the ball was passed to him, he ran so fast that no one could catch him. And it was fun watching the players falling in the snow.

A: You are coughing. Are you getting sick, too?

B: I guess I caught a cold at the game. But it was worth it!

New Words and Expressions

fever ['fi:və] *n*. 发烧
freeze [fri:z] *vi*. 结冰
bundle up 使穿得暖和
blanket ['blæŋkit] *n*. 毯子
heavy ['hevi] *adj*. 厚重的

player ['pleiə] *n*. 运动员
touchdown ['tʌtʃdaun] *n*. （橄榄球的）底线得分
cough [kɔf] *vi*. 咳嗽
catch a cold 感冒

Proper Names

Jenny ['dʒeni] （人名）詹尼
Jim [dʒim] （人名）吉姆
Jim Pullman [dʒim'pulmən] （人名）吉姆·普尔曼

Notes to the Dialogue

1. It must have been freezing sitting outside, I suppose. 我想坐在外面一定很冷。

   1) sitting outside 是动名词短语作主语，句中 it 是形式主语。
   2) must have done 表示对过去情况作肯定的猜测。例如：
      It must have rained yesterday, because the ground is wet. 昨天一定下雨了，因为地上很湿。
      如果表示否定，应该用 can't have done。例如：
      You can't have seen him yesterday because he went abroad two days ago. 你昨天不可能看到他，因为他两天前出国了。

2. We were all bundled up in blankets and heavy coats. 我们都裹着毯子和大衣。

3. It was fun watching players falling in the snow. 看到球手摔在雪里很

有趣。watching players falling in the snow 是动名词短语，作主语，it 是形式主语。

Grammar

动名词(The Gerund)

动名词在句中可以用作主语、表语、宾语、定语等。

1. 用作主语。例如：

   Though many people like receiving flowers, ***giving them*** is expensive. 虽然很多人喜欢收到花束，但送花可不便宜。

   Arranging your own flowers can save you money. 自己插花可以省钱。

   It was fun ***watching players falling in the snow***. 看到球手摔在雪里很有趣。

2. 用作表语。例如：

   The main thing is ***getting there on time***. 首要的事是及时赶到。

   His job is ***teaching English***. 他的工作是教英语。

3. 用作宾语，或介词宾语。例如：

   We were in the garden when he arrived and started ***talking***. 他到的时候，我们正在花园里，牧师便开始高谈阔论。

   The minister was proud of ***knowing*** Latin. 牧师以懂拉丁语为傲。

   I find ***swimming*** interesting. 我发现游泳很有趣。

   注意：1) 有些动词如 enjoy, finish, understand, admit, consider, avoid, deny(否认), keep, miss, mind, practise, suggest 等只能接动名词做宾语。例如：

   I haven't finished ***writing*** the report yet. 我还没有写完这篇文章。

   We enjoyed ***watching*** the football game. 我们喜欢看足球比赛。

2) 有些动词,如 love, like, begin, start, continue, 既可以用动名词作宾语,又可以用不定式作宾语,意义差别不大。例如:

Do you like *to play*(*playing*)chess? 你喜欢下棋吗?

The minister started *to talk*(*talking*)when he arrived. 牧师一到便开始高谈阔论。

但在 remember, regret, want, try, forget 等词的后面差别就比较明显,例如:

I remember *seeing* him before. 我记得以前见过他。

Please remember *to bring* your notebooks here. 记得下次把笔记本带来。

I regret not *accepting* your advice. 我很后悔没听你的建议。

I regret *to say* that I can't help you. 我很遗憾的告诉你我不能帮助你。

The room wants *cleaning*. 房间需要打扫。

He doesn't want to *go*. 他不想去。

Let's try *doing* the work some other way. 让我们用别的方法试一试。

We must try *to finish* the work on time. 我们必须设法按时完成工作。

I forget *having* told you that. 我忘了我已经告诉你了。

Don't forget *to take* the key with you. 别忘了带钥匙。

4. 用作定语。例如:

He spent the whole day in the *reading* room. 他一整天都呆在阅览室。

There are a lot of people in the *swimming* pool. 游泳池里有很多人。

Exercises

I. Which of the following statements are true or false? Write T for true and F for false.

(　)1) Father was different from most other lawyers because he was talkative.

(　)2) One year we spent part of the summer in Illinois.

(　)3) At midnight my mother screamed because there was a rat in the room.

( )4) Father knew nothing about the bat.
( )5) The minister came to visit us because he had something important to say to Father.
( )6) Father quarreled with the minister.
( )7) The minister fell into the ditch and was badly hurt.
( )8) The minister was embarrassed (尴尬) when he got to his feet.
( )9) Father comforted the minister in Latin because the minister only knew Latin.
( )10) Father laughed at the minister by saying "Easy is the road down to Hell".

II. Match each word in Column A with a similar meaning in Column B.

A	B
1) lawyer	a. close
2) shut	b. priest
3) scream	c. a person who gives advice about laws
4) minister	d. ready to sleep
5) ditch	e. cry out highly in fear
6) church	f. twelve o'clock at night
7) Latin	g. a building for public Christian worship
8) sleepy	h. to make someone feel calmer and more hopeful
9) midnight	i. a kind of language
10) comfort	j. a long narrow channel dug in the ground

III. A. Fill in the blanks with the words or expressions given below. Change the form where necessary.

in a way	different from	comfort	be proud of
in the face	in a low voice	keep on	hurt
all at once	get to one's feet	remember	wake up

1) He _____ asking stupid questions at the class.
2) _____ you are right, but I still have some different ideas.
3) His hat is _____ mine.
4) He said good night to me _____.
5) Please _____ me _____ at 6 o'clock.
6) The child _____ himself when playing with a hammer.
7) He _____ his father who is a policeman.
8) The boy was red _____ when the teacher praised him.
9) I tried to _____ him but it was no use.
10) _____ a man jumped out from the corner and I was scared to death.
11) The boy fell but he _____ at once.
12) _____ to turn off the lights when you leave the classroom.

B. Fill in each of the blanks with a proper word.

1) sleep, sleepy, asleep
   a. He grew _____ and went to bed.
   b. Be quiet! Baby is _____.
   c. She _____ for eight hours a day.
2) friend, friendly
   a. He soon made _____ with his neighbours.
   b. When he passed by, he gave me a _____ smile.
3) clear, clearly
   a. I could see _____ once I cleaned my glasses.
   b. Do you have a _____ idea of what has happened?
4) wonder, wonderful, wonderfully
   a. Walking on the moon is a great _____.
   b. He sang the song _____.
   c. What a _____ memory she has!

IV. A. **Put into Chinese and fill in the blanks with the suitable one.**

sleeping-car	English-speaking country
smoking-room	opening speech
sewing-machine	closing-ceremony

1) People can smoke in a _____.
2) Mother made me a beautiful skirt with the _____.
3) The mayor gave the _____ at the meeting.
4) There were wonderful performances (表演) at the _____.
5) In _____, people speak English.
6) It's quite comfortable in the _____ where you can have a rest.

B. **Point out the functions of the underlined parts in the following sentences.**

1) It will be nice <u>seeing you again.</u>
2) This is an <u>interesting</u> movie.
3) We are reading books at the <u>reading</u> room.
4) Let's stop <u>talking.</u> The teacher is coming.
5) The boy was found <u>promising.</u>
6) <u>After thinking everything over</u>, he decided to go.
7) I saw him <u>smoking.</u>
8) I dislike him <u>smoking.</u>
9) He was criticized for <u>being late.</u>
10) I call it <u>robbing Peter to pay Paul</u> (拆东墙补西墙).

C. **Put the verbs in the right form.**

1) They all enjoyed _____ (learn) to skate.
2) I hate _____ (lie) and _____ (cheat).
3) I'll never forget _____ (see) her for the first time.
4) I regret _____ (tell) you that your homework need _____ (rewrite).

5) It is no good _____ (smoke).

6) _____ (meet) you has been a great pleasure.

7) Take these pills before _____ (go) to bed.

8) Besides _____ (read) he is fond of _____ (dance) too.

9) She's responsible for _____ (operate) all the machines in the office.

10) They finished _____ (give) their employees on-the-job training.

11) He's afraid of _____ (drive) in traffic.

12) We're thinking about _____ (move) to the suburbs (郊区).

V. Complete the following sentences, using "could (not) have done".

1) You _____ (本来是可以通过考试的), if you had worked harder.

2) Her husband _____ (本来可以帮助她的), but he refused to.

3) You _____ (本来可以告诉我们的) about it.

4) She _____ (本来可以买车的), but she chose to lend the money to her brother.

5) Tom _____ (不可能把钢笔拿走). He was not there yesterday.

VI. Translation.

A. From Chinese to English.

1) 在某种程度上这家餐馆与众不同。

2) 整个晚上他一直唱同一首歌。

3) 你本可以把那件事告诉我,我可以帮助你。

4) 今晚我有几本书要看,就不能陪你看电影了。

5) 别总不说话,我们需要你的建议。

6）母亲坚持认为房间要粉刷一下。

B. From English to Chinese.

1) I have nothing to say on this problem.
2) Father said something in a sleepy voice but we couldn't quite hear his words.
3) Gone are the days when the black people are treated as slaves.
4) At midnight my mother woke us screaming: "There's a bat in this room."
5) He tried to speak French to us but we couldn't understand him. So he tried speaking English.
6) Tom could have come to the party yesterday but his mother was ill and he had to look after her.

Passage Reading

A Working Woman's Dilemma

Dear Doctor,

　　My husband and I got married in 1965 and for the first ten years of our marriage I was very happy to stay home and raise our three children. Then four years ago, our youngest child went to school and I thought I might go back to work.

　　My husband was very supportive and helped me to make decision. He emphasized all of the things I can do around the house, and said he thought I could be a great success in business.

　　After several weeks of job-hunting, I found my present job, which is working for a small public relations firm. At first, my husband was very proud of me and would tell his friends, "my clever little wife can run that company she's working for."

But as his joking remark approached reality, my husband stopped talking to me about my job. I have received several promotions and pay increases, and I am now making more money than he is. I can buy my own clothes and a new car. Because of our combined incomes, my husband and I can do many things that we had always dreamed of doing, but we don't do these things because he is very unhappy.

We fight about little things and my husband is very critical of me in front of our friends. For the first time in our marriage, I think there is a possibility that our marriage may come to an end.

I love my husband very much, and I don't want him to feel inferior, but I also love my job. I think I can be a good wife and a working woman, but I don't know how. Can you give me some advice? Will I have to choose one or the other or can I keep both my husband and my new career?

Please help.

"DISDRESSED"

New Words & Expressions

dilemma [di'lemə] *n.* 进退两难之境
marriage ['mæridʒ] *n.* 婚姻
raise [reiz] *vt.* 抚养
decision [di'siʒən] *n.* 决定
supportive [sə'pɔːtiv] *adj.* 支持的
hunt [hʌnt] *vt.* 追猎,寻找
   job-hunting 找工作
present ['preznt] *adj.* 现在的
relation [ri'leiʃən] *n.* 关系
firm [fəːm] *n.* 公司
at first 开始
run [rʌn] *vt.* 经营

joking ['dʒoukiŋ] *adj.* 开玩笑的
mark [mɑːk] *n.* 评价
reality [ri'æliti] *n.* 现实
promotion [prə'mouʃən] *n.* 提升
pay [pei] *n.* 工资
   pay increase 涨工资
because of 因为
combine [kəm'bain] *vt.* 合并
income ['inkʌm] *n.* 收入
unhappy [ˌʌn'hæpi] *adj.* 不高兴的
fight [fait] *vi.* 吵架
critical ['kritikəl] *adj.* 挑剔的

possibility [pəsə'biliti] n. 可能性
come to an end 结束

inferior [in'fiəriə] adj. 地位低下的
distressed [dis'trest] adj. 苦恼的

Notes to the Passage

1. A Working Woman's Dilemma 一个职业女性的困境。
2. After several weeks of job-hunting, I found my present job, which is working for a small public relations firm. 我开始找工作,几个月后,我找到现在的工作,在一家小的公共关系公司上班。job-hunting 是由名词和 v-ing 构成的合成词,意为"找工作",类似的合成词还有:horse-riding 骑马, bird-watching 赏鸟, book-keeping 簿记, window-shopping 逛街,等。
3. Because of our combined incomes, my husband and I can do many things that we had always dreamed of doing, but we don't do these things because he is very unhappy. 把我们的工资加一块儿,我和我丈夫可以做以前我们一直想做的事,但我们没有,因为我丈夫不高兴。combined 是过去分词,在句中做定语。because of 意为"因为",后面接名词或名词短语,不能接从句。例如:
Because of her illness, she did not go to school. 因为她病了,没能上学。
4. Will I have to choose one or the other or can I keep both my husband and my new career? 难道我不得不选择其一,我不能两者兼得吗? both...and...意为"不但…而且",连接两个并列成分。例如:
We visited both London and Washington. 我们不仅去了伦敦,还去了华盛顿。
Both Mary and Tom are good at singing. 玛丽和汤姆都擅长唱歌。

Answer the questions according to the passage.
1. When was the letter probably written?
2. Why did the woman want to go back to work?

3. Did her husband support her at first?
4. How did her husband feel when she found the job?
5. When did her husband stop talking to her about the job?
6. Why did her husband get angry with her?
7. Did the woman still feel that their marriage was perfect?
8. What choice did the woman have to make?

Unit 13

Text

Chance

(Part I)

No fewer than four hundred and ninety-one passengers were on board the *Central America*, a ship on her way from Havana to New York. Most of them were miners returning home with their gold. When they started off, the sky had been cloudless and the wind fair. But three days later the ship was rolling into a storm, which threw her about like a child's toy. It was not long before water found its way into the engine-room and put out the fires, leaving the ship helpless, with her engines stopped.

In spite of all efforts, more and more water came in. It was clear to all that nothing could save the ship, and that she would soon go to the bottom.

Unusual courage was shown by nearly all on board: even the women didn't give themselves up to useless tears. Captain Herdon moved about the ship, encouraging all and giving orders in attempt to save his ship. But all his efforts were in vain.

Fortunately, when all hope of safety had entirely gone, another ship, the *Marie of Boston*, appeared. The *Marie* had also suffered heavily in the storm, but her captain immediately moved the women and children in boats from the *Central America* to his own ship. Because of the mountainous sea, only a few people could be taken at one time. The work was very slow but there was no disorder: even the rough miners waited patiently, making no attempt to save themselves until the women and children were safe. When they had all been taken off, there was time for forty of the men to be taken to the *Marie* as well.

New Words & Expressions

passenger ['pæsindʒə] *n*. 乘客
on board 搭乘
miner ['mainə] *n*. 矿工
gold [gould] *n*. 黄金
start off 出发
cloudless ['klʌudlis] *adj*. 无云的
fair [fɛə] *adj*. （风）顺畅的
roll [roul] *vi*. 颠簸
storm [stɔ:m] *n*. 风暴

engine room 轮机室
put out 熄灭
helpless ['helplis] *adj*. 无助的
effort ['efət] *n*. 努力
bottom ['bɔtəm] *n*. 海底,底部
courage ['kʌridʒ] *n*. 勇气
captain ['kæptin] *n*. 船长
attempt [ə'tempt] *n*. 试图
  in attempt to 试图

vain [vein] *n*. 徒劳
 in vain 徒劳
fortunately ['fɔːtʃənitli] *adv*. 幸运地
heavily ['hevili] *adv*. 严重地
mountainous ['mauntinəs] *adj*. 像山一样的
at one time 一次

disorder [dis'ɔːdə] *n*. 混乱
rough [rʌf] *adj*. 粗鲁的
patiently ['peiʃəntli] *adv*. 耐心的
take off 带走
as well 也
give up 放弃

Proper Names

Central America ['sentrəl ə'merikə] (船名) 中美洲号
Havana [hə'vænə] (古巴首都) 哈瓦那
Herdon ['həːdən] (人名) 赫尔登
Marie of Boston [məˈriːəv'bɔstən] (船名) 波士顿·玛丽号

Notes to the Text

1. No fewer than four hundred and ninety-one passengers were on board the *Central America*, a ship on her way from Havana to New York. 至少 491 位乘客登上了一艘名为中美洲号的轮船，这艘船从哈瓦那出发，前往纽约。on board 意为"搭乘（船、飞机、火车等），在（船、飞机、车）上"。例如：

   There were 200 passengers on board the plane. 飞机上有 200 名乘客。

   As soon as we were on board, our ship left the port. 我们一上船，船就出港了。

2. Most of them were miners returning home with their gold. 乘客中大部分人是带着金子回家的矿工。most 意为"大多数的，几乎全部的"，后面可直接加名词。例如：

Most Americans own cars. 大多数美国人都有车。

most 还可以和 of 连用,后面可接人称代词或名词。例如:

Most of them want to go to the cinema. 他们中大部分人都想去看电影。

Most of her money is spent on books. 她把大部分钱花在买书上。

但名词前如果没有物主代词修饰,则必须加定冠词 the。例如:

可以说:Most cheese contains a lot of fat(脂肪).

可以说:Most of the cheese contains a lot of fat.

但不能说:Most of cheese contains a lot of fat.

3. When they started off, the sky had been cloudless and the wind fair. 他们出发时,天空万里无云,风平浪静。在 the wind 后省略了 had been。

4. But three days later the ship was rolling into a storm, which threw her about like a child's toy. 但三天后,船却在暴风雨中颠簸摇摆,暴风雨把船像儿童玩具一样来回抛甩。which threw her about like a child's toy 是非限制性定语从句,用来补充说明前面提到的 storm。

关于非限制性定语从句需要说明两点:

1) 在非限制性定语从句中,指人时用 who(m),指物时用 which,不能用 that,前面应用逗号隔开。例如:

The river, which is clean enough to swim in, was polluted for over a hundred years. 这条河现在很干净,可以游泳,它曾经被污染了一百多年。

The man, who(m) I met at a party last week, proved to be a famous professor. 我在上周聚会上遇到的那个人原来是一位著名的教授。

Alfred, who was selling meat, saw a man near the shop door. 艾尔弗雷德,他正在卖肉,看见了一个人在商店门口附近。

2) 非限制性定语从句也可以修饰前面整个部分。例如:

He drinks a lot of wine every day, which makes his wife very angry. 他每天喝很多酒,这使他的妻子非常生气。

5. It was not long before water found its way into the engine-room and put out the fires, leaving the ship helpless, with her engines stopped. 水很快就进了轮机舱,炉火灭掉了,发动机熄火了,船陷入了孤助无援的地步。

   1) It is not long before 意为"不久,很快"。例如:
      It won't be long before you get well. 不久你就会康复的。
   2) find one's way (to) 意为"流入,流进"。再如:
      The river finds its way to the sea. 这条河流入大海.
   3) put out 意为"熄灭(火、光、香烟等)"。例如:
      She put out all the lights before going to bed. 上床之前她把所有的灯都关掉了。
   4) stopped 是过去分词,在句中与 with her engine 组成复合结构,充当状语,表原因。

6. In spite of all efforts, more and more water came in. 尽管所有的办法都用了,但还是有越来越多的水涌进来。in spite of 意为"尽管,虽然",后面跟名词或名词词组,不可跟从句。例如:
   I went out in spite of the rain. 尽管下雨,我还是出去了。

7. Unusual courage was shown by nearly all on board; even the women didn't give themselves up to useless tears. 船上几乎所有人都显示了非凡的勇气,就连女人们也没有放弃,因为他们知道哭是无济于事的。give up 的主要意思有:

   1) 戒除(习惯),放弃(想法),可接名词或动名词。例如:
      My father decided to give up smoking. 我父亲决定戒烟。
      You should not give up hope. 你不应该放弃希望。
   2) 对某人放弃希望。例如:
      The doctors gave my father up two years ago, but he is still alive. 两年前医生对我父亲放弃了希望,但他现在还活着。
   3) 认输。例如:
      Don't give up halfway. 不要半途而废。

8. Captain Herdon moved about the ship, encouraging all and giving orders in attempt to save his ship. 赫尔登船长在船上四处走动,给大家鼓劲,发布指示,试图挽救他的船。in attempt to 意为"尝试,试图",后跟动词原形。例如:

He laughed loudly in attempt to catch her attention. 他大声笑着,试图引起她的注意。

注意 attempt 还可以用在 make an attempt to 短语中。例如:

He made an attempt to learn to swim. 他试图学游泳。

9. But all his efforts were in vain. 但他所做的努力都失败了。in vain 意为"徒劳无功的"。例如:

He tried to memorize the poem but in vain. 他试图把诗背下来,但未能成功。

10. Fortunately, when all hope of safety had entirely gone, another ship, the *Marie of Boston*, appeared. 幸运的是,当所有获救的希望都破灭时,另一艘船——波士顿·玛丽号出现了。

11. When they had all been taken off, there was time for forty of the men to be taken to the *Marie* as well. 所有的妇女和儿童被转移后,剩下的时间只够把四十个男人转移到玛丽号。as well 意为"也"。例如:

Tom went to the party; Peter came as well. 汤姆参加了晚会,彼得也去了。

Dialogue

A: Hello.

B: Hello. May I speak to Mary, please?

A: Speaking.

B: Hi, Mary. This is Tom Johnson.

A: Oh, hi, Tom. How've you been?

B: Just fine. Listen! Mary, I called to ask if you are busy tomorrow evening.
A: Let me see. No, I don't think I've got anything planned. Why?
B: Well, I thought we might have dinner together and go to the movies.
A: Oh, that sounds like fun.
B: I'll pick you up at 5:30 then.
A: Thanks! I'll see you tomorrow. Bye, Tom.
B: Bye, Mary.

Notes to the Dialogue

1. How've you been? 你好吗？相当于 How are you?
2. I don't think I've got anything planned. 我想我没有打算要做什么。
3. I'll pick you up at 5:30 then. 我五点半开车去接你。

Grammar

过去分词(The Past Participle)

过去分词在句中可以用作表语、定语、状语、补语。
1. 用作表语。例如：
   Are you *interested* in reading? 你喜欢读书吗？
   Father never got *excited*. 父亲从不激动。
2. 用作定语。例如：
   There are over 80 *known* pyramids in Egypt. 在埃及有 80 多个著名的金字塔。
   Her job is to take care of the *wounded* soldier. 她的工作是照顾受伤的士兵。
   过去分词短语作定语要放在所修饰的名词后面。

This is the book ***given by the teacher***. 这就是老师给的那本书。

She happened to see on the desk a big note book ***marked Minutes of Managers' meetings***. 她碰巧看到桌子上有个大笔记本,上面写着"经理会议记录"。

The great Pyramid was built thousands of years ago for a king ***called*** Khufu. 大金字塔是数千年前为一个叫胡佛的国王修建的。

3. 用作状语,表时间、原因、让步、条件、伴随情况等。例如:

Asked why he was late, he said that he missed the bus. 被问起为什么迟到,他说没赶上车。(时间)

Changed into his uniform, he looked younger. 换上了制服,他看上去年轻多了。(原因)

United we stand; ***divided*** we fall. 团结则存,分裂则亡。(条件)

Defeated, he did not feel sad. 尽管打败了,他也没难过。(让步)

He came into the classroom, ***followed*** by several students. 他走进教室,后面跟着几个学生。(伴随)

4. 用作宾语补语,其动词多为感觉动词或使役动词。例如:

He felt a bit uneasy when he heard his name ***called***. 当听到有人喊他的名字,他感到有点不自在。

He was friendly, but he was also a wonderful man for keeping his mouth ***shut***. 他平易近人,但又十分有趣,因为他常常缄口不言。

Exercises

I. Choose the best answer a, b, c or d to these questions about the text.

1) When the *Central America* started off, there were _____ passengers on board.

    a. four hundred and ninety-one

    b. fewer than four hundred and ninety-one

    c. exactly or more than four hundred and ninety-one

d. about four hundred
2) Most of the passengers were _____.
   a. tourists   b. miners   c. tradesmen   d. soldiers
3) What happened to the ship three days later?
   a. The ship crashed into another ship.
   b. The ship met a terrible storm.
   c. The ship lost her way.
   d. The passengers found toys in the sea.
4) When the ship was in trouble, the passengers _____.
   a. burst into tears
   b. tried to find another ship to save them
   c. did all they could to save the ship
   d. criticized the captain for his mistakes
5) When the *Marie of Boston* appeared, _____.
   a. she left because she had also suffered a lot in the storm
   b. she helped the people on the Central America although she had suffered a lot in the storm, too
   c. she helped the people on the Central America because she was in good condition
   d. she left although she was in good condition
6) _____ was (were) the first to be saved to the Marie.
   a. Women and children
   b. The captain
   c. Young miners
   d. Strong miners
7) Why was the work very slow?
   a. Because there was a great disorder.
   b. Because the rough miners pushed around.
   c. Because there were terrible waves.

d. Because there were only a few boats.

8) How many people were saved by the Marie?

   a. Only the women and children.

   b. Forty men.

   c. All the people.

   d. Women and children and forty men.

II. **Match each word in Column A with a similar meaning in Column B.**

   A   B

   1) rough   a. the ground under the sea or a river

   2) suffer   b. the leader of a ship

   3) attempt   c. no use

   4) bottom   d. a person traveling in a car, ship or airplane

   5) passenger   e. not stormy

   6) roll   f. almost

   7) captain   g. an effort made to do something

   8) vain   h. swing (摇摆) from side to side

   9) nearly   i. experience pain

   10) fair   j. not polite

III. A. **Fill in the blanks with the words or expressions given below. Change the forms where necessary.**

start off	put out	in spite of	give up
on one's way	in vain	as well	at one time
disorder	take off	find one's way	on board
effort	in (an) attempt to		

1) The police _____ searching the missing boy.

2) Every _____ is being made to deal with the issue (问题) you raised at the last meeting.

3) Remember to _____ all the lights before you leave.

4) Only one of her inventions has _____ into the shops.
5) He tried to pass the exam but _____.
6) _____ diffuse (缓解) the tension (紧张) I suggested that we break off for lunch.
7) It's a long trip. Let's _____ early.
8) Everything was in _____, but nothing seemed to be stolen.
9) We'll go to the cinema tonight. Why don't you come _____?
10) The ship went down with all its crew _____.
11) _____ his illness, he went to school on time.
12) The crew were _____ the wrecked ship by the lifeboat (救生艇).
13) You can only borrow five books _____.
14) I met an old friend _____ to school.

B. Fill in each blank with a different form of the word given in the bracket.

1) My teacher _____ me to work hard. (courage)
2) Because of the _____ sea, the ship could not reach the island. (mountain)
3) After the earthquake took place, the whole city was totally in _____. (order)
4) I felt that I was the most _____ person in the world after I won the first prize. (fortune)
5) It's _____ to cry over spilt milk. (use)
6) The sky is _____ and blue. Let's have a picnic (野餐). (cloud)
7) The _____ of the ship is the responsibility of the captain. (safe)
8) All his friends left and he was in a _____ situation. (help)

IV. A. Put the verbs into brackets in the correct form.
1) I'd like this dress _____. (wash)
2) I have heard the story _____ too often. (repeat)
3) Vegetables _____ in the hot-house are not rich in color. (grow)
4) A window of the hotel was _____; he saw a shadow move across the blinds. (light)
5) I have a _____ view of my future. (decide)
6) If you'd like it _____ (fix), I can have it _____ (do) for you.
7) When we got there, we found them all _____ out. (sell)
8) _____ at by everyone, he did not give up his dream. (laugh)

B. Join each of the following pairs of sentences, turning one of them into a participial phrase and making other necessary changes.
1) They were surprised at the suggestion. They began to discuss it among them.
2) The buses were driven in gas. The gas was carried in a large bag on the roof.
3) He was absorbed in the work. He forgot food and sleep.
4) That evening we were filled with excitement. We went to his home.
5) He was deeply moved. He thanked the audience again and again.

C. Replace the clauses in italics with past participial phrases and make other necessary changes.
1) *If the medicine is taken in time*, it will work.
2) *Because we were deeply attracted by the book*, we spent the whole day reading it.
3) *After he was asked several questions*, he left the office.
4) *Although we are defeated*, we will never give up.

5) *We were encouraged by his words* and went on working.

V. A. Rewrite the following sentences after the model.

Model 1: Although they made all efforts, more and more water came in.

→ In spite of all efforts, more and more water came in.

1) Although Captain Herdon attempted to save the ship, it sank to the bottom. (attempt)
2) Although it rained, he went fishing. (rain)
3) Although he was ill, he was determined to carry out his plan. (illness)
4) Although she is old, she is very active. (age)

Model 2: Because the sea was mountainous, only a few people could be taken at one time.

→ Because of the mountainous sea, only a few people could be taken at one time.

1) He had to resign (辞职) because he had family difficulties.
2) She couldn't take part in the Olympic Games because her leg got broken. (broken leg)
3) They only turned the water on for two hours a day because they were short of water. (water shortage)
4) He walked slowly because he was in poor health.

B. Make sentences after the model, using "It was not (or will not be) long before..." and the given words.

Model: water, find its way, into the engine room

→ It was not long before water found its way into the engine room.

1) all the students, get to know him
2) you, get used to (习惯于), the life here
3) the ship, sink to the bottom of the sea

4) all the passengers, be taken off

VI. Translation.

A. From Chinese to English.

1) 船上大部分人是美国人。
2) 很快你就会喜欢这里的生活。
3) 尽管做了种种努力,但船还是沉入了海底。
4) 他试图接住球,但失败了。
5) 虽然船在风暴中受了很大的破坏,但船长仍没有放弃。
6) 所有获胜的希望都破灭了。

B. From English to Chinese.

1) It was clear to all that nothing could save the ship.
2) No fewer than ten answers are right.
3) In spite of the bad weather, he went off as usual.
4) The plane took off after the last passenger was on board.
5) Even the rough miners waited patiently, making no attempt to save themselves until the women and children were saved.
6) Only a few people were taken off at one time.

Passage Reading

Chance

(Part II)

During this time, the *Central America* had been sinking lower in the water, and at eight o'clock on Saturday evening in September 1847, she disappeared forever in the roaring sea. Those who had not reached the *Marie* found themselves swimming in the water. Fortunately, the water was not too cold at first.

The night was dark. The miserable men held on to any bit of wood they could find. They called to the *Marie* for help, but she was far beyond the reach of the human voice. At one o'clock in the morning the water was getting colder, and a sharp wind had begun to blow.

Suddenly lights were seen in the distance. Another ship! The shouts of the swimmers were heard on board, and they were pulled out of the water. The name of the ship that had so fortunately arrived in time to save their lives was the *Ellen*. What had brought her to the exact spot through the darkness sea? Her captain had known nothing of the wreck and had attempted to sail away from it. But let him speak for himself.

"I was forced by the wind to change our course," he said, "Just as I changed it, a small bird flew across the ship once or twice and then flew at my face. I took no notice of this until exactly the same thing happened a second time, which caused me to think it rather unusual. While I was considering it, the same bird, for the third time, appeared and flew about in the same way as before. I was then persuaded to change my course back to the original one. I had not gone far when I heard strange noises; and when I tried to discover where they came from, I found I was in the middle of people who had been shipwrecked. I immediately did my best to save them."

New Words & Expressions

sink [siŋk] *vi*. 下沉
roaring ['rɔːriŋ] *adj*. 咆哮的
miserable ['mizərəbl] *adj*. 不幸的
bit [bit] *n*. 小块
beyond [bi'jɔnd] *pron*. 超过

in the distance 在远处
swimmer ['swimə] *n*. 游泳者
exact [ig'zækt] *adj*. 确切的
spot [spɔt] *n*. 地点
in time 及时

wreck [rek] n. 沉船
shipwrecked ['ʃiprekt] adj. 遇难的
sail [seil] vi. 航行
course [kɔːs] n. 航线
once or twice 一两次，几次
take no notice of 不注意

darkness ['dɑːknis] n. 黑暗
cause [kɔːz] vt. 引起
persuade [pə'sweid] vt. 说服
original [ə'ridʒənəl] adj. 原来的
do one's best 尽力

Notes to the Passage

1. During this time, the *Central America* had been sinking lower in the water, and at eight o'clock on Saturday evening in September 1847, she disappeared forever in the roaring sea. 在这期间，中美洲号渐渐沉入水中，在1847年9月星期六晚上8点，她永远地消失在咆哮的大海中。had been sinking 是过去完成进行时，表示过去某时以前一直做某事。例如：

   She had been expecting to get promoted. 她一直期待被提拔。

   They had been having trouble with their car until they took it to a mechanic. 他们的车子一直有点毛病，直到送给机修工才修好了。

2. Those who had not reached the Marie found themselves swimming in the water. 那些没能登上玛丽号的人在水里游着。find oneself + doing something/介词短语，意为"发现自己处于某种状态或某地"，含有不知不觉的意味。例如：

   When he woke up, he found himself (lying) in a hospital bed. 当他醒来时，发现自己躺在医院的床上。

   After wandering around, we found ourselves back at the hotel. 我们漫无目的地转了一会，发现又回到了旅馆。

3. The miserable men held on to any bit of wood they could find. 那些不幸的人紧紧抓住他们能找到的任何木头。hold on to 意为"紧紧抓住"。例如：

The little girl held on to the coat of her mother. 小女孩紧紧抓住她妈妈的衣服。

4. They called to the *Marie* for help, but she was far beyond the reach of the human voice. 他们向玛丽号求救,但船太远了,听不到他们的声音。beyond one's reach 意为"超过某人的能力范围"。例如:
   Please place the bottle beyond the reach of the child. 请把瓶子放在孩子够不到的地方。
   This question is beyond my reach. 这个问题我答不上来。

5. Her captain had known nothing of the wreck and had attempted to sail away from it. 船长对沉船一无所知,还曾想转舵离开这里。know nothing of 意为"对某事一无所知"。例如:
   I know nothing of the traffic accident. 我对车祸一无所知。

6. I took no notice of this until exactly the same thing happened a second time, which caused me to think it rather unusual. 我没在意这件事,后来同样的事又发生了,我才觉得它不同寻常。在序数词前一般加定冠词 the,但如果加的是不定冠词 a,则表示"再一,又一"的意思。例如:
   We'll have to do it a second time. 我们得重做一次。
   When I sat down, a fourth man rose to speak. 我坐下后,第四个人又起来发言。

7. While I was considering it, the same bird, for the third time, appeared and flew about in the same way as before. 当我在考虑这件事时,同一只鸟第三次出现了,像以前一样飞来飞去。the same...as... 意为"和…相同",指同一类事物。例如:
   He made the same mistake as he did last time. 他犯了和上次相同的错误。
   the same...that 也意为"和…相同",但指的是同一件事物。例如:
   This is the same wallet that I lost a week ago. 这就是我一星期前丢的钱包。

217

Which of the following statements are true or false? Write T for true and F for false.

( )1. The Central America went to the bottom early in the morning.
( )2. The passengers were all saved to the Marie.
( )3. The Marie did not save the people in the water because there was no room on the ship.
( )4. In the morning the water was very cold and the people were in danger.
( )5. The Ellen arrived in time because she heard the strange noise.
( )6. A small bird flew across the Ellen for some food.
( )7. The captain realized that something unusual happened when the bird appeared for the first time.
( )8. It was the bird that led the Ellen to save the people who had been shipwrecked.

Unit 14

Text

A Case of Mistaken Identity

One of the qualities that most people admire in others is the willingness to admit one's mistakes. It is extremely hard sometimes to say a simple thing like "I was wrong about that," and it is even harder to say, "I was wrong, and you were right about that." Perhaps the reason we admire this quality so much in others is that we all know first-hand how difficult it can be. Some people find it so difficult that it takes years to get to the point where they are able to admit a mistaken judgment.

I had an experience recently with someone admitting to me that he had made a mistake fifteen years ago. It came as a complete surprise to me, and I had no idea what he was talking about. He told me he had been the manager of a certain grocery store in the neighborhood where I grew up, and he asked me if I remembered the egg cartons. Then he related an incident that took place in the store years ago. As he talked, I began to remember vaguely the incident he was describing.

I was about eight years old at that time, and I had gone into the store with my mother to do the weekly grocery shopping. On that particular day, I must have stopped in front of the display of eggs to wonder what it would be like if all those cartons of eggs came tumbling down. Just then, a woman came by pushing her grocery cart. She must have steered too close because, all of a sudden, the bottom rows of cartons popped out and the stacks collapsed to the floor. For some reason, I decided it was up to me to put the display back together so I went to work.

The noise of the cartons falling had attracted the attention of the manager. When he appeared, I was on my knees inspecting some of the cartons to see if any of the eggs were broken, but to him it looked as though I was the culprit. Conveniently, there was no one else near the area. He severely reprimanded me and said I was going to have to pay for any broken eggs. I protested my innocence and tried to explain about the woman with the cart, but it did no good. Even though I quickly forgot all about the incident, apparently, the manager did not.

New Words & Expressions

quality ['kwɔliti] *n*. 品质
willingness ['wiliŋnis] *n*. 自愿
admit [əd'mit] *vt*. 承认
first-hand *adv*. 首先
point [pɔint] *n*. 程度

mistaken [mis'teikən] *adj*. 错误的
judgment ['dʒʌdʒmənt] *n*. 判断
experience [iks'piəriəns] *n*. 经验
certain ['sə:tən] *adj*. 某个
grocery ['grousəri] *n*. 杂货店

carton ['kɑ:tən] *n*. 纸板箱(盒)
relate [ri'leit] *vt*. 叙述,说
incident ['insidənt] *n*. 事件
take place 发生
vaguely ['veigli] *adv*. 模糊地
weekly ['wi:kli] *adj*. 每周的
display [dis'plei] *n*. 陈列,陈列品
tumble ['tʌmbl] *vi*. 跌落,滚落
steer [stiə] *vt*. 驾驶,引得
all of a sudden 突然间
row [rou] *n*. (一)排,(一)行
pop out 忽然突出来
stack [stæk] *n*. (一)推
collapse [kə'læps] *vi*. 倒塌

up to 取决于
attract [ə'trækt] *vt*. 吸引
appear [ə'piə] *vi*. 出现
knee [ni:] *n*. 膝,膝盖
inspect [in'spekt] *vt*. 检查
culprit ['kʌlprit] *n*. 导致不良后果的人
conveniently [kən'vi:niəntli] *adv*. 近处地
severely [si'viəli] *adv*. 严厉地,严重地
reprimand ['reprimɑ:nd] *vt*. 申斥
protest [prə'test] *vt*. 申明,声言
innocence ['inəsns] *n*. 无辜
apparently [ə'pærəntli] *adv*. 明显地

Notes to the Text

1. Perhaps the reason we admire this quality so much in others is that we all know first-hand how difficult it can be. 大概,我们十分赞赏别人身上这种品质的理由是因为我们首先明白认错该有多么的艰难。句中"it"指上文提到的"to admit one's mistakes"; first-hand 意为"首先","直接的"。例如:

   The government had to deal first-hand with the social problems of the area. 政府必须首先处理该地区的社会问题。

2. Some people find it so difficult that it takes years to get to the point where they are able to admit a mistaken judgment. 一些人认为认错非常困难,以至于要过许多年才能做到承认自己有过误判。

   1) 句中前一个"it"代替前文提到的"admit one's mistakes",后一个"it"代替不定式 to get to the point where...

   2) get to the point where they are able to admit a mistaken judgment

达到能够承认有过误判的地步。句中 point 意为"程度,地步"。

3. a certain grocery store 某一个杂货店。certain 意为"某(一)个"的。例如:

   for a certain reason 为了某种理由。

4. I must have stopped in front of the display of eggs to wonder what it would be like if all those cartons of eggs came tumbling down. 我肯定在鸡蛋展位前停过,心里想要是这些蛋箱倒下来不知道会是什么样子。

5. For some reason, I decided it was up to me to put the display back together, so I went to work. 不知是何缘故,我决定由我来把展位摆回原处。因此,我动手干了。up to 意为"该由,取决于"。例如:

   It is up to you to take care of him. 该由你来照顾他了。

6. The noise of the cartons falling. 蛋箱往下掉的声音。falling 为现在分词,作后置定语,修饰 cartons。

7. When he appeared, I was on my knees inspecting some of the cartons to see if any of the eggs were broken, but to him it looked as though I was the culprit. 当他走到我跟前的时候,我正跪在地上查看蛋箱看看是否有鸡蛋摔破。可是,在他看来我却像是个罪魁祸首。

8. ...the manager did not = the manager did not forget all about the incident. 此句中省略了 forget all about the incident。

Dialogue

A: Well, London looks very pleasant.

B: Yes, it's a good thing the sun's shining for your first day here. You may never see it again.

A: It's not that bad, surely.

B: No. I'm pulling your leg.

A: What's this place?

B: This is Hyde Park.

A: Oh, yes, I know. I've heard of it in Sweden. This is where people make speeches on Sundays.

B: That's right. Politicians of all kinds, religious people and one or two madmen.

A: Look, would you like to go round by Buckingham Palace? It's not much further.

B: Yes, please. That would be nice.

New Words & Expressions

surely [ˈʃuəli] *adv.* 肯定地
pull one's leg 愚弄某人，同某人开玩笑
hear of 听说

politician [ˌpɔliˈtiʃən] *n.* 政客
religious [riˈlidʒəs] *adj.* 宗教的
madman [ˈmædmən] *n.* 疯子

Proper Names

Hyde Park [haid pɑ:k] 海德公园
Sweden [ˈswi:dən] *n.* 瑞典
Buckingham Palace [ˈbʌkiŋəm ˈpælis] 白金汉宫

Notes to the Dialogue

1. It's not that bad, surely. 当然不会那么糟糕。that 在句中是副词，意为"那么"，相当于"so"。例如：
I don't like him all that much. 我根本没那么喜欢他。

2. Look, would you like to go round by Buckingham Palace? 嗨，绕道走白金汉宫好吗？look 在此处用来引起对方注意，不是"看"的意思。

Grammar

带引导词 It 的常用结构

1. 形式主语 It (The Formal Subject "It")

   当不定式、动名词或主语从句用作主语时,常用 It 在句首作形式主语,把真正的主语移到句后,以免头重脚轻。如:

   It is extremely hard sometimes to say something like "I was wrong". 要说句像"我错了"这样的话有时候是极其困难的。

   It is no use talking without doing. 光说不做是没有用的。

   It is still a question whether we can fulfill our task in time. 我们能否及时完成任务还是个问题。

   It's a good thing (that) the sun's shining for your first day here. 你来这儿的第一天就出太阳,真是不错。

2. 形式宾语 It (The Formal Object "It")

   在"动词 + 宾语 + 宾语补足语"结构中,如果宾语是不定式、动名词或宾语从句,而后面又常以名词或形容词作宾语补足语时,常需要在原来宾语位置上用 it 作形式宾语,把真正的宾语移到后面。例如:

   They found it necessary to go on with the training. 他们发觉继续进行训练很有必要。

   I think it no good learning without practice. 我认为光学习,不实践没有好处。

   Do you think it possible that the computer will replace man? 你认为计算机有可能代替人吗?

3. 强调 It (The Emphasis "It")

   当需要强调句中某一部分时,可用此句型:It is (was) + 被强调部分 + that (who) + 其余部分。被强调部分可以是主语、宾语或状语,也可以是从句。例如:

It was my little sister who gave me a snake for my birthday. 我小妹把一条蛇送给我作为生日礼物。(强调主语)

It was a snake that my little sister gave me for my birthday. 我小妹送我的生日礼物是一条蛇。(强调宾语)

It was three minutes later that Alfred saw him coming to the door. 三分钟后艾尔弗雷德看到他朝门口走去。(强调状语)

It was because some thief was taking things from their shop that the manager told him to watch people. 正是因为有人在偷商店里的东西，经理才告诉他监视着人们。(强调原因状语从句)

It was not until he finished his homework that he went to bed. 他直到做完家庭作业才去睡觉。(强调时间状语从句)

Exercises

I. Choose the best answer a, b, c or d to these questions about the text.

1) The author's purpose of writing this passage is to tell us that _____.

   a. it is too difficult for some people to admit a wrong judgment.

   b. it is easy for some people to say "I was wrong about that".

   c. we admire the quality so much in others, for we all have it in ourselves.

   d. it takes years for some people to find a place to admit one's mistake.

2) How old is the author now?

   a. Eight.   b. Twelve.   c. Fifteen.   d. Twenty-three.

3) _____ came as a complete surprise to the author.

   a. That the manager admitted his mistake to him

   b. That the manager related the incident

   c. What had happened fifteen years ago

    d. That the cartons suddenly fell to the ground

4) The phrase "weekly grocery shopping" means _____.

    a. to buy things at the store everyday

    b. to buy things at the store once a week

    c. to buy things at the store every weekend

    d. to buy things at the store all the week

5) Which of the following statements is true?

    a. The cartons collapsed to the floor, but no eggs were broken.

    b. The manager forgot all about the incident.

    c. I didn't admit to having broken the eggs.

    d. I didn't hear the sound of the cartons falling.

6) The expression "pop out" means _____.

    a. to make sound   b. to burst open

    c. to stand up   d. to come out suddenly

7) Even though the author quickly forgot all about the incident, the manage remembered it _____.

    a. vaguely   b. uncertainly   c. unclearly   d. distinctly

8) Which sentence best expresses the main idea?

    a. The author quickly forgot all about the incident.

    b. When the author was young, he often went to the grocery store with his mother.

    c. Most people admire those who are willing to admit their mistakes.

    d. Someone admitted that he had made a mistake fifteen years ago.

II. A. Match each word in Column A with a similar meaning in Column B.

        A   B

1) willingness   a. whole

2) judgment   b. show

3) complete   c. strict
4) relate   d. at that time
5) display   e. ready to do what is needed
6) stack   f. free from moral mistake
7) then   g. decision of a judge
8) innocent   h. fall down
9) severe   i. tell someone about events that have happened
10) tumble   j. a pile of things

B. Match the words with opposite (相反的) meaning in Column A and B.

A   B
1) find   a. leave
2) unhappy   b. pull
3) purchase   c. guilty
4) clearly   d. take apart
5) beautiful   e. vaguely
6) stay   f. sell
7) hard   g. pleased
8) put together   h. lose
9) innocent   i. easy
10) push   j. ugly

III. Fill in the blanks with the words or expressions given below. Change the form where necessary.

put	grow up	admit	collapse	pay for
steer	take place	attract	reprimand	start out
certain	relate	up to	all of a sudden	

1) Tom _____ that he hadn't done his duty.
2) The accident _____ on the corner of the street.

227

3) Everyone else, the sick excepted, must _____ at once.

4) Smith wants to be a teacher when he _____.

5) The film shown recently _____ a large audience.

6) Sometimes you have to _____ your mistakes.

7) He was _____ for insufficient (不充分的) control.

8) The boat _____ for the harbor.

9) We followed the directions but could not _____ the machine together.

10) The walls of the burning house _____.

11) It's _____ you whether you decide to take the job.

12) _____, the lights went out.

13) When my friend returned from Asia, he _____ many stories about her trip.

14) A _____ Mr. Jones phoned you today.

IV. Point out the function of "it" in the following sentences.

1) It is no good trying to raise its temperature.

2) It is a fine day though it is cold.

3) They found it necessary to use new methods.

4) We think it useful to do some more research work on it.

5) It was at that moment that he changed his mind.

6) It is quite clear who is the oldest of the three.

7) It will take you two hours to go there by bike.

8) It feels like it's going to rain.

9) We think it possible that the ordinary students can become top students if they work hard.

10) It is an exciting experience just to walk down a New York street.

V. A. Complete the following sentences, using "must have done".

1) That sounds like an ambulance (救护车). _____ (是的,一定

有事故了。)

2) _____ （我一定是在鸡蛋的展位前停了下来）to wonder what it would be like if all those cartons of eggs came tumbling down.

3) _____ （你一定是见到过他的），he lives next door to you.

4) My sister has just come back from abroad. _____ （她这趟旅行一定非常愉快。）

B. Complete the following sentences, using "What will (would) it be like if..."

1) _____ I am late for class?

2) _____ there was an accident?

3) _____ he made a mistake?

4) _____ she refused to accept the job.

VI. Translation.

A. From Chinese to English.

1) 小偷承认偷了老人的钱。

2) 有些人认为承认错误很难。

3) 我们是否现在出发取决于你。

4) 我花了三年才写成这本小说。

5) 突然，一个孩子从左边跑到公路上。

6) 地面是湿的，昨晚一定是下雨了。

B. From English to Chinese.

1) What are you up to?

2) I had an experience recently with someone admitting to me that he had made a mistake fifteen years ago.

3) I protested my innocence and tried to explain about the woman with the cart, but it did no good.

4) What would it be like if all those cartons of eggs came tumbling down?

5) We heard the news first hand.

6) Then he related an incident that took place in the store years ago.

Passage Reading

Guilty or Not Guilty

Fred Wilks was arrested and taken to court. The police accused him of stealing.

"Are you guilty or not guilty?" the judge asked.

"Not guilty," Fred said.

"I'll hear the evidence," the judge said. "Call the first witness."

The first witness was a woman.

"I saw that man go into the shop," She said, pointing at Fred, "and come out carrying a TV set. A few minutes later the shopkeeper ran out and shouted 'Stop thief' and ran after him."

The second witness was a man.

"I was in the shop," the man said. "I saw that man come in, pick up a TV set and carry it out of the shop. I told the shopkeeper what I had seen."

The third witness was the shopkeeper.

"I was in my shop," he said, "When a man came up to me and told me that man," he pointed at Fred, "had carried a TV set out of the shop. I knew he had not paid for it so I ran after him."

The fourth witness was a policeman.

"I was walking along the street," he said, "When a shopkeeper ran up to me. He said that that man", he pointed at Fred, "had walked out of his shop with a TV set he had not paid for. I, therefore, arrested him."

At this moment, Fred stood up.

"I'm guilty," he said.

"Why did you say you were not guilty earlier?" the judge asked him angrily.

"I hadn't heard the evidence then," Fred said.

New Words & Expressions

arrest [ə'rest] vt. 逮捕
court [kɔ:t] n. 法院
accuse [ə'kju:z] vt. 控告
 accuse sb of 控告(某人)
guilty ['gilti] adj. 有罪的

judge [dʒʌdʒ] n. 法官
evidence ['evidəns] n. 证据
witness ['witnis] n. 见证人
shopkeeper ['ʃɔpˌki:pə] n. 店员
run after 追赶

Notes to the passage

1. ...taken to court. 被起诉。
2. The police accused him of stealing. 警方起诉他偷东西。"accuse sb of"后面接名词或动名词。如:
He was accused of being a spy. 他被控告充当了间谍。
3. "I saw that man go into the shop," she said, pointing at Fred, "and come out carrying a TV set." 我看见这个男人进入商店, 她指着弗雷德说:"出来时抱着一台电视。"

Answer the following questions according to the passage.

1. Why was Fred arrested and taken to court?
2. Who was the first witness? What had he (she) seen?
3. What had the second witness seen?
4. What was the third witness?
5. What had the fourth witness seen?
6. Did Fred admit that he was guilty at first? Why?

Unit 15

Text

Dolores Silva, Small Business Co-owner

(Part I)

When people ask me to name my profession, I can't answer. My job is too complicated to sum up in a word.

My husband and I own an import company, Silva Enterprises. Our business is so small that we have to do all the work ourselves. What is my profession? I'm a co-owner, business manager, secretary, buyer, salesperson, accountant, and even janitor!

On some days I'm in only one of these professions. For example, I sometimes spend the whole day on the phone talking to buyers from gift shops. (We import arts and crafts objects from South America, and sell them wholesale to gift shops in the city.) Or perhaps I might type correspondence in the morning and go over the books in the afternoon.

But other days are much busier and my professions multiply. Yesterday was one of the busiest days I've ever had. My husband woke up sick, so I began the day as a nurse. I gave him aspirin and took his temperature. Then I became a chef and prepared his breakfast. He said I was a good chef, but he was too sick to eat. I became a wife and kissed him goodbye.

At the office, after I opened the mail and paid a few bills, both of the phones started ringing. On the first phone, a man said that he wanted to speak to the business manager. I asked him to hold the phone for a minute, and I answered the second one. On the line was a man with one of the deepest voices I've ever heard. He said he owned a gift shop and wanted to make a business appointment with the owner of the company. I was intimidated by his deep voice. I don't know why, but suddenly I felt very confused, so when he asked me if I was the secretary, I quickly said yes.

Then I felt ashamed. Was I frightened by his deep voice? What a coward! I was really mad at myself for not telling him that I was the co-owner of the company. He made an appointment to come at 3:30 that afternoon and I told him that he would meet one of the owners then. I said the owner's name was Silva.

New Words & Expressions

co-owner [kou'ounə] n. 合伙人
own [oun] vt. 拥有
profession [prə'feʃən] n. 职业
complicated ['kɔmplikeitid] adj. 复杂的
sum up 概括
in a word 总而言之，一言以蔽之
import ['impɔ:t] n. 进口
enterprise ['entəpraiz] n. 企业
buyer ['baiə] n. 购买者，买主
salesperson ['seilzpə:sn] n. 销售人员
accountant [ə'kauntənt] n. 会计员
janitor ['dʒænitə] n. 看门人
arts and crafts 工艺品
object ['ɔbdʒikt] n. 物品

wholesale ['houlseil] adv. 大批地，批发地
correspondence [ˌkɔris'pɔndəns] n. 通信
go over 仔细检查
aspirin ['æspərin] n. 阿司匹林
temperature ['tempəritʃə] n. 温度
chef [ʃef] n. 厨师长
mail [meil] n. 邮件
bill [bil] n. 账单
confuse [kən'fju:z] vt. 使困惑
confused [kən'fju:zd] adj. 困惑的
ashamed [ə'ʃeimd] adj. 惭愧
frighten ['fraitən] vt. 使惊吓
coward ['kauəd] n. 胆小鬼

Proper Names

Dolores Silva ['dɔlərəs'silvɑ:] （人名）多洛雷斯·席尔瓦
Silva Enterprises ['silvɑ:'entəpraisiz] 席氏企业
South America [sauθə'merikə] 南美洲

Notes to the Text

1. My job is too complicated to sum up in a word. 我的工作太复杂,不能用一句话来概括。

   1) sum up 意为"概括"。例如：

The last chapter sums up the arguments. 最后一章概括了所有的论点。

2) in a word 意为"一句话,简言之"。例如:

"Did you enjoy the film?" "In a word—no." "你喜欢这个电影吗?""一句话——不喜欢。"

2. On some days I'm in only one of these professions. 有些日子里,我仅仅从事这些职业中的一种工作。

3. Or perhaps I might type correspondence in the morning and go over the books in the afternoon. 或者很可能上午打信件,下午查看账本。情态动词 might 这里不表示过去,只表示说话人对所说之事把握很小,所以用一种保留的口气表述。例如:

What you say might be true. 你说的话也许是真的。

4. My husband woke up sick, so I began the day as a nurse. 我丈夫醒来的时候生病了,所以这一天我先当护士。句中 sick 作主语补足语。此句相当于 My husband woke up and he was sick. 再如:

It's impossible for young children to sit still. 要让小孩子坐着不动是不可能的。

The famous writer married very young. 这位著名作家很年轻的时候就结了婚。

类似的还有: stand silent, lie awake, etc.

5. On the line was a man with one of the deepest voices I've ever heard. 电话那头是一个男子,他的声音是我听过的最低沉的。由于主语"a man"后边有很长的修饰语,故采用倒装。例如:

Around the lake are 50 villages with 950 families. 湖的四周有 50 个村庄 950 户家庭。

6. I was really mad at myself... 我实在对自己很生气…。句中"mad"意为"生气的,愤怒的",是俗语用法。仅用于非正式场合。

7. He made an appointment to come at 3∶30 that afternoon... 他约定那天下午三点半来…

Dialogue

A: You're late. Are you ready to leave?

B: In a minute or two. I was making out lesson plans, and then the father of one of my students came in.

A: Trouble?

B: He wanted to know why his daughter wasn't reading better.

A: What did you tell him?

B: The truth, of course. Her health is part of the problem. She's absent too often, and when she does come to class, she can't concentrate.

A: What's the matter with her?

B: I'm not sure why she gets sick so often.

A: Did you ask the father?

B: Yes, but he isn't sure either, even though he's taken her to the doctor.

A: Is there anything you can do to help the girl?

B: I sent some work that her father can help her with at home. But what about you? You're here late too.

A: Oh, I was doing the usual things—correcting homework and making out lesson plans.

B: Well, let's go now. It's been a long day.

New Words and Expressions

make out 制定
matter ['mætə] n. 问题

concentrate ['kɔnsəntreit] vi. 集中精力
either ['aiðə] adv. 或者

Notes to the Dialogue

1. In a minute or two 再过一会儿。in 可用在将来时态中表示一段时间之后。例如：
   He'll come back in three days. 他将在三天之后回来。
   如果是过去时态应用 later。例如：
   He came back three days later (after three days). 他是三天后回来的。
   如果表示具体某一时刻之后，应用 after。例如：
   Please tell me the reason after super. 请晚饭后告诉我原因。
   They went to bed after nine o'clock. 九点钟以后，他们上床睡觉。
2. When she does come to class, she can't concentrate. 她就是来上课，也不能集中精力学习。does 在这里表示强调，do 有时可以放在谓语动词前，用于加强语气，时态随谓语变。例如：
   I did tell him the truth. 我的确把真实情况跟他讲了。

Grammar

直接引语与间接引语
(The Direct Speech & Indirect Speech)

引述别人的讲话有两种方式。一种叫直接引语，即直接重复说话人的原话，并用引号引上；另一种叫间接引语，即由引述者转达说话人的内容，同时要有相应的变化。例如：

直接引语：She said, "I like light music".

间接引语：She said that she liked light music.

1. 引述陈述句时，开头用 that 引导，并根据意思改变相应的人称、时态和时间地点等。例如：

{ She said, "I have been playing volleyball this afternoon."
{ She said that she had been playing volleyball that afternoon.
{ He said, "I will come here again tonight."
{ He said that she would go there again that night.
{ Tom said to me, "This is the house where my father was born."
{ Tom told me that that was the house where his father had been born.

具体的变化规律见下表：

指示代词	this these	that those
时间	ago now this week yesterday last week	before then that week the day before the week before
地点	here	there
动词	come	go
时态	一般现在时 现在进行时 一般将来时 现在完成时	一般过去时 过去进行时 过去将来时 过去完成时

但在下列情况下，尽管引述动词为过去时，间接引语中的动词时态无需变化。

1) 当引述的是客观事实、科学真理或习惯性行为时。例如：
   { He said, "The earth moves round the sun."
   { He said that the earth moves round the sun.

2) 动词所表示的状态或动作在引述时仍在继续。例如：
   { "I'm eighteen", she said.
   { She said that she is eighteen.

3) 当谓语动词属无过去时形式的情态动词时。例如：

{ She said, "I had better not do it."
{ She said that she had better not do it.

2. 引述疑问句时,除要注意前边所说的变化外,要变疑问句语序为陈述语序。句中没有疑问词时,需用连词 whether(if)引导。例如:

{ He asked, "Where does she live?"
{ He asked where she lived.

{ He asked, "How are you getting along?"
{ He asked us how we were getting along.

{ "Do you want to go by ship or by plane?" Mary asked.
{ Mary asked whether I wanted to go by ship or by plane.

{ "You've already got well, haven't you?" she asked.
{ She asked whether he had already got well.

3. 引述祈使句时,要把祈使对象变为直接宾语,将祈使句改成不定式短语作宾语补足语。谓语动词可根据句子的口气决定。

{ "Come in, please." he said.
{ He asked me to go in.

{ He said, "Don't work too long time."
{ He told me not to work too long time.

{ He said, "Get everything ready at once."
{ He ordered us to get everything ready at once.

Exercises

I. Choose the best answer a, b, c or d to these questions about the text.

1) Dolores' job is too complicated to sum up in a word because _____.

   a. her job is too difficult
   b. she has to play several parts in her daily life
   c. she herself is the owner of the import company

    d. she has to make a lot of business appointments
2) When Dolores goes over the books, she is doing the work of _____.
    a. an accountant
    b. a salesperson
    c. a buyer
    d. a secretary
3) Dolores goes over the books _____.
    a. every morning
    b. the whole day
    c. in the afternoon
    d. every afternoon
4) When she typed correspondence, she was doing the work of _____.
    a. an accountant
    b. a salesperson
    c. a buyer
    d. a janitor
5) When Dolores's husband was ill, she had to _____.
    a. be a nurse to care for him
    b. be a chef to cook food
    c. stay at home
    d. both a and b
6) Silva Enterprise is a company that _____.
    a. imports books from homeland
    b. imports aspirin from homeland
    c. buys toys from homeland
    d. buys arts and crafts objects from abroad
7) Dolores was very angry with herself because _____.
    a. the gift shop owner had a deep voice
    b. the man made an appointment to come
    c. her husband was ill in bed
    d. she told a lie to the man

II. Match each word in Column A with a similar meaning in Column B.

       A   B
1) import   a. mix up in the mind

2) wholesale　　　　　　b. a present
3) confuse　　　　　　　c. low
4) gift　　　　　　　　　d. a person who controls a business
5) correspondence　　　e. bring in from abroad
6) own　　　　　　　　　f. cook
7) deep　　　　　　　　　g. in large amounts
8) manager　　　　　　　h. increase a number
9) chef　　　　　　　　　i. letters
10) multiply　　　　　　j. belong to oneself

III. Fill in the blanks with the words or expressions given below. Change the form where necessary.

sell	spend	wake up	in a word	go over
start	import	own	sum up	frighten
make an appointment		wholesale	ashamed	confuse

1) I _____ attending the remedial reading class in the evening.
2) John is smart, polite and well-behaved. _____ he is admirable (讨人喜欢的).
3) When he _____ the sea became calm again.
4) The doctor _____ the girl carefully, but could find no broken bones.
5) It is the chairman's duty _____ at the end of the meeting.
6) He _____ a number of shops and several factories abroad.
7) The manager _____ to see me that evening.
8) The students _____ three nights practicing the group-singing for Teacher's Day.
9) Hundreds of stalls (货摊) _____ special articles (商品) for the lunar (阴历) New year.
10) All these arts, crafts and small articles _____ from Africa

241

last year.

11) He felt _____ that he should have hit a small child.

12) They sold arts and crafts objects _____ to department stores in the city.

13) The man _____ the old lady into signing the paper.

14) They had _____ me with their conflicting (互相矛盾的) advice.

IV. A. **Put the following questions into indirect speech.**

1) Where did you leave the key? (She wanted to know...)

2) What are the plans for today? (She asked me ...)

3) May I use your phone? (The man asked me...)

4) Did you meet him yesterday? (He asked me ...)

5) Who is his father? (She wondered ...)

6) How many novels have you read this term? (He asked me ...)

7) Is he going to swim this afternoon? (He asked me ...)

8) When will you be here again? (She wanted to know...)

9) Shall I go with you? (She asked me...)

10) Have you seen our new machine? (He asked us ...)

B. **Put the following into indirect speech.**

1) He said, "I haven't seen this film before."

2) "You must do it on your own", he told me.

3) She said, "My doctor won't let me drink anything but champagne."

4) I said, "He didn't tell me the good news yesterday."

5) He told Henry, "Write that exercise out carefully."

6) "Don't get your shoes dirty, boy," she said.

7) He said, "I would do the same if I were in your place."

8) The teacher said, "I'll try to give you some easier examples tomorrow morning."

9) He asked her, "Please change seats with me."

10) The teacher told the students, "You will learn two lessons this week."

V. A. **Rewrite the following sentences after the model.**

Model: My job is so complicated that I cannot sum up in a word.

My job is too complicated to sum up in a word.

1) My husband was so sick that he could not eat.
2) He was so tired that he could not go away further.
3) It was so cold that we did not go swimming.
4) Everyone says we are so young that we can't get married.

B. **Complete the following sentences, using the expressions given below in their proper forms.**

wake up sick	come true	sit still	marry young
lie awake	turn green	go wrong	fall ill

1) His dream _____ at last. He became a general(将军).
2) Leaves(树叶) _____ in spring.
3) My husband _____, so I began the day as a nurse.
4) It is impossible for a small child to _____ in class.
5) Professor Li _____, because of overwork.
6) She's now a mother of five children. It is said that she _____.
7) The engine isn't working properly. Something must have _____.
8) He _____, thinking what it would be like if he declined (拒绝) the invitation to the dinner party.

VI. **Translation.**

A. **From Chinese to English.**

1) 这台机器的结构太复杂而没能找到问题。
2) 我跟出口部经理约定中午见面。

3) 我哥哥直到35岁才结婚。(remain unmarried)

4) 10月30日公司开始检查账目。

5) 别挂电话,我去叫他。

6) 由于不愿意在恶劣的环境中工作,所以他的工作量增加了。

B. From English to Chinese.

1) I always confused the meaning of the two words.

2) I was really mad at myself for not telling him that I was the co-owner of the company.

3) I was ashamed when I couldn't remember his name.

4) He is too much of a coward to tell her he loves her.

5) Our business is so small that we have to do the work ourselves.

6) If you don't pay your bills, you will probably have to be taken to court.

Passage Reading

Dolores Silva, Small Business Co-owner

(Part II)

We hung up, and I returned to the first phone. It was a man named Tomas Martin, from Nicaragua, I said that I was the business manager and asked if I could help him. He replied that he was calling about the marimbas.

"What marimbas?" I asked.

"Oh, you know," he said , "the 200 marimbas your husband ordered last week, during our spring sale."

"Two hundred marimbas?" I couldn't believe it. "Are you sure?" I asked.

"Oh, yes," he said. "I have the purchase order right here. I was just beginning to fill out the invoice. The reason I am calling is to make a special offer: 325 marimbas for the price of 250. A terrific bargain! There's almost no profit margin at all on this one for me."

Three hundred and twenty-five marimbas! What could we do with 325 marimbas? For that matter, what could we do with 200?

I politely turned down his offer, and we hung up. For the rest of the morning, I worked as a salesperson, trying to sell marimbas to retail musical instrument companies. I sold only forty-five.

After lunch I wrote letters to some gift shops. In the letters, after describing the beautiful, handmade Nicaraguan marimbas, I claimed that they were very unusual gifts.

At 3:30 I met the gift shop owner with the deep voice. He was short and nervous, and he seemed very surprised to find a woman in the position of owner. He looked over our inventory, but bought nothing.

I cleaned up the office and went home with a bad headache and a sudden cough. My husband hadn't eaten all day and was very hungry. But I was exhausted, and I told him that he must become a chef. Also a nurse. Also a marimba player.

While he stood there, looking hopelessly confused, I took two aspirin, then sneezed. Some days it's better just to stay in bed.

New Words & Expressions

hung up 挂断(电话)
marimbas [mə'rimbəs] n. 马林巴(木琴的一种)
purchase ['pɜːtʃəs] n. 购买
order ['ɔːdə] n. 定货单
fill out 填写
invoice ['invɔis] n. 发票,清单
make an offer 提议
terrific [tə'rifik] adj. 极好的
bargain ['bɑːɡin] n. 交易

profit ['prɔfit] n. 利润,收益
margin ['mɑ:dʒin] n. 盈余,毛利
politely [pə'laitli] adv. 客气地
turn down 拒绝
retail [ri'teil] adj. 零售的
handmade ['hændmeid] adj. 手工的
claim [kleim] vt. 声称
nervous ['nə:vəs] adj. 神经质的,紧张的
position [pə'ziʃən] n. 位置

look over 逐一检阅,检查
inventory ['invəntəri] n. 存货目录(清单)
headache ['hedeik] n. 头疼
sudden ['sʌdn] adj. 突然的
exhaust [ig'zɔ:st] vt. 使筋疲力尽
exhausted [ig'zɔ:stid] adj. 筋疲力尽的
hopelessly ['houplisli] adv. 不抱希望地
sneeze [sni:z] vi. 打喷嚏

Proper Names

Tomas Martin ['tɔməs'mɑ:tin] (人名) 托马斯·马丁
Nicaragua [ˌnikə'rægjuə] (国名) 尼加拉瓜
Nicaraguan [nikə'rægjuən] adj. 尼加拉瓜的

Notes to the Passage

1. There's almost no profit margin at all on this one for me. 按这个价我几乎根本不赢利了。
2. For that matter 就那种情况而论。
3. retail musical instrument companies 零售乐器公司。
4. ..., and he seemed very surprised to find a woman in the position of owner. 他似乎很惊奇地发现一个女人坐在店主的位置上。
5. ...he must become a chef. Also a nurse. Also a marimba player. 相当于：...he must become a chef. He must also become a nurse, and he must also become a marimba player.

Answer the following questions according to the passage.

1. Why did Tomas Martin call?

2. Who ordered the 200 marimbas?
3. What was Tomas Martin's special offer?
4. Did Dolores accept the offer?
5. To whom did Dolores try to sell the marimbas?
6. What was the gift shop owner like?
7. Did he buy anything?
8. How did she feel on her exhausting day?

Unit 16

Text

It's Never Too Late

(Part I)

What is it you want to do, but haven't done yet?

Is it because you think it's too late, or too scary, or because maybe you might fail?

Yesterday, while walking the beach with our dog, Sasha, (who usually manages to draw people into conversation) I met a retired couple from the Midwest. They kept saying how much they love visiting the Oregon coast.

"We're both crazy about the ocean," the woman said, "and we're kicking ourselves that we didn't buy some property here 10 years ago."

"Do you think it's too late now?" I asked.

"Well, uh, no," she said, "but it would have been a lot cheaper then."

So—will they stay stuck in an area they dislike, or will they dare to try something that feels exciting and challenging?

If I'd known them better, I would have mentioned the old line about the lady who waited so long for her ship to come in that her pier collapsed.

Someone once said, "Most people go through life in a state of quiet desperation." Going through life in a state of "quiet expectation" sounds a lot better to me.

What it takes is a conscious change in attitude.

Look how many people talk about making changes—but talk is all they're good at. For example:

"Things would really be different if I could just:
- change my job
- get married
- have kids
- get rid of the kids
- move somewhere else."

You hear this stuff all the time.

I've enjoyed contesting as a sub-hobby for years, and occasionally suggest to friends that they try it because surprises are such fun. When an old friend in Nebraska found out that the 4th Polaroid camera had arrived at our house, she said, "Oh, that would never happen to me, I'm just not the type of person who ever wins anything."

"Why not change your attitude?" I suggested. "Sometimes you have to make things happen and see yourself as a winner."

This gal never calls long distance, so I was surprised to hear her voice when the phone rang.

"Guess what?" she yelled into the phone. "I decided to try changing how I think about myself. I saw this contest notice in a store window, so I walked in and signed up and then really tried to picture myself as a winner," At this point she sounded breathless. "They just called to tell me I've won a HUNDRED DOLLARS!" Then she added, "so I figured I could afford to call and say your philosophy works."

New Words & Expressions

scary ['skɛəri] *adj*. 令人惊恐的
manage ['mænidʒ] *vt*. 设法,对付
  manage to do 设法做某事
retired [ri'taiəd] *adj*. 退休的
couple [kʌpl] *n*. 一对(夫妇)
coast [koust] *n*. 海岸
crazy ['kreizi] *adj*. 热衷的,热爱的
  be crazy about 喜欢
ocean ['ouʃən] *n*. 海洋
dislike [dis'laik] *vt*. 不喜欢
dare [dɛə] *v. aux*. 敢,敢于
challenge ['tʃælindʒ] *vt*. 挑战
challenging ['tʃælindʒiŋ] *adj*. 有挑战性的
line [lain] *n*. (非正式)故事

pier [piə] *n*. 码头
go through 经历,忍受
state [steit] *n*. 状态
  in a state of 处于…状态
desperation [ˌdespə'reiʃən] *n*. 绝望;拼命
expectation [ˌekspek'teiʃən] *n*. 期待,期望
kick [kik] *vt*. 抱怨
  kick oneself 严厉自责
property ['prɔpəti] *n*. 地产,资产
stick [stik] (stuck, stuck) *vt*. 粘,不离开
get rid of 摆脱,消除
stuff [stʌf] *n*. 废话

contest [kən'test] *vi*. 竞赛
occasionally [ə'keiʒənəli] *adv*. 偶尔地
conscious ['kɔnʃəs] *adj*. 明白的,清醒的
attitude ['ætitjuːd] *n*. 态度
be good at 擅长于
kid [kid] *n*. 小孩
gal [gæl] *n*. (口语)女孩,少女

sign up 签名
picture ['piktʃə] *vt*. 在心中描绘,想象
winner ['winə] *n*. 获胜者
breathless ['breθlis] *adj*. 气喘吁吁的
figure ['figə] *vt*. 想象,估计
philosophy [fi'lɔsəfi] *n*. 哲理,人生观

Proper Names

Midwest ['midwest] 美国中西部
Nebraska [nə'bræskə] 内布拉斯加(美国中部之一州)
Oregon ['ɔrigən] 俄勒冈(美国中西部之一州)
Polaroid ['poulərɔid] 宝丽来一次成像照相机

Notes to the Text

1. While walking the beach with our dog 当我在海滩上领着狗散步时…。此句中 walk 作及物动词。
2. "We're both crazy about the ocean," the woman said, "and we're kicking ourselves that we didn't buy some property here 10 years ago." "我们俩都迷恋海洋,"那女的说,"我们在责怪自己十年前没在这里置些房产。"
    1) be crazy about(on) 对…着迷,对…狂热。例如:
       The boy is crazy about swimming. 这男孩特别喜欢游泳。
    2) kick oneself 意为"严厉自责"。例如:
       He is always kicking himself every time he makes a mistake. 每次犯错误,他总是严厉自责。
3. "but it would have been a lot cheaper then." 此句为虚拟语气,它省略

了从句"If we had bought some property"。

4. So—will they stay stuck in an area they dislike, or will they dare to try something that feels exciting and challenging? 如此说来,他们还将固守在他们不喜欢的地方吗？或者说他们敢于尝试那些令人激动或是具有挑战性的事情吗？

   1）stay 在这里是系动词, stuck 是过去分词做表语, 表示继续处于粘着固定的状态。

   2）注意 dare 的用法。dare 既可作情态动词, 也可作行为动词。例如：
   My new car is meant to go at 120 miles an hour, but I daren't try it at that speed. (= but I don't dare to...) 我的新车可以以一小时 120 英里的速度行驶, 但我不敢以那样的速度试行。
   How dare you speak to me in that rude way? (= How do you dare to...) 你怎么敢这么粗鲁地跟我讲话？
   Everyone was silent. No one dared breathe. (= dared to) 大家一言不发, 没人敢喘气。

5. If I'd known them better, I would have mentioned the old line about the lady who waited so long for her ship to come in that her pier collapsed. 如果我对他们更了解的话, 我就会提起关于那个女士的往事——她久久等待来船, 结果却是码头塌毁, 一事无成。

   1）the old line 意为"往事"。

   2）...waited so long for her ship to come in that her pier collapsed 这是个比喻。实际意思是：人生就是在等待中虚度光阴, 一事无成。句中 that 引导的是结果状语从句。

6. Someone once said, "Most people go through life in the state of quiet desperation." "Going through life in a state of quiet expectation" sounds a lot better to me. 有人曾经说过"多数人都是在无奈绝望中默默地度过人生。"我要说"在期待中默默地度过人生", 听起来要顺耳得多。

7. sub-hobby 表示"业余爱好中的一部分"。此处 sub 意为"a part of",

再如：subcommittee 小组委员会；subgroup 小小组等。

8. the 4th Polaroid camera 第四代宝丽来牌照相机。第一代宝丽来诞生于 1948 年。

9. "Why not change your attitude?" I suggested. "为什么不改变一下态度呢？"我提议道。本句是省略句，相当于 Why don't you change your attitude? 后面的"Guess what?"也是省略句。应是 Guess what I'm going to say?

10. "So I figured I could afford to call and say your philosophy works." 因此，我估计我能付得起电话费，对你说声你讲的道理真的很管用。此句中 work 意为"起作用"。再如：
    Your plan is rather difficult, but it might work. 你的计划有相当的难度，但也可能行的通。

Dialogue

It's January and two women friends are on the phone complaining about the weather.

A: It's freezing out there today. Are you going out?

B: Yes, but I'm wearing three layers of clothes and heavy boots to keep warm.

A: At least it's not snowing. It could be worse!

B: It's bad enough. I had trouble starting my car this morning. My neighbor had to give me a jump. I'm taking my car in for a new battery today.

A: My car is running, but there's something wrong with the heat in the house. My husband's trying to fix it now. We're both wearing jackets in the house. I wish it were summer.

B: In summer you always complain about how hot and humid it is!

New Words & Expressions

layer ['leiə] *n*. 层
boot [bu:t] *n*. 靴子
jacket ['dʒækit] *n*. 夹克衫
humid ['hjumid] *adj*. 潮湿的

jump [dʒʌmp] *n*. 跨接起动
battery ['bætəri] *n*. 蓄电池
heat [hi:t] *n*. 暖气

Notes to the Dialogue

1. I'm wearing three layers of clothes and heavy boots to keep warm. 我穿了三层衣服和棉靴子保暖。heavy boots 意为"棉靴子"，heavy 还有其他解释，例如：
   heavy heart 沉重的心情　　heavy rain 大雨
   heavy smoker 烟鬼　　　　heavy sea 波涛汹涌的海面

2. It could be worse! 可能会更糟!

3. I have trouble starting my car this morning. 今天早晨我的车子都发动不了。have trouble (in) doing something 意为"很难做某事"。例如：
   I had trouble (in) working out this question. 我无法做这道题。
   We had trouble (in) finishing the task on time. 我们无法按时完成工作。

4. My neighbor had to give me a jump. 我的邻居不得不来帮我起动汽车。give somebody a jump 意为"帮某人起动汽车"。原句的意思是 B 的汽车打不着火，只好求助邻居，用邻居汽车的蓄电池跨接 B 的蓄电池，以启动发动机。

5. I wish it were summer. 现在要是夏天就好了。wish 后跟虚拟语气。例如：
   I wish I were a bird. 我希望我是一只鸟。
   I wish I had seen the film yesterday. 我希望我昨天看了那场电影。

Grammar

虚拟语气(The Subjunctive Mood)

虚拟语气是谓语动词的一种形式,用来表示与事实相反的,或不可能实现的假设,或表示建议、请求或愿望等。虚拟语气常用于虚拟条件句中。其使用形式如下:

	条件状语从句	主句
与现在事实相反的假设	动词过去式,were	would(should, might, could) + 动词原形
与过去事实相反的假设	had + 过去分词	would(should, might, could) + have + 过去分词
将来不能(或难以)实现的假设	should + 动词原形(或were + 不定式)	would(should, might, could) + 动词原形

1. 虚拟语气现在式

    If he <u>had</u> a motorcycle, he <u>would ride</u> it to school. 如果他有了机械脚踏车,他就会把它骑到学校来。

    If I <u>were</u> you, I <u>would go</u> with your uncle. 假如我是你,我就会跟你叔叔一起去。

    Things <u>would</u> really <u>be</u> different if I <u>could change</u> my job. 如果我能够变换一下工作的话,事情可能就真的不同了。

2. 虚拟语气过去式

    If I'<u>d known</u> them better, I <u>would have mentioned</u> the old line. 如果我更了解他们的话,我就会提起那件往事的。

    If we <u>had bought</u> some property here ten years ago, it <u>would have been</u> a lot cheaper then. 如果我们十年前在这里买下些产业的话,那可要便宜多了。

3. 虚拟语气将来式

If the rain <u>should not stop</u>, what <u>would</u> you <u>do</u>? 要是雨不停的话,你怎么办?

If I <u>were to make</u> the design, I <u>might do</u> it in a different way. 如果我做这个设计,我可能用不同的方法去做。

4. 虚拟条件句有时省略 if, 后边使用倒装语序

<u>Were he here</u>, he would help me (If he were here) 假如他在这儿的话,他就会帮助我。

<u>Had he worked hard,</u> he would have succeeded. (If he had worked hard) 如果当初努力工作的话,他就会取得成功了。

<u>Should it rain,</u> the crops would be saved. (If it should rain) 倘若天下雨的话,庄稼就可得救了。

Exercises

I. **Choose the best answer a, b, c or d to each of the questions about the text.**

1) What is the author's attitude towards what we want to do but haven't done yet?

   a. It's too late.　　　　b. It's too scared.
   c. It's never too late.　　d. It's a failure.

2) The word "scared" in the second line means _____.

   a. confused   b. failed   c. worried   d. frightened

3) "But it would have been a lot cheaper then" implies (隐含) _____.

   a. the price was too dear at that time
   b. the price was more expensive ten years ago
   c. the price is increasing a lot
   d. the price is very cheap at present

4) "The lady waited so long for her ship to come in that her pier col-

lapsed" means _____.

   a. She waited so long that she lost patience

   b. She waited for her ship, but it did not come

   c. There happened an accident when she waited for her ship

   d. She expected to succeed but accomplished nothing (一事无成)

5) "Going through life in a state of quiet expectation" shows that _____.

   a. the author is optimistic (乐观) about life

   b. the author is pessimistic (悲观) about life

   c. the author lives a hopeless life

   d. the author likes dreaming during daytime

6) In the author's opinion, talking about making changes is _____.

   a. helpful   b. useful   c. useless   d. meaningful

7) The girl never calls long distance because _____.

   a. she lived far from the post office

   b. she was short of money

   c. she didn't like to disturb others

   d. she didn't like to phone a distant call

8) The girl was very much excited because _____.

   a. she had won a contest

   b. the author's philosophy had worked

   c. she had won a hundred dollars

   d. all of the above

II. Match each word in Column A with a similar meaning in Column B.

   A   B
   1) beach   a. wildly excited
   2) draw   b. to call to have a fight

3) crazy   c. imagine
4) property   d. attract
5) challenge   e. coastline (海岸) covered with sand
6) mention   f. propose
7) expectation   g. area of land and buildings
8) picture   h. think
9) suggest   i. future prospects
10) figure   j. refer to

III. **Fill in the blanks with the words or expressions given below. Change the form where necessary.**

afford	find out	retire	go through	have trouble
kick	occasionally	breathless	figure	manage
draw	get rid of	be crazy about	stick	

1) You'll _____ yourself when I tell you the answer.
2) How can I _____ this unwelcome guest?
3) The detective (侦探) couldn't _____ anything about the suspect (嫌疑犯).
4) General Zhang _____ from the army at 60.
5) Jane lives far away from here. She _____ stops by to see us.
6) He sounded _____ after running up the stairs.
7) The cat usually manages to _____ people into conversation.
8) The math problem is so difficult that I _____ (work) it out.
9) You'll have to _____ a severe test before you get this job.
10) Ling's family is very poor. She cannot _____ to go to school.
11) I _____ that he was drunk and shouldn't be allowed to drive.
12) She _____ walking the beach with the dog.

13) Please _____ a map on the letter before you post it.

14) They finally _____ to get there in time.

IV. A. Put the verbs in brackets in the subjunctive mood.

1) If I _____ (have) the money, I _____ (buy) my son one of the cape recorders.

2) If everyone _____ (take) a little more exercise, then we _____ (have) more life years.

3) If they _____ (arrive) ten minutes earlier they _____ (catch) the plane.

4) If I _____ (be) you, I _____ (take) a degree in Modern Languages.

5) If you _____ (have) a lot of money, _____ you _____ (buy) a car?

6) _____ he _____ (study) more, he _____ (be) able to pass the examination.

7) _____ there _____ (not be) the computer, the design _____ (not make) within a few hours.

8) If I _____ (be) to do the test, I _____ (do) it in a easy way.

B. Rewrite the following sentences after the model.

Model: I did not know you were coming, so I did not wait.

If I had known you were coming, I would have waited.

1) I believed him, so I lent him some money.

2) I shall not have a holiday this summer.

3) He can't go back to work because he doesn't have the chance.

4) I shall not be able to go to Europe with you.

5) I walked home because I missed the last bus.

6) I understand what you said. I don't need to listen to it again.

V. A. Rewrite the following sentences after the model.

Model 1: Why don't change your attitude?

<u>Why not</u> change your attitude?

1) Your friend is in a bad mood. Why don't you send her some flowers?
2) She is alone at home. Why don't you invite her out?
3) Why don't you make your own Christmas cards instead of buying them?
4) Why don't you go to the cinema? The film is very interesting.

Model 2: While I was walking the beach with the dog, I met a retired couple.

While walking the beach with the dog, I met a retired couple.

1) While I was having supper, I heard someone shouting "Help".
2) While I was taking a walk in the street, I met an old friend.
3) While I was looking out of the window, I found a man lying on the ground.
4) While the policeman was watching people in the shop, he noticed a man taking things from the shelf.

B. Complete the following sentences.

1) Your suggestion _____ (听上去不错).
2) _____ (我感到惭愧) of my behavior.
3) _____ (我感到很茫然), so when he asked me if I was the secretary, I quickly said yes.
4) He is ill in bed. _____ (他看上去脸色苍白。)
5) The green leaves _____ (在雨后似乎更美了).
6) This soup (汤) _____ (气味很香).

VI. Translation:

A. From Chinese to English.

1) 这对退休夫妇喜爱音乐。
2) 我上大学时打不起长途电话。
3) 如果我能摆脱孩子们的纠缠,情况就会大不一样。
4) 她向我建议道"天色已晚,何不马上动身呢?"
5) 听见他死于交通事故,我感到吃惊。
6) 他们终于及时赶到了那儿。

B. From English to Chinese.

1) He feels it challenging to be a supermarket manager.
2) I've enjoyed contesting as a sub-hobby for years, and occasionally suggest to friends that they try it because surprises are such fun.
3) It's not necessary to kick yourself. Everyone makes mistakes.
4) She managed to pass her driving test on her fifth attempt.
5) If I had known them what I know now, how different my life would have been.
6) I'm just not the type of person who ever wins everything.

Passage Reading

It's Never Too Late

(Part Ⅱ)

Have you ever noticed that people who are failures attract others who are failures, and that they tend to hang out together? My belief is if you want to know about success, hang out with successful people. If you want to radiate health, don't hang out with people who focus only on their aches and pains.

In my classes at Oregon Coast Community College I've encouraged students to go for their dreams, to be passionate about something, (anything!) and, above all, to have faith in themselves.

One woman said, "I've got some fears about seeing if I can write, but it's also something I've always wanted to try." (She is now one of 7 students whose work has been accepted for publication.)

And on the subject of faith, did you hear about the two nuns who were driving down the highway, ran out of gas, and had to walk to the nearest gas station?

"Did you bring a container to put gas in?" asked the attendant.

"Oh, no," said the nuns, "there wasn't one in the car."

"Well, I'm sorry," the attendant said, "we're all out of containers, but there's an old antique bedpan in the back room that'll hold enough gas to get you going. You're welcome to use it."

"That'll be fine," said the nuns, and soon they were trudging back to their car carefully carrying the bedpan. Just as they were pouring gas into the tank of their car, an 18-wheeler went by.

"Well, I'll be—," muttered the truck driver, "Now, that's what I call faith!!"

New Words and Expressions

tend [tend] *vi.* 倾向,趋于
    tend to 倾向于
hang out 聚集
belief [bi'li:f] *n.* 信心,信条
radiate ['reidieit] *vt.* 发射,表现
focus ['foukəs] *vi.* 使聚集于焦点,集中
    focus on 集中于⋯上

ache [eik] *n.* 疼痛
pain [pein] *n.* 痛苦,疼痛
community [kə'mju:niti] *n.* 社区,社会
go for 追求,寻求
passionate ['pæʃənit] *adj.* 热情的,易动情的
    be passionate about 热爱⋯

above all 尤其,特别是
faith [feiθ] *n*. 信心,信仰
　have faith in 信任…
fear [fiə] *vt*., *n*. 担心
publication [pʌbli'keiʃən] *n*. 出版,发行
subject ['sʌbdʒikt] *n*. 被讨论的对象
nun [nʌn] *n*. 修女
highway ['haiwei] *n*. 公路,交通要道
put in 把…放入(装进)
attendant [ə'tendənt] *n*. 服务员

antique [æn'ti:k] *adj*. 古代的
bedpan ['bedpæn] *n*. 尿盆
trudge [trʌdʒ] *vi*. 步履艰难地走
pour [pɔ:] *vt*. 倒,灌
tank [tæŋk] *n*. 油箱
wheeler ['wi:lə] *n*. 有轮的东西(如车辆)
mutter ['mʌtə] *vi*. 喃喃自语,轻声低语

Notes to the Passage

1. Have you ever noticed that people who are failures attract others who are failures, and that they tend to hang out together? 你曾注意到失败的人爱吸引失败的人,而且他们还喜欢混在一起吗？"tend to"意为"往往会,易于"。例如：
I tend to go to bed earlier during the winter. 在冬天,我往往很早睡觉。

2. If you want to radiate health, don't hang out with people who focus only on their aches and pains. 如果你想表现健康,就不要跟那些只把注意力集中在这儿疼那儿痛的人混在一起。

3. "I've got some fears about seeing if I can write…" 我有些担心,想弄明白我是否会写作…

4. We're all out of containers 我们都没有盛油的家伙(容器)。

5. You're welcome to use it. 要用就随便吧。

6. an 18-wheeler went by 一台 18 个轮子的大卡车开了过去。

7. "Well, I'll be—," muttered the truck driver. "Now, that's what I call faith!!"
作者在本文最后引出 the subject of faith。有了 faith, 就 "It's never

too late"。大卡车司机看到两位修女用小便盆装汽油,不禁脱口说出:"真他妈的。"(I'll be 之后还有"———",即"damned"这字,因不雅,故没有说出口。)这可算得是 faith 了!"faith"这里是双关语:两位修女对上帝的虔诚和坚信者事必成。天主教的圣职人员,都穿着道袍,一看就知道是嬷嬷。

Answer the following question according to the passage.
1. What is the author's belief?
2. What did the author encourage students to do in his class?
3. What happened to the nuns who were driving down the highway?
4. Did the nuns bring a container to put gas in?
5. What happened just as they were pouring gas into the tank of their car?
6. How do you understand the title "It's never too late"?

Vocabulary List 词汇表

A

a bit 一点，一些   2
*above all 尤其，特别是   16
*according to 根据   6
accountant [ə'kauntənt] n. 会计员   15
*accuse [ə'kju:z] vt. 控告   14
    *accuse somebody of 控告（某人）
*ache ['eik] n. 疼痛   16
acre ['eikə] n. 英亩   4
act [ækt] n., vi. 行为，行动   9
*activity [æk'tiviti] n. 活动   5
*add [æd] vt. 加法   8
*addition [ə'diʃən] n. 附加物   5
    in addition to 除了…之外
admire [əd'maiə] vt. 赞美，称赞   5
admit [əd'mit] vt. 承认   14
*advertise ['ædvətaiz] vt. 登广告
*advertising ['ædvətaiziŋ] n. 广告   5
advice [əd'vais] n. 建议   10
advise [əd'vaiz] vt. 建议   8
*after all 毕竟   8
*agree [ə'gri:] vt., vi. 同意   2
*a large number of 大量的，许多   5
all at once 突然   12
all of a sudden 突然间   14

allow [ə'lau] vt. 允许，同意   5
alone [ə'loun] adj. 独自一人   9
already [ɔ:l'redi] adv. 已经   5
*although [ɔ:l'ðou] conj. 虽然   2
*amateur ['æmətə] n., adj. 业余爱好者，业余的   9
amazed [ə'meizd] adj. 惊奇的   11
America [ə'merikə] n. 美洲，美国   6
*amount [ə'maunt] n. 数量   11
ancient ['einʃənt] adj. 古代的，远古的   4
anger ['æŋgə] n. 生气   10
animal ['æniməl] n. 动物   6
announce [ə'nauns] vt. 宣布   8
*another [ə'nʌðə] prep., adj. 另一个   3
    *one another 互相
*antique [æn'ti:k] adj. 古代的   16
*anyway ['eniwei] adv. 无论如何   8
apparently [ə'pærəntli] adv. 明显地   14
appear [ə'piə] vi. 出现   14
appointment [ə'pɔintmənt] n. 约会   8
approach [ə'proutʃ] vt. 走近，靠近   3
*area ['ɛəriə] n. 地区   5
*arithmetic [ˌæriθ'metik] adj. 数学的   8

注：表中带 * 号的均为阅读材料中的单词。

arrange [əˈreindʒ] vt. 安排 5
　arrange for 安排…做…
*arrest [əˈrest] vt. 逮捕 14
*art [ɑːt] n. 艺术 9
*article [ˈɑːtikl] n. 文章 5
arts and crafts 工艺品 15
ashamed [əˈʃeimd] adj. 惭愧 15
ask [ɑːsk] vt. 提问 3
asleep [əˈsliːp] adj. 睡着 3
as long as 只要,在…条件下 10
aspirin [ˈæspərin] n. 阿司匹林 15
assistant [əˈsistənt] n. 助手,店员 1
*associate [əˈsouʃieit] vt. 把…联系在
　一起 6
　*associate...with 与…有关
as well 也 13
*at first 开始 12
at last 最后 1
at least 至少 3
at one time 一次 13
at the end 最后 3
attempt [əˈtempt] n., vt. 试图 13
　in (an) attempt to do sth 试图做某事
attend [əˈtend] vt. 参加 2
*attendant [əˈtendənt] n. 服务员 16
*attention [əˈtenʃən] n. 主意 10
　pay attention to 主意
attitude [ˈætitjuːd] n. 态度 16
attract [əˈtrækt] vt. 吸引 14
average [ˈævəridʒ] adj. 平均的 4
　n. 平均
awfully [ˈɔːfuli] adv. 非常 9

B

back [ˈbæk] vt. 使后退 6
backward [ˈbækwəd] adv. 向后 12
*ballpark [ˈbɔːlpɑːk] n. 棒球场 9
*band [ˈbænd] n. 带,箍带 11
bank [bæŋk] n. 河岸 4
*bargain [ˈbɑːgin] n. 交易 15
*bark [bɑːk] vi. 犬叫 1
base [beis] n. 根基,底面 4
*baseball [ˈbeisbɔːl] n. 棒球 9
*basic [ˈbeisik] adj. 基本的 11
bat [bæt] n. 蝙蝠 12
battery [ˈbætəri] n. 蓄电池 16
be good at 擅长于 16
*beach [biːt] n. 海滩,海滨 5
bear [bɛə] vt. 忍受 10
*because of 因为 12
*bedpan [ˈbedpæn] n. 尿盆 16
before long 不久 8
beginning [biˈginiŋ] n. 开始 4
be good at 善于 16
*belief [biˈliːf] n. 信心,信条 16
belong [biˈlɔŋ] vi. 属于 5
　belong to 属于
*be sure of 知道,确信 6
*between [biˈtwiːn] prep. 在…之间 5
*beyond [biˈjɔnd] prep. 超过 13
bill [bil] n. 账单 15
*bit [bit] n. 小块 13
black [blæk] adj. 黑色的 7

blanket ['blæŋkit] n. 毯子	12
block [blɔk] n. (木、石等之)块	4
blood [blʌd] n. 血	1
boat [bout] n. 小船	4
body ['bɔdi] n. 尸体	4
boot [bu:t] n. 靴子	16
*boss [bɔs] n. 老板,上司	7
bottom ['bɔtəm] n. 海底,底部	13
*bouquet [bu'kei] n. 花束	11
brain [brein] n. 脑,脑髓	7
break [breik] vt. (broke, broken) 打破	2
breathless ['breθlis] adj. 气喘嘘嘘的	16
*bright ['brait] adj. 聪明的	10
*brighten ['braitən] vt. 点亮,使…明亮	11
brighten up 使…生辉	
*bud [bʌd] n. 花蕾	11
*builder ['bildə] n. 建设者	2
bullet ['bulit] n. 子弹	7
bunch [bʌntʃ] n. 束	11
bundle up 使穿得暖和	12
bury ['beri] vt. 埋葬	4
butterfly ['bʌtəflai] n. 蝴蝶	5
button ['bʌtn] n. 按钮	6
*buy [bai] n. 便宜货	11
buyer ['baiə] n. 购买者	15

C

cabinet ['kæbinit] n. 外壳	2
cafeteria [ˌkæfi'tiəriə] n. 自助餐馆	5
*calculation [ˌkælkju'leiʃən] n. 计算	2
*calendar ['kælində] n. 日历	6
call at 造访	3
can [kæn] n. 罐子	6
captain ['kæptin] n. 船长	13
car [kɑ:] n. 火车车厢	6
card [kɑ:d] n. 卡片,扑克牌	1
*career [kə'riə] n. 生涯	8
careful ['kɛəful] adj. 仔细的	1
carefully ['kɛəfuli] adv. 仔细地	1
carton ['kɑ:tən] n. 纸板箱	14
case [keis] n. 盒子,事例	5
in case 万一	
casual ['kæʒuəl] adj. 随便的	11
catch a cold 感冒	12
*cause [kɔ:z] vt. 引起	13
*celebrate ['selibreit] vt. 庆祝	6
*central ['sentrəl] adj. 中央的	5
certain ['sə:tən] adj. 确定的	14
challenge ['tʃælindʒ] vt. 挑战	16
challenging ['tʃælindʒiŋ] adj. 具有挑战性的	
chance ['tʃɑ:ns] n. 机会	1
by any chance 可能	
cheap [tʃi:p] adj. 便宜的	2
cheat [tʃi:t] vi., vt. 欺骗	9
check [tʃek] vt. 检查	3
n. 支票	8
chef [ʃef] n. 厨师长	15
*choose [tʃu:z] vt. (chose, chosen) 选择	6

267

*Christ [kraist] n. 基督	6
Christmas ['krisməs] n. 圣诞节	6
church [tʃəːtʃ] n. 教堂	12
*citizen ['sitizn] n. 公民	8
*claim [kleim] vt. 声称	15
clean [kliːn] adj. 干净的	2
clear [kliə] adj. 清楚的	2
*close [klouz] vt. 关门	1
clothesbrush ['klouðbrʌʃ] n. 衣服刷	12
cloudless ['klaudlis] adj. 无云的	13
club [klʌb] n. 俱乐部	2
clue [kluː] n. 线索	11
coast [koust] n. 海岸	16
*coffin ['kɔfin] n. 棺材,柩	4
collapse [kə'læps] vi. 倒塌	14
colleague ['kɔliːg] n. 同事	11
*collect [kə'lekt] vt. 拿来,接来	1
collection [kə'lekʃən] n. 收集	5
*combine [kəm'bain] vt. 合并	12
*come to an end 结束	12
common ['kɔmən] adj. 普通的	8
*community [kə'mjuːniti] n. 社会,社区	16
company ['kʌmpəni] n. 陪伴	2
compare [kəm'pɛə] vt. 比较	4
compare...to 把…比做	
complain [kəm'plein] vi. 抱怨	6
complete [kəm'pliːt] adj. 完整的	8
complicated ['kɔmplikeitid] adj. 复杂的	15
concentrate ['kɔnsentreit] vi. 集中精力	15
*conceptional [kən'sepʃənəl] adj. 理想的	8
condition [kən'diʃən] n. 条件	5
on condition that 条件是,不过得要	
conference ['kɔnfərəns] n. 会议	8
confuse [kən'fjuz] vt. 使困惑	15
confused [kən'fjuzd] adj. 困惑的	
congratulate [kən'grætjuleit] vt. 祝贺	5
conscientiously [ˌkɔnʃi'enʃəsli] adv. 谨慎地	11
conscious ['kɔnʃəs] adj. 明白的,清醒的	16
*contain [kən'tein] vt. 包含,含有	5
*container [kən'teinə] n. 容器	11
contest ['kɔntest] n. 比赛	9
[kən'test] vi. 竞赛	16
control [kən'troul] vt., n. 控制	2
convenient [kən'viːnjənt] adj. 方便的	2
conveniently [kən'viːnjəntli] adv. 方便地,近处	14
co-owner [kou'ounə] n. 合伙人	15
copy ['kɔpi] vt. 抄	9
correspondence [ˌkɔris'pɔndəns] n. 通信	15
cost [kɔst] n. 费用	8
cough [kɔf] vi. 咳嗽	12
couple [kʌpl] n. 一对(夫妇)	16
courage ['kʌridʒ] n. 勇气	13
*course [kɔːs] n. 航线	13

*court [kɔːt] n. 法院   14
cover ['kʌvə] vt. 遮盖…的表面,
   遮盖   4
coward ['kauəd] n. 胆小鬼   15
cram [kræm] vt. (为考试)死记
   硬背   7
crazy ['kreizi] adj. 热衷的,热爱的   16
   be crazy about 热衷于
*creativity [ˌkriːeiˈtiviti] n. 创造力   11
credit ['kredit] n. (学科的)学分   7
*critical ['kritikəl] adj. 苛刻的   12
crowded ['kraudid] adj. 拥挤的,
   挤满人的   5
crush ['krʌʃ] vt. 压碎   1
culprit ['kʌlprit] n. 导致不良
   后果的人   14
*curious ['kjuəriəs] adj. 好奇的   7
*curl [kəːl] vi. 卷曲   9
   *curl up 蜷缩
*current ['kʌrənt] adj. 现代的   9
*custom ['kʌstəm] n. 习惯   6

D

dangerous ['deindʒrəs] adj. 危险的   9
dare [dɛə] v. aux. 敢   16
*dark [dɑːk] adj. 黑的,颜色深的   11
*darkness ['dɑːknis] n. 黑暗   13
day in and day out 整日整夜   11
daytime ['deitaim] n. 白天   3
dead [ded] adj. 死的   4
dean [diːn] n. 系主任   8

dean of studies 教务主任
dear [diə] adj. 亲爱的   1
decide [diˈsaid] vt. 决定   1
*decide on 选定   5
*decision [diˈsiʒən] n. 决定   12
*decorate ['dekəreit] vt. 装饰   6
   *decoration [ˌdekəˈreiʃən] n. 装饰;
    装饰品
*deficiency [diˈfiʃənsi] n. 缺陷   8
describe [disˈkraib] vt. 描述,描写   3
*desert ['dezət] n. 沙漠,荒地   4
desperation [ˌdespəˈreiʃən] n. 绝望,
   拼命   6
detective [diˈtektiv] n. 侦探   3
difficult ['difikəlt] adj. 困难的   3
*dilemma [diˈlemə] n. 进退两难
   之境   12
directive [diˈrektiv] n. 指示   11
dirty ['dəːti] adj. 肮脏的   12
disappear [ˌdisəˈpiə] vi. 消失   3
discover [disˈkʌvə] vt. 发现   8
dishonest [disˈɔnist] adj. 不诚实的   9
dislike [disˈlaik] vt. 不喜欢   16
dismiss [disˈmis] vt. 解散   9
disorder [disˈɔːdə] n. 混乱   13
display [disˈplei] n. 陈列   14
distance ['distəns] n. 距离   2
   in the distance 在远处   13
*distressed [disˈtrest] adj. 苦恼的   12
ditch [ditʃ] n. 小沟   12
*divide [diˈvaid] vt. 除法   8
*do one's best 尽力   13

*do's and don'ts 注意事项 11
dormitory (dorm) ['dɔmitəri] n.
    (集体)宿舍 5
*doze [douz] vi. 打瞌睡,打盹 3
*dozen ['dʌzn] n. 一打,十二个 11
Dr. (doctor 的缩写) 医生 7
*drafty ['drɑːfti] adj. 通风的 11
*drag [dræg] vt. 拖,拽 3
*dream ['driːm] vi. 梦,梦见 7
    dream of 梦见
drop [drɔp] vt. 放下,投入 6
*dull [dʌl] adj. 呆笨的 9
duty ['djuːti] n. 职责 10

E

each [iːtʃ] pron., adj. 每一(个) 3
easy ['iːzi] adj. 简单的 3
edge [edʒ] n. 边缘 7
*editor ['editə] n. 编辑 5
education [edjuˈkeiʃən] n. 教育 11
effort ['efət] n. 努力 13
*Egyptian [iˈdʒipʃən] adj. 埃及的 2
*Egypt ['idʒipt] n. 埃及
either ['aiðə] adv. 或者 15
*elder ['eldə] adj. 年长的 6
electric [iˈlektrik] adj. 用电的,电动的 6
electricity [iˌlekˈtrisiti] n. 电,电学 3
else [els] adj. 其余的 2
emphasize ['emfəsaiz] vt. 强调 9
encourage [inˈkʌridʒ] vt. 鼓励 5
end [end] n. 尽头 1

enemy ['enimi] n. 敌人 10
engine room 轮机室 13
English Department 英语系 8
*enjoyment [inˈdʒɔimənt] n. 娱乐 9
enroll (in) [inˈroul] vi. 参加 8
enterprise ['entəpraiz] n. 企业 15
*entertainment [ˌentəˈteinmənt] n.
    娱乐 9
enthusiasm [inˈθjuːziæzəm] n. 热情 11
enthusiastic [inˌθjuːziˈæstik] adj.
    热情的 11
*equal ['iːkwəl] adj. 同样的 11
*Europe ['juərəp] n. 欧洲 6
*eve [iːv] n. 前夜,除夕 6
*evidence ['evidəns] n. 证据 14
*exact [igˈzækt] adj. 正好的 13
exam [igˈzæm] n. 考试 3
excellent ['eksələnt] adj. 优秀的 2
excitedly [ikˈsaitidli] adv. 兴奋地 3
*excitement [ikˈsaitmənt] n. 兴奋 3
*exclaim [iksˈkleim] vi. 惊叫 2
*exhaust [igˈzɔːst] vt. 使筋疲力尽 15
    exhausted [igˈzɔːstid] adj. 精疲力竭的
exhibit [igˈzibit] n. 展品 4
expect [iksˈpekt] vt. 期望 11
expectation [ˌekspekˈteiʃən] n. 期
    待,期望 16
expensive [iksˈpensiv] adj. 昂贵的 2
experience [iksˈpiəriəns] n. 经验 14
*expose [iksˈpouz] vt. 使暴露 4
*express [iksˈpres] vt. 表达 3
*expression [iksˈpreʃən] n. 表达 9

extra ['ekstrə] adj. 额外的   9

F

*fail [feil] vi. 失败   8
*failure ['feiljə] n. 失败者,失败   7
fair [fɛə] adj. (风)顺畅的   13
fairly ['fɛəli] adv. 相当地   10
*faith [feiθ] n. 信心,信仰   16
  *have faith on 对…有信心,信任
fall in love 坠入爱河   5
*fall on 落到   9
*fashionable ['fæʃənəbl] adj. 高级的,
  上流社会的   5
*favourite ['feivərit] adj. 最喜欢的   3
*fear [fiə] vt., n. 担心   16
*fee [fi:] n. 费用   8
*feeling ['fi:liŋ] n. 感受   11
fever ['fi:və] n. 发烧   12
*fight [fait] vi. 吵架   12
*figure ['figə] n. 数字   5
  vt. 想象,估计   16
*fill out 填写   15
*fill up 填满   9
final ['fainl] adj. 最后的   9
finish ['finiʃ] vt. 完成   3
*firm [fə:m] n. 公司   12
first-hand adv. 首先   14
flashlight ['flæʃlait] n. 手电筒   6
flood [flʌd] n. 洪水   4
flunk [flʌŋk] vt. (某学科)考试不
  及格   7

flute [flu:t] n. 长笛   2
*focus ['foukəs] vi. 集中,使集中于
  焦点   16
  *focus on 集中于…上
follow ['fɔləu] vt. 跟从   5
following ['fɔlouiŋ] adj. 下列的   5
*fond [fɔnd] adj. 喜欢   6
  *be fond of 喜欢
foot [fut] n. 英尺 (复) feet   4
*forever [fə'revə] adv. 永远   4
form [fɔ:m] vt. 形成,组成   2
*formal ['fɔ:məl] adj. 正式的   11
fortunately ['fɔ:tʃənitli] adv. 幸运地
  13
*freedom ['fri:dəm] n. 自由   5
*free [fri:] adj. 自由的   5
freely ['fri:li] adv. 自由地   11
freeze [fri:z] vi. 结冰   12
fresh [freʃ] adj. 新鲜的   11
freshman ['freʃmən] n. 大学一
  年级学生   8
frighten ['fraitən] vt. 使惊吓   15
Frisbee ['frizbi:] n. 飞盘   9
front [frʌnt] n. 前面   6
  in front 前面
  in front of 在…前面
full of 充满   10
fun [fʌn] n. 乐趣   5

G

gal [gæl] n. (口语)女孩   16

general ['dʒenərəl] adj.总的	11
general manager 总经理	11
get in trouble 惹麻烦	9
get rid of 摆脱,消除	16
give up 放弃	13
glance [glɑ:ns] vi.瞥	11
glance at 瞥见	
*go for 追求,寻求	16
go over	15
go through 经历,忍受	16
gold [gould] n.金子	13
grade [greid] n.年级	9
graduate ['grædjuit] vi.毕业	11
graduation [ˌgrædju'eiʃən] n. 毕业典礼,毕业	5
*grammar school 小学	8
greet [gri:t] vt.问候	11
grind [graind] vi.刻苦	11
grocery ['grousəri] n.杂货店	14
ground [graund] n.地面,场所	1
*grow up 成长,发展	6
*guarantee [ˌgærən'ti:] vt.保证	8
guess [ges] vt.猜,认为	2
*guest [gest] n.客人	5
*guilty ['gilti] adj.有罪的	14
Guinness ['ginis] n.吉尼斯	2
gun [gʌn] n.枪,炮	7

H

hand in 递交	11
handbag ['hændbæg] n.手提袋	3
*handmade ['hændmeid] adj.手工的	15
*hang out 聚集	16
happen to 碰巧	9
*happily ['hæpili] adv.高兴地	1
hard [hɑ:d] adv.努力地	1
*hardly ['hɑ:dli] adv.几乎不	3
*head [hed] n.头,头部	4
*headache ['hedeik] n.头痛	15
hear of 听说	14
heat [hi:t] n.暖气	16
heavily ['hevili] adv.严重地	13
heavy ['hevi] adj.厚重的	12
hedge [hedʒ] n.树篱(用于田地、花园周围)	3
heel [hi:l] n.足跟	12
*height [hait] n.高度	11
hell [hel] n.地狱	12
*helpful ['helpful] adj.有帮助的	11
helpless ['helplis] adj.无助的	13
*hemisphere ['hemisfiə] n.半球	6
hide [haid] vi.躲藏	3
*higher learning 高等教育	8
*highway ['haiwei] n.公路,交通要道	16
history ['histəri] n.历史	4
hit [hit] vt.打,碰撞	1
hobby ['hɔbi] n.爱好	2
*hold [hould] vt.(held, held) 拿着,握住,保存	2
*hold up 举起…展示	
hold on to 紧紧抓住	13

honesty ['ɔnisti] n. 诚实 9
hope [houp] vt. 希望 9
*hopelessly ['houplisli] adv.
  没希望地 15
*hot [hɔt] adj. 热的 2
how long 多久 3
huge [hju:dʒ] adj. 巨大的 4
*human ['hju:mən] adj., n. 人的,
  人类的 4
humid ['hju:mid] adj. 潮湿的 16
*hung up 挂断(电话) 15
*hunt [hʌnt] vt. 狩猎 12
*job-hunting 找工作 12
husband ['hʌzbənd] n. 丈夫 2

I

ice [ais] n. 冰 6
if [if] conj. 是否,如果 3
illiterate [i'litərit] n. 文盲 8
  *imagine [i'mædʒin] vt. 想象 9
immediately [i'mi:diətli] adv. 立即,
  马上 2
import ['impɔ:t] n. 进口 15
in a word 总而言之,一言以蔽之 15
in one way 某种程度上 12
inch [intʃ] n. 寸 2
incident ['insidənt] n. 事件 14
include [in'klu:d] vt. 包括 2
*income ['inkʌm] n. 收入 12
*inferior [in'fiəriə] adj. 地位低下的
  12

inform [in'fɔ:m] vt. 告知 8
innocence ['inəsns] n. 无辜 14
*inside [in'said] prep. 在…里面 3
inspect [in'spekt] vt. 检查 14
*inspector [in'spektə] n. (英)警察;
  巡官 3
*in spite of 尽管 5
*instead of 而不是 9
*institution [ˌinsti'tju:ʃən] n. 惯例,
  制度 8
*instrument ['instrumənt] n. 乐器 9
interest ['intrist] n. 兴趣 2
interesting ['intristiŋ] adj. 有趣的 5
*in the distance 在远处 13
*in time 及时 13
into prep. 到…内,到…里 1
  look into 检查
*introduce [ˌintrə'dju:s] n. 介绍 6
*in use 在使用的,在用的 6
*inventory ['invəntri] n. 存货目录
  (清单) 15
*invoice ['invɔis] n. 发票,清单 15

J

jacket ['dʒækit] n. 夹克衫 16
janitor ['dʒænitə] n. 看门人 15
jewelry ['dʒuəlri] n. 珠宝 3
*job-hunting 找工作 12
joke [dʒouk] vi. 开玩笑 11
*joking ['dʒoukiŋ] adj. 玩笑的 12
joyfully ['dʒɔifuli] adv. 高兴地 11

*judge [dʒʌdʒ] n. 法官　14
judgment ['dʒʌdʒmənt] n. 判断　14
jump [dʒʌmp] vi. 跨接起动　16

K

keep a record of 将…记录下来　3
keep in high spirit 保持高昂情绪　11
keep on 一致,继续　12
kick [kik] vt. 抱怨　16
　kick oneself 严厉自责
kid [kid] n. 小孩　16
*kind [kaind] n. 种类　2
kill [kil] vt. 消磨　11
king [kiŋ] n. 国王　4
knee [ni:] n. 膝盖　14
known [noun] adj. 著名的　4

L

lake [leik] n. 湖　9
large [lɑ:dʒ] adj. 大的　2
last [lɑ:st] vi. 延续,持续　2
late [leit] adj. 新近的　2
later ['leitə] adv. 较迟的,较后的　1
Latin ['lætin] n. 拉丁语　12
lay out 布局　4
layer ['leiə] n. 层　16
lazy ['leizi] adj. 懒惰的　5
lean [li:n] vi. 倾斜,倚　9
least [li:st] adj. 最小的,最少的　2
　(little 的最高级)

*leisure ['leʒə] n. 空闲　9
*length [leŋθ] n. 长度　11
lesson ['lesn] n. 功课　5
lift [lift] vt. 举起　4
*limestone ['laimstoun] n. 石灰石　4
line [lain] n. (非正式)故事　16
*lion ['laiən] n. 狮子　4
list [list] n. 名单表　3
literature ['litəritʃə] n. 文学,文艺　7
*local ['loukəl] adj. 本地的　11
locate [lou'keit] vt. 在…地点设置　4
　be located on/in 位于
log [lɔg] n. 圆木　6
*look after 照看　1
*look over 逐一检阅,检查　15
lucky ['lʌki] adj. 幸运的　5

M

*machinery [mə'ʃi:nəri] n. 机器　2
mad [mæd] adj. 疯狂的　12
madman ['mædmən] n. 疯子　14
*magazine [ˌmæɡə'zi:n] n. 杂志　5
mail [meil] n. 邮件　15
*make [meik] vt. 赚(钱),发财　5
*make an offer 提议　15
make out 制定　15
manage ['mænidʒ] vt. 设法,对付　16
　manage to do something 设法做某事
management ['mænidʒmənt] n.
　管理　11
*margin ['mɑ:dʒin] n. 盈余,毛利　15

词条	页码
*marimbas [mə'rimbəs] n. 马林巴（木琴的一种）	15
*mark [mɑːk] vt., n. 做记号；记号	10
n. 评价	12
*market ['mɑːkit] n. 市场	11
*marriage ['mæridʒ] n. 婚姻	12
*mathematical [ˌmæθə'mætikəl] adj. 数学的	2
matter ['mætə] n. 问题	15
maybe ['meibiː] adv. 也许	9
mean [miːn] vt. 意思是	7
meantime ['miːntaim] n. 在这期间	10
mention ['menʃən] vt. 提及	9
*merry ['meri] adj. 欢乐的，快乐的	6
*message ['mesidʒ] n. 信息	11
*messenger ['mesindʒə] n. 信使	11
meter ['miːtə] n. （计量单位）米	2
midnight ['midnait] n. 午夜	12
mid-term [mid təːm] n., adj. 期中的	7
*mile [mail] n. 英里	4
million ['miljən] num. 百万	2
*millionaire [ˌmiljə'nɛə] n. 百万富翁	7
mind [maind] n. 主意	2
vt. 介意	8
miner ['mainə] n. 矿工	13
minister ['ministə] n. 牧师	12
minutes ['minits] n. 会议记录	11
*miserable ['mizərəbl] adj. 不幸的	13
mistaken [mis'teikən] adj. 错误的	14
model ['mɔdl] n. 型号	2
modern ['mɔdən] adj. 现代化的	4
moment ['moumənt] n. 片刻	4
mountainous ['mauntinəs] adj. 像山一样的	13
*multiply ['mʌltiplai] vt. 乘法	8
*music ['mjuːzik] n. 音乐	5
*musical ['mjuːzikəl] adj. 音乐的	9
musician [mjuː'ziʃən] n. 音乐家	2
*mutter ['mʌtə] vt. 喃喃自语，轻声低语	16
mysteriously [mis'tiəriəsli] adv. 神秘地，难理解地	3

N

词条	页码
*natural ['nætʃərəl] adj. 自然的	11
nearby ['niəbai] adj. 附近的	3
adv. 在附近	
nearly ['niəli] adv. 几乎	3
*nervous ['nəːvəs] adj. 神经质的	15
*no longer 不再	4
nobody ['noubədi] prop. 没有人	3
noise [nɔiz] n. 吵闹声	1
*northern ['nɔːðən] adj. 北部的	6
nose [nouz] n. 鼻子	1
not at all 根本不	8
nothing ['nʌθiŋ] prop. 没有东西，没有什么	3
no wonder 难怪，一点都不奇怪	6
number ['nʌmbə] n. 数字	2
*nun [nʌn] n. 修女	16

O

object ['ɔbdʒikt] *n*. 物品   15
occasionally [ə'keiʒənəli] *adv*. 偶尔地 16
ocean ['ouʃən] *n*. 海洋   16
o'clock [ə'klɔk] …点钟   5
of course 当然   2
offer ['ɔfə] *vt*. 提供   10
on board 搭乘   13
*once [wʌns] *adv*. 一次   5
*once or twice 不时地   13
onto ['ɔntu] *prep*. 到…上   6
open up 开足（马力）   6
operate ['ɔpəreit] *vi*. 动手术   7
  operate on 给…动手术
opportunity [ɔpə'tjuniti] *n*. 机会   10
*opinion [ə'pinjən] *n*. 观点   2
optimistic [ɔpti'mistik] *adj*. 乐观的 8
*order ['ɔ:də] *vt*. 命令   7
  n. 订货单   15
*origin ['ɔridʒin] *n*. 起源   6
*original [ə'ridʒənəl] *adj*. 原来的 13
*outdo [aut'du:] *vt*. 胜过   4
overjoyed [ouvə'dʒɔid] *adj*. 非常
  高兴的   11
own [oun] *adj*. 自己的   9
  vt. 拥有   15
*owner ['ounə] *n*. 主人   1

P

*pain [pein] *n*. 疼痛   16
*paint [peint] *vt*. 画画   9
part [pɑ:t] *n*. 部分   5
participate [pɑ:'tisipeit] *vi*. 参加   8
particular [pə'tikjulə] *adj*. 特别的   2
pass [pɑ:s] *vi*., *vt*. 合格, 通过   3
pass up 错过   10
passage ['pæsidʒ] *n*. （文章的）一段   3
passenger ['pæsindʒə] *n*. 乘客   13
*passionate ['pæʃənit] *adj*. 热情的,
  易动情的   16
  *be passionate about 热爱
patiently ['peiʃəntli] *adv*. 耐心地   13
*pay [pei] *n*. 工资   12
  *pay increase 涨工资
perfect ['pə:fikt] *adj*. 完美的   2
period ['piəriəd] *n*. 时期, 期间   2
person ['pə:sn] *n*. 人   2
*persuade [pə'sweid] *vt*. 说服   13
philosophy [fi'lɔsəfi] *n*. 哲理,
  人生观   16
piano [pi'ænou] *n*. 钢琴   2
picture ['piktʃə] *n*. 图画   2
  vt. 在心中描述, 想象 16
pier [piə] *n*. 码头   16
place [pleis] *vt*. 放置   2
play up to 拍马屁   11
player ['pleiə] *n*. 运动员   12
please [pli:z] *vt*. 使满足   6
plus [plʌs] *prep*. 加   7
pocket ['pɔkit] *n*. 衣袋   1
*point [pɔint] *n*. （尖）端   4
  vt., *vi* 指, 指出   10

n. 要点	
n. 程度	14
point out 指出	10
*politely [pə'laitli] *adv*. 客气地	15
politician [ˌpɔli'tiʃən] *n*. 政客	14
*poorly-dressed ['puəli drest] *adj*. 衣着破旧的	7
pop out 忽然突出来	14
popular ['pɔpjulə] *adj*. 受欢迎的	2
*position [pə'ziʃən] *n*. 位置	15
possession [pə'zeʃən] *n*. 拥有, 所有物	5
*possibility [ˌpɔsə'biliti] *n*. 可能性	12
pottery ['pɔtəri] *n*. 陶器	9
pour [pɔː] *vt*. 倒进, 灌	16
*present ['preznt] *n*. 礼物	6
adj. 现在的	12
*preserve [pri'zəːv] *vt*. 维持, 使不损坏	4
pretend [pri'tend] *vt*. 假装	11
pretty ['priti] *adv*. 相当, 非常	5
prevent [pri'vent] *vt*. 阻止, 预防	3
price [prais] *n*. 价格	2
*principal ['prinsəpəl] *n*. 校长	8
*private ['praivit] *adj*. 私人的, 个人的	5
probably ['prɔbəbli] *adv*. 可能地	2
problem ['prɔbləm] *n*. 问题	8
profession [prə'feʃən] *n*. 职业	15
*profit ['prɔfit] *n*. 利润, 收益	15
*program ['prougræm] *n*. 节目	9
promise ['prɔmis] *vt*. 答应, 承诺	5

n. 征兆	6
*promotion [prə'mouʃən] *n*. 提升	12
property ['prɔpəti] *n*. 地产, 资产	16
protest [prə'test] *vt*. 申明	14
proud [praud] *adj*. 骄傲的	10
psychologist [sai'kɔlədʒist] *n*. 心理学家	11
public ['pʌblik] *adj*. 公共的	8
*publication [ˌpʌbli'keiʃən] *n*. 出版, 发行	16
*pull [pul] *vt*. 拉	3
pull one's leg 愚弄某人, 同某人开玩笑	14
pupil ['pjuːpl] *n*. 小学生	5
*purchase ['pəːtʃəs] *n*. 购买	15
push [puʃ] *vt*., *n*. 推进	6
*put in 把…放入(装进)	16
put out 熄灭	13
*put up 搭起	6
*pyramid ['pirəmid] *n*. 金字塔	2

Q

quality ['kwɔliti] *n*. 品质	14
quarter ['kwɔːtə] *n*. 一刻钟	5
question ['kwestʃən] *n*. 问题	3
quickly ['kwikli] *adv*. 快的, 急速地	1
quiet ['kwaiət] *adj*. 静静的, 安静的	1
quietly ['kwaiətli] *adv*. 静静地	
quite a few 不少	1

R

*radiate ['reidieit] n. 发射,表现 16
*radio station 广播站 6
*rage [reidʒ] n. 生气 8
　*fly into a rage 勃然大怒
*raise [reiz] vt. 抚养 12
range [reindʒ] n. 范围 2
ready ['redi] adj. 准备好的 5
real [riəl] adj. 真正的 6
*reality [ri'æliti] n. 现实 12
realize [riə'laiz] vt. 了解 4
*reason ['ri:zn] n. 理由 6
record ['rekɔ:d] n. 纪录 2
　keep a record of 将…记录下来 3
*recorder [ri'kɔ:də] n. 录音机 6
refuse [ri'fju:z] vt. 拒绝 10
relate [ri'leit] vt. 叙述,说 14
*relation [ri'leiʃən] n. 关系 12
*relax [ri'læks] vi. 放松,使放松 5
religious [ri'lidʒəs] adj. 宗教的 14
remain [ri'mein] vi. 留下 5
remedial [ri'mi:djəl] adj. 补救的 8
*remember [ri'membə] vt. 记得 2
*rent [rent] vt. 租,租用 5
replace [ri'pleis] vt. 代替 11
reprimand ['reprima:nd] vt. 申斥 14
responsibility [ris,pɔnsə'biliti] n.
　责任 8
*responsible [ris'pɔnsəbl] adj.
　有责任的 5

*be responsible for 对…负责
rest [rest] n. 其余 1
*rest [rest] vi. 安息 4
retail [ri:'teil] adj. 零售的 15
retired [ri'taiəd] adj. 退休的 16
*reunion ['ri:'ju:njən] n. 团聚 6
rise [raiz] vi. 升起 4
rising ['raiziŋ] n. 升起 4
*roaring ['rɔ:riŋ] adj. 咆哮的 13
roll [roul] vi. 颠簸 13
*rose [rouz] n. 玫瑰 11
rough [rʌf] adj. 粗鲁的 13
row [rou] n. (一)排,(一)行 14
*rubber ['rʌbə] n. 橡皮 11
*run [rʌn] vt. 经营 12
　*run after 追逐 14
run away 逃走 9
run out of 用尽 6
rush [rʌʃ] n. 仓促,匆忙 4

S

safe ['seif] adj. 安全的 4
*safely ['seifli] adv. 安全地 2
*sail [seil] vi. 航行 13
*sale [seil] n. 销售 5
salesperson ['seilzpə:sn] n. 销售
　人员 15
same [seim] adj. 同样的 2
save [seiv] vt. 把…(从危险中)救出 7
*saying [seiiŋ] n. 谚语 9
scared [skɛəd] adj. 惊吓的,可怕的 15

scary ['skɛəri] *adj*. 令人惊恐的,可怕的	16
*scissor ['sizə] *n*. 剪刀	11
scream [skri:m] *vi*. 尖叫	12
screen [skri:n] *n*. 屏幕	2
*second ['sekənd] *n*. 秒	2
*section ['sekʃən] *n*. 阶层,地区	5
sell [sel] *vt*., *vi*. 卖出,销售	1
semester [si'mestə] *n*. 半学年,学期	7
sender ['sendə] *n*. 赠送者	11
sentence ['sentəns] *n*. 句子	8
seriously ['siəriəsli] *adv*. 严肃地	9
set [set] *vt*. 设置	3
vi. 落下	4
setting ['setiŋ] *n*. 落下	4
several ['sevərəl] *adj*. 几个的	3
severely [si'viəli] *adv*. 严重地	14
*shape [ʃeip] *n*. 形状	11
share [ʃɛə] *vt*. 分享	2
*sharp [ʃɑ:p] *adj*. 尖的	4
*shipwrecked ['ʃiprekt] *adj*. 沉船的	13
*shopkeeper ['ʃɔpˌki:pə] *n*. 店员	14
shortcoming [ʃɔ:t'kʌmiŋ] *n*. 缺点	10
show [ʃou] *vt*. 展示	5
shower [ʃauə] *n*. 淋浴	2
shut [ʃʌt] *vt*. 关上	10
side [said] *n*. 边,面	4
sight [sait] *n*. 看见	11
catch sight of 看见	
sign up 签名	16
similar ['similə] *adj*. 相似的	2
*simple ['simpl] *adj*. 简单的	2
*sink ['siŋk] *vi*. 下沉	13
siren ['saiərin] *n*. 警笛	6
size [saiz] *n*. 尺寸	2
slave [sleiv] *n*. 奴隶	4
sleepy ['sli:pi] *adj*. 昏昏欲睡的	12
*slip [slip] *vi*. 悄悄移动,潜行	3
slow [slou] *adj*. 慢的	1
slow down 放慢速度	6
slowly ['slouli] *adv*. 缓慢地	1
smell [smel] *vi*. 闻	11
*smooth [smu:ð] *adj*. 光滑的	4
*sneeze [sni:z] *vi*. 打喷嚏	15
*soft [sɔft] *adj*. 柔软的	7
solid ['sɔlid] *adj*. 固体的	4
*sometimes ['sʌmtaimz] *adv*. 有时	3
soon after 不久	8
special ['speʃəl] *adj*. 特别的,特殊的	1
*spectator [spek'teitə] *n*. 观众	9
speech [spi:tʃ] *n*. 演讲,讲演	5
*spirit ['spirit] *n*. 精神	6
*sports [spɔ:ts] *n*. 运动	9
*football sports 足球运动	
*basket ball sports 篮球运动	
*spot [spɔt] *n*. 地点	13
stack [stæk] *n*. (一)堆	14
stadium ['steidiəm] *n*. 体育馆	9
stamp [stæmp] *n*. 邮票	9
*stand [stænd] *vi*. 站立	2
*stare [stɛə] *vi*. 盯着,凝视	7
*stare at 盯着看,目不转睛	
start off 出发	13

state [steit] n. 状态 16
  in a state of 处于某种状态
station ['steiʃən] n. 局,所 1
  police station 警察局
*statue ['stætju:] n. 塑像 4
steal [sti:l] vt. 偷 3
steer [stiə] vt. 驾驶,引得 14
*stem [stem] n. 花茎 11
*step [step] n. 台阶 4
stick [stik] (stuck, stuck) vt. 粘, 不离开 16
storm [stɔ:m] n. 风暴 13
strange [streindʒ] adj. 奇怪的 9
stranger ['streindʒə] n. 陌生人 2
strong [strɔŋ] adj. 坚固的 4
strongly ['strɔŋli] adv. 强烈地 8
*struggle ['strʌgl] n. 搏斗 3
study ['stʌdi] vi., vt. 学习 3
stuff [stʌf] n. 材料,废话 16
*subject ['sʌbdʒikt] n. 被讨论的 对象 16
*subtract [səb'trækt] vt. 减法 8
suburb ['sʌbə:b] n. 郊区,市郊 6
*succeed [sək'si:d] vi. 成功 5
  *succeed in 成功于
*success [sək'ses] n. 成功 5
*successful [sək'sesful] adj. 成功的 5
such as 例如 11
*sudden ['sʌdn] adj. 突然的 15
suggest [sə'dʒest] vt. 建议 8
suitable ['sju:təbl] adj. 适合的 3
*sum [sʌm] n. 数目 8

sum up 概括 15
*supportive [sə'pɔ:tiv] adj. 支持的 12
suppose [sə'pəuz] vt. 设想 5
  be supposed to 被期望,应该
sure [ʃuə] adj. 确信的 3
  for sure 确信,毫无疑问
  be sure of 知道,确信 6
surely ['ʃuəli] adv. 肯定地 14
*surface ['sə:fis] n. (任何物体的) 表面 4
*surprise [sə'praiz] vt. 使…惊奇 2
*swiftly ['swiftli] adv. 敏捷地 3
*swimmer ['swimə] n. 游泳者 13
*symbol ['simbəl] n. 象征 6

T

*take no notice of 没注意 13
take off 带走 13
take place 发生 14
*tank [tæŋk] n. 油箱 16
taxi ['tæksi] n. 出租车 7
tear [tiə] n. 眼泪 10
television ['teliˌviʒən] n. 电视 2
  television set 电视机
temperature ['tempəritʃə] n. 温度 15
*tend [tend] vi. 倾向,趋于 16
  tend to 倾向于
*tennis ['tenis] n. 网球 5
*terrace ['teris] n. 露天平台 5
*terrible ['terəbl] adj. 糟糕的, 很坏的 7

*terrific [təˈrifik] adj. 极好的		15
test [test] n. 测试		9
test paper 试卷		
than [ðæn] prep., conj. 比		2
*theater [ˈθiətə] n. 戏院		9
theft [θeft] n. 偷窃行为		3
thief [θi:f] n. 贼,小偷		1
thin [θin] adj. 瘦弱的		10
though [ðou] conj., adv. 虽然		4
thousand [ˈθauzənd] num. 千		2
throw away 扔掉		8
*time [taim] n. 倍数		11
*tip [tip] n. 提示		11
tomb [tu:m] n. 坟墓		4
ton [tʌn] n. 吨		4
*tool [tu:l] n. 工具		2
*top [tɔp] n. 顶部		4
touchdown [ˈtʌtʃdaun] n. (橄榄球的) 底线得分		12
tough [tʌf] adj. 倔强的,难对付的		7
track [træk] n. 轨道		6
side track (美)(铁路的)侧线,岔道		
transistor [trænˈsistə] n. 晶体管		3
trap [træp] n. 圈套,陷阱		3
treasure [ˈtreʒə] n. 金银财宝		4
*trick [trik] n. 计谋		3
*trudge [trʌdʒ] vi. 步履艰难地走		16
truth [tru:θ] n. 真相		10
tuition [tjuˈiʃən] n. 学费		8
tumble [ˈtʌmbl] vi. 倒下		14
*turn down 拒绝		15
turn in 上交,交出		9

U

understand [ˌʌndəˈstænd] vt. 理解		8
*unhappy [ʌnˈhæpi] adj. 不高兴的		12
uniformed [ˈju:nifɔ:md] adj. 穿制服或军服的		3
unusual [ʌnˈju:ʒuəl] adj. 特别的,不寻常		2
up to 取决于		14
*urgent [ˈə:dʒənt] adj. 紧急的		8
*used to 过去常常		4
*useful [ˈju:sful] adj. 有用的		10
*useless [ˈju:slis] adj. 无用的		
usual [ˈju:ʒuəl] adj. 平常的		5

V

vaguely [ˈveigli] adv. 模糊地		14
vain [vein] n. 徒劳		13
in vain 徒劳		
*valley [ˈvæli] n. 山谷,河谷		4
*variety [vəˈraiəti] n. 变化		11
*a variety of 各种各样的		
vase [vɑ:z] n. 花瓶		11
*VCR 摄像机		9
victim [ˈviktim] n. 受害者		1
*view [vju:] n. 看,眺望		5
voice [vɔis] n. 声音		7

W

waiting room 候诊室		7

wallet ['wɔlit] n. 钱包	3
watch for 寻找,等待	1
weak [wi:k] adj. 虚弱的,脆弱的	7
weekly ['wi:kli] adj. 每周的	14
weigh [wei] vt. 称…的重量	4
welcome ['welkəm] adj. 受欢迎的, vt. 欢迎	8
west [west] n. 西方	4
wet [wet] adj. 湿的	1
*wheeler ['wi:lə] n. 有轮的东西	16
whenever ['wenevə] conj. 无论何时	11
wherever [wɛə'revə] adj. 不管在哪里	9
*whether ['weðə] conj. 是否	2
*while [wail] conj. 当…的时候	1
whisper ['wispə] vi. 小声地说	9
whistle ['wisl] n. 汽笛声	6
*white [wait] adj. 白色	4
wholesale ['houlseil] adv. 大批地,批发地	15
willingness ['wiliŋnis] n. 自愿	14
win [win] vt., vi. 赢得	9
winner ['winə] n. 胜利者	16
wiring ['waiəriŋ] n. 接线,配线工程	3
wish [wiʃ] vt. 希望	8
without [wi'ðaut] prep. 没有	4
*witness ['witnis] n. 见证人	14
*wonder ['wʌndə] n. 奇迹	2
wood [wud] n. 木材,木料	6
workroom ['wə:krum] n. 工作室	6
*worth [wə:θ] n., adj. 值得	10
*wreck [rek] n. 沉船	13

Y

yard [jɑ:d] n. 工作场,专用围地	6
yell [jel] vi. 喊叫	1